W9-AOV-294

Massacre at the Yuma Crossing

Massacre at the

MARK SANTIAGO

Yuma Crossing

Spanish Relations with the Quechans, 1779–1782

THE UNIVERSITY OF ARIZONA PRESS   TUCSON

Publication of this book is made possible in part by a grant from the
Soldwedel Family Foundation and in part by the proceeds of a permanent
endowment created with the assistance of a Challenge Grant from the
National Endowment for the Humanities, a federal agency.

The University of Arizona Press
This book is printed on acid-free, archival-quality paper.
Manufactured in the United States of America

03   02   01   00   99   98   6   5   4   3   2   1

Library of Congress Cataloging-in-Publication Data
Santiago, Mark, 1959–
    Massacre at the Yuma Crossing: Spanish Relations with the Quechans,
1779–1782 / Mark Santiago.
        p. cm.
    Includes bibliographical references and index.
    ISBN 0-8165-1824-6 (acid-free, archival-quality paper)
    1. Spaniards—Arizona—Yuma Region—History—18th century.
2. Yuma Region (Ariz.)—History. 3. Land settlement—Arizona—Yuma
Region—History—18th century. 4. Yuma Indians—Missions—Arizona—
Yuma Region—History—18th century. 5. Massacres—Arizona—Yuma
Region—History—18th century. I. Title.
F819.Y9S26   1998
979.1'71—dc21   98-8867
CIP

British Library Cataloguing-in-Publication Data
A catalogue record for this book is available from the British Library.

To Dawn,

forever and always

I have brought about the erection of two pueblos
of Spaniards among the Yumas so that these fortunate
Indians may embrace, voluntarily and happily, religion
and vassalage. . . . I do not doubt they will be happy,
because the respectable union of the two pueblos
of Spaniards offers the advantage of attracting docilely
the heathen Indians to reduction and vassalage.

TEODORO DE CROIX, 1781

Contents

Maps

Preface

Over three days—July 17, 18, and 19, 1781—Quechan Indians destroyed two Spanish mission-pueblos at the junction of the Gila and Colorado Rivers, at what would come to be known as the Yuma Crossing. The results of this "Yuma Massacre" were to prove one of the most crucial events of borderlands history. Indeed, one historian has asserted that "the Yuma disaster still stands as the greatest calamity to befall the Spanish on the northwestern frontier of New Spain."[1]

The impact of the Yuma revolt on the development of Spanish California was especially significant. The renowned historian Charles Edward Chapman characterized it as a crucial event in the development of Alta California:

> The Yuma Massacre closed the overland route to Alta California, and with it passed Alta California's chance for early populous settlement. It meant that gold was reserved for discovery in 1848. . . . Alta California settled down to an Arcadian existence, able to live happily and well, and to keep out

the casual foreigner but not populous enough to thrust back up the river valleys where lay the magic gold, which, had it been discovered, would at once have changed everything.[2]

Although Chapman's assessment may have been mixed with a bit of historical speculation, borderlands scholar David J. Weber detailed the actual effect of the uprising on California's development. "After the Yuma revolt of 1781 . . . no large influx of soldiers or colonists arrived, no additional presidios were built, and only one more town was established. . . . The closing of the Sonora road in 1781 had made California dependent once again on the sea for all communication with New Spain, and the province offered no attractions that would prompt immigrants to make the arduous ocean voyage."[3]

Spanish Arizona was also profoundly affected by the event. Weber notes: "Much as the Comanche attack on San Sabá a generation before had dashed Franciscan plans to build a chain of missions from San Antonio to Santa Fe, the Yuma rebellion of 1781 had brought an abrupt halt to . . . dream[s] of extending missions up the Lower Colorado River and into central Arizona."[4]

Although the importance of the Yuma Massacre has often been acknowledged, curiously relatively little has been written about the actual event itself, and even less about the Spanish settlements that precipitated the uprising. Indeed, much of what has been written is often of a summary nature, and at times incorrect. This is not surprising given the fact that most of the works that have touched on this subject were primarily concerned with broader historical themes or were biographies of famous individuals.

I have tried in this work to tell the complete story of the Spanish attempt to settle and control the Yuma Crossing from beginning to end, with the primary focus on the planning, execution, and disastrous unfolding of the two hybrid mission-pueblos sent out in December 1780. Parts of the story, such as the two expeditions of Juan Bautista de Anza through the Yuma Crossing to Alta California and the missionary wanderings of Father Francisco Garcés, are familiar and have been dealt with extensively elsewhere. However, other facets have been virtually unknown.

For example, the missions and/or settlers were actually at Yuma between August 1779 and July 1781, a period of time much longer than is usually portrayed. Furthermore, in the wake of the destruction of these establishments, the Spanish launched four punitive expeditions, which were among the largest and most complex military operations seen on the frontier. Several hundred Spanish soldiers and Indian auxiliaries battled against like numbers of Quechan and Mohave warriors in an extremely bloody campaign that resulted in a series of wars that raged along the lower Colorado River for more than fifty years.

As history is, by its most common definition, the interpretation of past events through written accounts, I have, of necessity, relied on sources that primarily present the points of view of the Spanish participants. Nevertheless, I have attempted to interpret the motivations and actions of the Indian participants in these events when possible, especially in regard to the nature of leadership within Quechan society and the hostility between the Quechan and Maricopa leagues. I have also attempted to examine the personality of the Quechan chieftain Salvador Palma.

As to the names of Indian tribal groups, I have for the most part utilized historical Spanish terms as being the most recognizable. For example, I have employed the names *Papago* and *Apache* rather than the more correct usage of *O'Odham* or *N'de*. The most notable exception is that I have consistently used *Quechan* for the people the Spaniards identified as *Yumas*. Given the number of references to the geographic locality of the *Yuma* Crossing, as well as the anthropological *Yuman* language groups, this seemed not only correct, but expedient.

In writing this story, much information was available in previously published primary and secondary works or in university dissertations and theses. For those sections I have acted merely as compiler and organizer. However, other aspects have required original research, translation, and personal interpretation. I hope that I have done these accurately and correctly.

Acknowledgments

I would like to thank my friends and fellow historians Rick Collins and Jeff Coleman for their help in reading and critiquing the manuscript in its early phases. Thanks also to Ron Beckwith for his accurate and graceful maps, and Joanne O'Hare and the staff of the University of Arizona Press for their guidance and support. I would especially like to thank my sons, Edward, Alexander, and Justin, for bearing with me during the research and writing of this book. Their filial piety and constant good humor have brought me great joy. Finally, to my wife, Dawn Moore Santiago, for her superb historical and editing skills. Without her constant and consistent help, this book would not have been possible.

Massacre at the Yuma Crossing

1

Wayfarers and Rivalries

*First Contacts between the Spaniards
and the Quechans, 1540 to 1771*

As THE GRAY-ROBED PRIEST trudged along, he did not realize that he
was lost. He had been following the Gila River for many days, knowing
that it emptied into the mighty Colorado. However, heavy rains had
swollen the waterways, thus causing the priest to miss the junction. As
he moved southwest along the Colorado, he believed that he was still
following the Gila.[1]

As he continued on, he met a man he thought was a member of the
Pima nation that lived along the Gila. In reality, his new companion was a
Quechan, or Yuma, Indian. The two began to converse in the Papago
language and the priest identified himself as Padre Francisco Garcés, from
the Spanish mission of San Xavier del Bac. The other introduced himself
as Olleyquotequiebe, "the one who wheezes." As they talked, neither
could have known the consequences of their meeting. The man would

3

cause the death of the priest; the priest would shatter the man's life. Both would change the course of their peoples' history.[2]

However, on this particular day Father Garcés simply wanted to know where he was and asked his new acquaintance where the Colorado River lay. Perplexed, "the one who wheezes" replied that the priest was standing next to it. But Garcés did not believe him.[3] Nevertheless, the two men quickly became friends. Olleyquotequiebe led the priest to nearby villages, where the residents entertained Garcés with feasting and dancing. Then, over the next two days, Olleyquotequiebe escorted the Franciscan among his people. Impressed by the amount of wheat, melons, and squash the Quechans produced, Garcés concluded that they might be ready for conversion to Christianity.[4]

But pleasant diversions aside, the priest had to finish his journey. When Garcés again asked where the junction of the Gila and Colorado lay, "the one who wheezes" indicated that they had passed it and suggested that they return the way they had come. The priest still refused to believe he had missed the confluence of the rivers and insisted on heading south. The Quechan gave up trying to convince the Spaniard, and the two men bid each other farewell.[5]

Father Garcés continued his journey, following the Colorado downstream. A few days later, a group of Indian warriors found the Franciscan praying on the banks of the river and helped him cross by building a raft. Garcés continued on, vainly seeking what he had already found. He wandered westward, then northward. He still believed Olleyquotequiebe and his people had deceived him. Eventually, he found another Indian settlement. The residents told him of more padres, "seven days distant." Although he was tempted to try to reach them, Garcés decided to turn eastward, where he soon located the Colorado River. Having finally found his original destination, he returned home to San Xavier del Bac.[6]

To many, Father Francisco Garcés seemed more comfortable among Indians than among Spaniards. Since his arrival in the northern frontier in 1768, he had demonstrated a willingness to listen to the Indians and to learn their ways, an invaluable asset in converting them to Christianity. As did many other missionaries, Father Garcés regarded the Indians as lost in the darkness of sinfulness and ignorance, from which only the faith of Jesus Christ could lead them. Many of these same missionaries demonstrated pastoral and fraternal love for the Indians, but Garcés went one step further. He genuinely liked them.[7]

Combined with this affection, Father Garcés demonstrated an apostolic wanderlust that sent him visiting and preaching to Indian peoples far beyond his mission of San Xavier. He dreamed of advancing the faith and expanding Spanish power northward from Sonora into Alta California. Spanish expansionism and Christian missionary zeal dovetailed in Father Garcés, and when he turned his gaze toward the junction of the Gila and Colorado Rivers, later known as the Yuma Crossing, both forces followed. As a result, this Franciscan, more than any other single individual, would determine Spanish relations with the Quechans. Thus, the chance meeting between the gray-robed priest and Olleyquotequiebe in August 1771 launched the Spanish Empire on a collision course with the Quechan nation.[8]

It was not until after Father Garcés returned home that he realized he had opened a route across the Sonoran Desert to California. The news of his journey reawakened the dreams of generations of Spanish explorers. Since the 1600s, both the Spanish crown and religious missionaries had plans to occupy the coasts of Alta and Baja California. For the crown, controlling California was strategically important in the face of English, Dutch, and Russian incursions into the waters of the Pacific. In fact, after Sebastián Vizcaíno discovered Monterey Bay in 1603, the government developed plans to establish bases in California to protect and supply the passage of the Manila Galleon's yearly excursion, carrying Spanish wealth from the Philippines. But, these plans were not implemented and no permanent occupation occurred.[9]

Where the crown did not succeed, missionaries made progress. In 1697, members of the Society of Jesus led by Father Juan María Salvatierra established themselves on the sterile peninsula of Baja California, a thousand miles south of Monterey Bay. The black-robed Jesuits began to build missions and slowly crept inland. Difficulties in supplying these new foundations led to several attempts to open a passage from the mainland of Sonora to the Baja California missions. For example, in 1701/1702 the renowned Jesuit explorer Eusebio Kino traveled from his mission outpost in the Pimería Alta of northwest Sonora, down the Gila River to its junction with the Colorado. He then followed the great river to its mouth and down into lower (Baja) California. Though many believed California to be an island, Kino satisfied himself that it was a peninsula and that supplies from Sonora could sustain the Baja California missions.[10]

To open this new route, Kino advocated the advance of Spanish control northward to the Gila and Colorado Rivers. From this point, links between Sonora and the missions of Baja California could be forged, and also future settlements in Alta California, perhaps at Monterey Bay, could be both established and supplied. The Spaniards might also be able to move eastward and connect with the colony of New Mexico. Kino even went so far as to muse that if the Gila and Colorado Rivers linked California, Sonora, and New Mexico, the three provinces could establish trade with Japan and the remainder of the Orient.[11]

Father Kino's idea struck home with many black robes, resulting in a new wave of Jesuit exploration between 1730 and 1750. Most notable was the Bavarian Jacobo Sedelmayr. Between 1743 and 1750, he explored regions north and south of the Gila and Colorado Rivers. His findings confirmed Kino's earlier accounts of the feasibility of supplying the lower Baja California missions from Sonora and the possibility of contacting New Mexico as well. The results of Sedelmayr's journeys spurred both the Spanish government and the Jesuit order to make new preparations for pushing the frontier north to the Gila and Colorado. However, plans came to an abrupt halt when Sonora suffered a series of revolts by the Yaqui, Mayo, Pima, and Seri Indians. The disruption caused by these uprisings, coupled with the constant raids of the Apache Indians, stifled all attempts at expansion.[12]

In the 1760s, the Spanish crown renewed its interest in a northward expansion, this time spurred by long-standing European rivalries rather than Jesuit activities. As the Seven Years' War came to a close in 1763, Spain suffered a humiliating defeat at the hands of Great Britain. The British seizure of Cuba and the Philippines, two vital regions, made manifest the vulnerability of the Spanish Empire to foreign attack. King Charles III of Spain, convinced of the inevitability of another war with Britain, prepared for the coming conflict. He set about to overhaul completely the military structure of Spain and her colonies.[13]

Within the larger, empirewide scheme of Charles's reforms, Sonora and California were distinctly secondary. The 1763 Peace of Paris left Spain and Britain as the only remaining major colonial powers in North America. The Spanish acquisition of Louisiana from France placed her in the position where her territory directly bordered onto the British possessions east of the Mississippi River. Furthermore, in the Caribbean, Britain's gain of Florida exposed Spanish Cuba to the threat of a renewed assault.[14]

To Charles III and his ministers, the nexus of Spain's North American defense was the silver-producing provinces of the Viceroyalty of New Spain, in central Mexico. Thus, fortifications in Cuba and along the Caribbean coastline as well as the formation of a dependable standing army were crucial to ensure the flow of Mexican silver; these were, therefore, the primary areas of the government's concern. Yet the vast northern frontier of the viceroyalty, stretching from California east to Illinois, and south to Florida, offered opportunities for Spain's rivals; even if the frontier were not to see a full foreign invasion, it at least might be the focus of diversionary attacks. To forestall this likelihood, Charles III dispatched several of his ablest advisers to the region. As part of developing their plans, they assessed the frontier situation as well as the entire military and financial capabilities of the viceroyalty. The most powerful and influential of these advisers was the *visitador* José de Gálvez.[15]

Gálvez ultimately initiated two complementary programs that dealt directly with the viceroyalty's northern boundaries. The first called for the reorganization and retrenchment of the frontier zone between the Gulf of California and the Gulf of Mexico, known as the Interior Provinces of New Spain. This area was to be placed under a unified military command better to cope with the incursions of hostile Indians. Second, Gálvez recommended a drive northward along the Pacific coast into the region of Monterey Bay. Together, Gálvez hoped that these two projects would advance Spanish power into areas claimed but now unoccupied, produce new wealth for the crown, and provide an effective defensive buffer against both European and indigenous enemies.[16]

Gálvez saw Spain's primary enemies along the Interior Provinces not as Europeans but as the numerous Indian peoples. Such groups as the Apaches and Comanches had continuously resisted Spanish religious and military pressures and in many areas had even halted or reversed expansion. Although these peoples did not actually threaten Spain's hold along the northern frontier, they did drain financial and military resources that were needed elsewhere. Furthermore, the Indians' proximity to British colonies created the specter of hostile tribes directly assisting the British, or at least acting as surrogates throughout the region.[17]

In addition, Spain's European rivals might use the unoccupied Pacific coastline against her: Since 1741, the Russians had been moving from their bases in Alaska, southward toward territory claimed by Spain. The British, having taken over Canada from the French, might also now present a potential threat to this area, if they moved westward across the Rocky Mountains from their trading stations along Hudson's Bay and the Great Lakes. Gálvez, therefore, planned the occupation of Alta California as another buffer against Spain's European foes. Like Kino before him, he also envisioned a lucrative increase in Spanish trade with the Orient.[18]

But Gálvez soon found his plans beset by changing governmental policies. For more than two centuries, the Spanish crown had expected the regular missionary orders of the Roman Catholic Church to lead the way in establishing control over new areas by converting the natives to Christianity. However, the reforms of Charles III in the 1760s meant that the military, not the religious, began to dominate Spain's Indian policies. The power of the missionary orders waned.[19]

Gálvez and other bureaucrats assumed that in pressing the Sonoran frontier northward, military and religious personnel together would demonstrate to the natives the self-evident superiority of Spanish arms and the Christian faith. But they soon found themselves in the center of a paradox: although they favored religious conversion of the Indians, they opposed the institutions charged with implementing them. As a man of the Enlightenment, José de Gálvez criticized both the methods and the results of acculturation that the religious orders used to convert the Indians. Foremost among these was the process of missionization.[20]

Since the sixteenth century, Spanish monarchs had allowed Roman Catholic religious orders to congregate some indigenous peoples into self-sufficient communities, popularly called missions. Theoretically, these communities would allow for the most rapid religious conversion and cultural assimilation of the natives into Spanish society. Once they had been converted to Christianity and had absorbed European social and cultural values, the mission communities would be dissolved and the Indians would be independent tax-paying and revenue-producing members of the republic. The religious orders would then reestablish the missions among new, unassimilated indigenous peoples, repeating the cycle.[21]

In spite of numerous setbacks, the mission system achieved remarkable results; its worth to both the Roman Catholic Church and the Spanish crown was self-evident. But, by the eighteenth century, if not before, critics of the system emerged. They claimed that the missions kept some Indians isolated in a state of perpetual dependence, rather than integrating them into society. Furthermore, the critics maintained that the religious orders that ran the missions did so in order to exploit the wealth the communities produced.[22]

José de Gálvez and many other Spanish bureaucrats, deeply resenting the independence the religious orders displayed in operating the missions, favored curtailing the power of the orders. They wanted to "reform" the old systems of religious conversion with more pragmatic policies, such as stripping the missionaries of their control over mission property and finances. They also favored a general move toward what was termed secularization. This position held that after ten years the religious orders and their regular priests should be replaced at the missions by secular priests who answered to a local bishop. The mission would then become a new parish within the diocesan organization of the church. The lands formerly held in common by the missions would be distributed in individual parcels to the Indians living there; the natives would then be subject to normal tithes and taxes, which would support the resident priest and the machinery of government.[23]

Those who favored reform of the missions never really questioned the need for the conversion and assimilation of Indians, but they did question who controlled the machinery of conversion, especially the personnel and the supporting funds.[24] The advocates of reform were especially critical of the Jesuit mission system, and they used this as a rationalization to suppress the order. The international connections and material power of the Society of Jesus both alarmed the absolutist tendencies of Charles III and offended the Enlightenment sensibilities of his ministers. In 1767, following the lead of Portugal and France, the Spanish king ordered the Jesuits out of all his possessions. In New Spain, Gálvez enthusiastically oversaw the expulsion of the black robes. The following year, the government turned Jesuit missions in Baja California and Sonora over to the Franciscan order. Spanish expansion toward Alta California and the Gila and Colorado Rivers was now to be advocated by the sons of St. Francis as vigorously as it had been by the disinherited sons of St. Ignatius.[25]

But when the Franciscans took over the Jesuit mission territories in lower California and Sonora, they found themselves constrained by a new set of regulations designed to enhance the agenda of reform and secularization at the expense of the traditional system of missionization. Naturally, the Franciscans resented these moves, complaining that they inhibited their ability to convert the Indians successfully.[26]

Both the Franciscan order and the Spanish government advocated expansion northward toward the Gila and Colorado Rivers, but the methods to be used for that expansion were in dispute. The Franciscans hoped to convert the region with the traditional mission system. Many Spanish administrators believed that by curtailing the power of the Franciscans, the perceived abuses of missionization could be eliminated and the conversion and assimilation of the Indians hastened. Both sides strove for the same end, but their means often seemed mutually exclusive. In advancing the frontier to the Gila and Colorado, the Spaniards carried with them a confusion of power and authority.[27]

Despite their differences, the ambitions of José de Gálvez and the missionary zeal of the Franciscans merged into a common desire to push Spanish power northward from Sonora into Alta California. However, the geographical and cultural complexities of the region were unknown to both Spanish bureaucrats and priests, and in the grand scheme of empire, the natives of the Colorado River region were only dimly recognized, let alone considered. To the power brokers in Madrid and Mexico City, the Quechan Indians were a little known and insignificant group, yet they would prove to be the crucible in which lay Spain's plans for northern expansion.[28]

The home of the Quechans was a natural gateway controlling the route to California. This location, the Yuma Crossing, was a bottleneck in the Colorado River, where it narrowed as it passed between a series of hills, allowing it to be forded easily. Directly upstream from the crossing, the Gila River emptied into the Colorado. The Indians since time immemorial had followed the course of the Gila as they traveled eastward and westward. This route, "the Gila Trail," as it would come to be called, was one of the few perennial sources of water when traversing the vast Sonoran Desert; it funneled human traffic inexorably to the Gila's junction with the Colorado. Therefore, if the Spaniards were to fulfil their plans for expansion into California, they had to pass through the Yuma Crossing. But use of the crossing required the acquiescence of the Quechans.[29]

The Quechans had occupied this region for an indeterminate period of time. According to their traditions, the creator Kwikumat sent all the Yuman-speaking peoples to populate the Colorado River region. Unlike their neighbors, the Quechans followed a special path to their new homeland. From this journey, called *xam kwatcan* (another way going down) the Quechans drew their name. Eventually they occupied a large area, with their villages spread out for many miles on both banks of the Colorado, on either side of the junction, and eastward up the Gila.[30]

For more than two centuries before Father Garcés and Olleyquotequiebe met in 1771, the Quechans had been aware of the Spaniards' presence. The first encounter between the two cultures occurred in 1540 when two ancillary expeditions supporting Francisco Vásquez de Coronado's search for the famed Seven Cities of Gold reached the Yuma Crossing. Hernando de Alarcón, a lieutenant of Coronado, sailed up the Gulf of California to the mouth of the Colorado River and then ascended in small boats as far as the Quechan villages in an attempt to resupply the expedition. A few months later, another of Coronado's officers, Melchor Díaz, and his party rode overland to the Yuma Crossing, but failed to locate Alarcón. Both Spanish expeditions had prolonged contact with the Quechans and their neighbors before departing.[31]

Sixty-five years later, in 1604/1605, Juan de Oñate, the Spanish conqueror of New Mexico, visited the Quechan. Oñate, lured by fables of rich kingdoms somewhere in the interior of North America, had set out westward to locate them. His expedition traveled across what is now northern Arizona, then followed the Bill Williams River to the Colorado. Oñate and his thirty men moved downstream, passing the Yuma Crossing to reach the mouth of the river at the Gulf of California.[32]

Though Alarcón, Díaz, and Oñate had extensive, though brief, contacts with the Quechans, they did not have any permanent effects on the natives. Indeed, it was not until the end of the seventeenth century that the Spanish presence influenced the natives of the Colorado River region to any great degree, and then only indirectly. As the Jesuits spread their missions among the Indian groups of Sonora, European crops, especially wheat, diffused northward.[33] The Jesuits also brought European animals to the missions of Sonora, and the practice of raising livestock also spread; by the first half of the eighteenth century, horses evolved into a valued commodity among the natives of the Colorado and Gila Rivers. When Father Jacobo Sedelmayr visited the Yuma Crossing in 1749 and 1750, he found the Quechans fascinated with the horses and saddles of his military escort. The priest was able to maintain peaceful relations with the Quechans, but other neighboring Indians attempted to seize the Spanish horses by force. In the resulting skirmish, several natives were killed.[34]

Father Sedelmayr's experience heralded the rapid expansion of live-

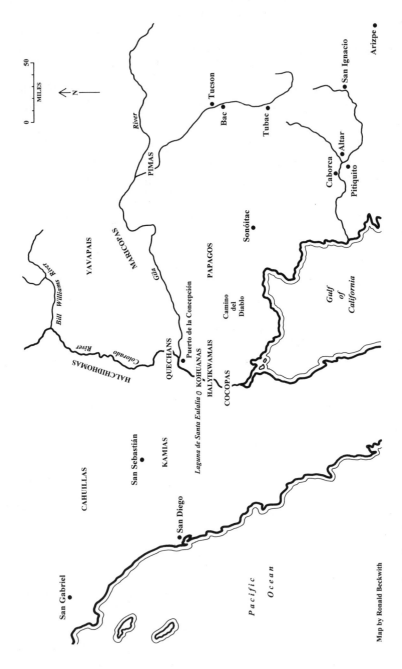

MAP 1. Indian tribes of the Lower Colorado River region in the late eighteenth century.

Map by Ronald Beckwith

stock into the region. Between 1730 and 1770, numerous Indian groups throughout Sonora rebelled against Spanish expansion. During these conflicts the natives acquired horses from the Spaniards through combat or theft and came to view the animals as a necessity. To get horses of their own, the Colorado River tribes dealt with groups such as the Papagos, who through direct contact with the Spaniards had developed breeding stock. By the 1770s, the Quechans and other peoples along the Colorado also raised their own herds of horses.[35]

As the novelty of European crops and livestock changed the traditional cultural patterns of the aboriginal peoples of the region, the proximity of the Spaniards exacerbated long-standing rivalries and hatreds among them. Warfare, long a part of the natives' lifestyle, apparently accelerated. One of the major reasons may have been their desire to obtain slaves, which could be bartered for European goods, food, and horses. The Papagos and Pimas traded horses and other goods to the Quechans and other Indians of the Colorado and Gila Rivers in exchange for slaves. The slaves were then resold to the Spaniards in Sonora, who employed them as cheap labor. As this demand for slaves increased, so did warfare among the Quechans and their neighbors.[36]

Gradually, two federations of mutually hostile tribes emerged—the Quechan League and the Maricopa–Gila Pima League. Yuman tribes of the lower Colorado and middle Gila Rivers, all of whom were racially and culturally akin to each other, formed the core of each league. Over the centuries, the two factions forged links with other neighboring peoples, and these ancient friendships coalesced into the federations. The rival River Yumans allied themselves with the Pimas and Papagos of northwestern Sonora, the Upland Yumans and Paiutes of the Colorado Plateau, and several California groups. The resulting patchwork of long-standing enmity stretched from southern California east through Arizona, and from the delta of the Colorado River north to the Grand Canyon.[37]

The core of each federation lay with the most powerful tribe of that faction. The Quechan League centered on the Quechan nation with their close kinsmen, the Mohaves, as second in power. The Mohaves lived up the Colorado River, along both banks north of the Bill Williams River. The Quechans and the Mohaves linked themselves with the Yavapais, an Upland Yuman people who lived southeast of the Mohaves. The league also contained several Piman-speaking groups: the Desert or Sand Papagos, the Western Papagos, and the Upper Pimas from the region near

Caborca, Sonora, southeast of the Yuma Crossing. Rounding out the federation were the Kamias of southern California, a Yuman-speaking people with close cultural links to the Quechans, and the Chemehuevi Paiutes, living at this time near present-day Lake Mead, Nevada.[38]

Opposed to the Quechan League was the Maricopa–Gila Pima League, which was led by the Maricopas, another River Yuman tribe. In the 1770s, the Maricopas were divided into two major groups, the Maricopas proper (or Opas, as the Spaniards called them), and the Kaveltcadomas (or Cocomaricopas). Their stronghold lay in the middle Gila River region, near present-day Gila Bend. Directly to the east of the Maricopas lived their most powerful supporters, the Pimas of the upper Gila River. Although ethnically distinct, both peoples had developed similar agricultural lifestyles, fostering mutual interdependence.[39]

The rich croplands cultivated by the Maricopas and the Pimas were coveted and constantly raided by numerous aboriginal enemies, including members of the Quechan League. As a result, the two tribes sought alliances with other native groups. Prominent among these were the River Yuman Cocopas of the Colorado River delta, who held a traditional and fierce hatred of the Quechans, as well as the Paipais of northern Baja California, close kinsmen of the Cocopas. North of the Yuma Crossing, the Maricopa League included the Halchidomas, River Yumans residing between the Gila and the Bill Williams Rivers and sandwiched by the Quechans and the Mohaves. Other members of the alliance included the Cahuillas, a Uto-Aztecan-speaking people who occupied the area to the northwest of Yuma in the San Bernardino Mountains, and the Walpais, Upland Yumans who lived to the northeast on the fringes of the Grand Canyon. South of the Gila River, the federation included the Eastern Papagos, whose settlements bordered on Spanish territory.[40]

Militarily, the two leagues were roughly equal, resulting in indecisive and endemic warfare. Small-scale raids for plunder or for revenge were interspersed with major campaigns in which several hundred warriors per side participated. League "armies" traveled more than a hundred miles to attack enemy villages. Although the elevated social status generated by successful combat enriched many warriors, the slaves garnered and sold directly or indirectly to Spaniards resulted in more immediate tangible benefits.[41]

Both federations realized that contact with the Spaniards provided material advantages in the form of horses and iron to use for weapons. As a result, many of the tribes displayed a willingness to maintain friendly relations with the white men. Therefore, contact between the members of both federations and the Europeans was common. If the Spaniards could be induced to become allies of one side or the other, that federation's power would undoubtedly prove decisive.[42]

Although some Spaniards in Sonora obviously understood the complexities of the rivalry between the Quechan and Maricopa leagues, these nuances were totally lost on government officials in Madrid or Mexico City as plans for expansion moved forward. On the other hand, the Quechans and their neighbors were just as unaware of the division among the Spaniards over the policies of missionization and methods of acculturation.[43] Thus when Father Garcés encountered the Quechan Olleyquotequiebe in August 1771, their meeting presaged a historical turning point. For the Spaniards, it opened up the prospect of controlling the Yuma Crossing, the linchpin of their planned expansion into California. For the Quechans, it promised a potential ally, more powerful than any tribal league. The ambitions and desires of both nations were fueled by the hopes of gain from the other. However, the ulterior motives of each were obscure and mutually unintelligible. Father Francisco Garcés and "the one who wheezes" had set their nations down the same path. As they walked together along the banks of the Colorado River in the sweltering August heat, neither man could know whether their peoples would journey as friends or part as enemies.

2

The Gate Unlocked

Opening the Road to California,
August 1771 to May 1774

WHEN FATHER GARCÉS turned his gaze toward the junction of the Gila and Colorado Rivers, Spanish expansionism and Christian missionary zeal followed. Consequently, this Franciscan more than any other single individual determined Spanish relations with the Quechans. His new acquaintance, Olleyquotequiebe, for his part viewed the Spaniards as the key to helping the Quechans in their wars with the members of the Maricopa federation. In their common desire, Garcés and "the one who wheezes" worked to bring a permanent Spanish presence to the Yuma Crossing.

Perhaps it was Garcés's peasant origins that sparked his affection for the Indians of the northern frontier. To him they were simple and unsophisticated people, inured to the vagaries of nature. He had grown up in the hills of his native Aragón among such people, simple and unsophisticated farmers and herders. Born on April 12, 1738, he was the fourth child of Juan Garcés and Antonia Maestra. His parents lived in the small village of Morata del Conde, south of Zaragoza, as tenant farmers of the count of Morata, like almost all the other inhabitants. He was baptized on the day after his birth in the parish church which sat next to the count's palace. The infant's uncle Francisco Garcés, the count's personal chaplain, stood as godfather. In his honor Juan and Antonia named their newborn son Francisco Tomás Hermenigildo.[1]

From an early age, young Garcés showed an inclination toward a religious life. A second uncle, Domingo Garcés, served as rector of the nearby village of Chodes and apprenticed the boy as a helper in the parish chores. By fifteen, Francisco determined he would enter religious life and petitioned the local bishop to join the Order of Friars Minor, commonly known as the Franciscans. Once approved, Garcés entered the Convento de San Cristóbal de Alpartir, whose members, the Recollects, observed a strict version of the rule of the order as originally laid down by St. Francis of Assisi. Though other Franciscans, known as Conventuals, felt the rule to be too harsh and impractical, Brother Francisco found the discipline to his liking.[2]

For several years Garcés studied, first classics and philosophy at Alpartir and later theology in the city of Calatayud. By age twenty-four, he completed his studies, and in 1762 he was ordained a priest. Late in that same year, he volunteered for ten years of missionary service in Mexico and joined a group of twenty-three recruits bound for the Franciscan College of Santa Cruz in the city of Querétaro, north of Mexico City. On August 1, 1763, Father Francisco Garcés embarked at the port of Cádiz for America, never again to see the hills of Aragón.[3]

During the four years following his arrival in Querétaro, he prepared to become a missionary. The Santa Cruz College was one of several autonomous Franciscan institutions in Mexico that maintained missions among the Indians of the far north. In imitation of their founder, the Querétaran friars wore habits of undyed gray wool, symbolizing that they, like St. Francis of Assisi, had dedicated themselves to "Lady Poverty." They practiced a strict asceticism designed to harden the body and the soul for the rigors of the frontier. To prepare for the day when the recruits would go out among the heathen, the Santa Cruz friars occasionally sent out "home missions" to preach and minister to the citizens of Querétaro and the surrounding regions. The college superiors felt Father

Garcés was "simple and artless" and too young to hear the confessions of the worldly women of Querétaro. Therefore, they relegated him to ministering to the young, where he soon became known as "the Children's Padre." Like his fellow recruits, Garcés hoped for the day when he might be sent to the college's frontier missions in Coahuila and Texas.[4]

In 1767, the members of the Santa Cruz College were stunned by the news of the expulsion of the Society of Jesus from the kingdom. Viceroy the Marqués de Croix asked the Franciscan order to reoccupy the scores of vacant Jesuit missions in Baja California, Sonora, and the Tarahumara country. Eventually, fifty-one friars went forth. For the College of Santa Cruz de Querétaro, its portion to minister was "part of the region of Sonora and the Pimería."[5]

On August 5, after a solemn religious service, fifteen volunteers, including Francisco Garcés, left for the northern frontier. At the town of Tepic, 123 miles north of Guadalajara, they got their first hint of the momentous changes occurring in Sonora and California, into which they were to be thrust. The *visitador* José de Gálvez was organizing a major military campaign. His primary purpose was to crush a rebellion of the Seri Indians along the Sonoran coast, but in addition he planned to use the operation to advance the frontier northward into Alta California. The visitador ordered the Franciscans to join his troopers at the port of San Blas by late August. To conserve resources, the friars and soldiers would together take ships north to Guaymas, Sonora, and Loreto, Baja California. However, Gálvez's grand plans had not reckoned with a shortage of vessels and contrary winds in the Gulf of California. The last of the Franciscan friars and Spanish soldiers did not reach their destinations until April 1768.[6]

Those Franciscans heading for the Sonoran missions disembarked at Guaymas and traveled several more weeks to their assignments. For Father Garcés, the Santa Cruz College superiors selected the most northern of all posts, the Mission of San Xavier del Bac. Garcés first stopped at the presidio of San Miguel de Horcasitas to receive last-minute instructions and load up on provisions before journeying the final two hundred and fifty miles. On June 30, 1768, he finally reached his station on what was literally "the rim of Christendom."[7]

San Xavier lay in the midst of what the Spaniards labeled the "Pimería Alta," the land of the Upper Pima Indians. Located in the vast Sonoran Desert, the Pimería Alta contained eight missions with about three thousand Indians congregated around them. The Jesuits had founded all of these missions in the late seventeenth and early eighteenth centuries, and at least a veneer of Christianity had been established throughout the area. Most of Father Garcés's flock at San Xavier were "river Pimas"— agriculturists who cultivated the valleys of the Santa Cruz and San Pedro Rivers, tributaries of the Gila River. Several miles north of the mission lay a subpost, or *visita*, at the Pima village the Spaniards called Tucson. At these two places, Garcés found several hundred men, women, and children over which he had been granted spiritual authority.[8]

Besides his duties at his post, Garcés longed to proselytize the many Indian peoples in the surrounding region among whom Christianity had never been established. To the north, resided the Pimas of the Gila River, kinsmen to the villagers at San Xavier. To the west lived the Papagos, who, ethnically linked to the Pimas, had developed a unique culture within the heart of the deserts and mountains of the region. Beyond the Papagos lay the Yuman peoples, the Maricopas, the Quechans, and others, of the lower Gila and the Colorado Rivers, all still only vaguely known to the Spaniards. To the east, ranged the dreaded Western and Chiricahua Apaches, whose raids on the riverine Pimas pre-dated the coming of the Europeans and whom the Spaniards knew far too well. The Apaches now preyed regularly on the Spanish missions and not even an idealist like Father Garcés hoped to convert them.[9]

On August 29, almost two months to the day after he reached San Xavier, Francisco Garcés set out on his first of six missionary journeys into the unknown, which ultimately triggered Spain's attempt to expand northward to the Colorado River and into Alta California. This time he went out to preach to the Papagos and Pimas, accompanied only by a single Indian companion.[10] After several weeks, Garcés returned favorably impressed, especially with the Gila River Pimas. He felt that they were prime candidates for conversion to Christianity. Two years later, in October of 1770, he again left San Xavier to preach to the Papagos and the Pimas. Determined to cover new ground, the Franciscan traveled down the Gila River until he came upon the Maricopas, the first of the Yuman peoples he would meet.[11]

From the Maricopas he heard some exciting news. They told him of a party of white men operating to the west, beyond the great Colorado River. Garcés realized that this report was of an expedition sent out by José de Gálvez. The visitador's plans of 1768 to defeat quickly the rebellious Seri Indians of Sonora and to organize Baja California to serve as a base for occupying Alta California had not turned out as Gálvez had predicted. By 1769 the Seri's remained defiant, holed up in Cerro Prieto, their mountain stronghold, while the sterility of Baja California mocked the idea of using it as a supply line to the north.[12]

In the midst of these setbacks, there had been one notable success. In 1769/1770, a combined land and sea expedition under the command of Captain Gaspar de Portolá founded a mission and presidio at San Diego, in the southernmost portion of Alta California. Portolá then pushed far to the north and set up a second outpost at the long-dreamed-of Monterey Bay, which he grandiloquently labeled as the capital of Alta California. Portolá enhanced his success by discovering an even greater natural harbor north of his ramshackle capital, which he named San Francisco. Although the settlements at Monterey and San Diego existed tenuously, they had finally established Spain's presence in Alta California.[13]

Upon hearing the stories of the Maricopas, Garcés knew they were about Portolá's men. When the priest returned to San Xavier in November, he no doubt sent word of these reports of white men to Captain Juan Bautista de Anza, commander of the presidio of Tubac, located forty miles to the south of the mission. However, Captain Anza had already received the news through his own Indian informants. Both Anza and Garcés immediately grasped the significance of the news the Indians had brought. If word of Portolá's men had come to Sonora, men from Sonora could retrace the path and reach California. The problem consisted of exactly where the path lay and who could find it.[14]

José de Gálvez was determined that the Spanish presence in Alta California remain permanent. Though the viceroy gave his full support, Gálvez was the one who had to provide the solution. Gálvez realized that his initial plan of using Baja California as the supply base for the new settlements at San Diego and Monterey was not feasible. He had only two alternatives: one, he could send supplies by ship from the port of San Blas, but this option was risky as the vessels would have to navigate more than one thousand miles in contrary winds; two, he could supply the California settlements overland from the province of Sonora. The reports from Captain Anza and Father Garcés proved that communication between Sonora and California was possible, and for Gálvez they raised the hope of establishing the lifeline the new settlements desperately needed.[15]

Establishing a new supply route required a measure of peace and stability in Sonora. Originally, Gálvez planned to crush the Seri Indians quickly and then lead his forces against the Apaches, but the Seri campaign had developed into a protracted guerrilla war with no end in sight. In the meantime, the Apaches took advantage of most of the Spanish troops' concentration in the Cerro Prieto to raid the rest of the province almost unopposed. Despite his assumption of personal command of Spanish forces in May 1769, Gálvez could not bring the campaign to a successful close.[16]

Late in that same year, the idea of establishing a new route to the California settlements lost momentum when Gálvez suffered a mental breakdown that left him fighting bouts of temporary insanity. Viceroy Croix, convinced that Gálvez's failures had caused the breakdown, insisted that the visitador return to Mexico City. Once in the capital, Gálvez's health gradually improved. Then both he and Croix sent to the Spanish crown proposals to develop an overland route from Sonora to Alta California. However, in 1771 both Gálvez and Viceroy Croix were recalled to Spain; without their presence, the plans for California seemed to evaporate.[17]

While Gálvez struggled in vain against the Seris, the Franciscans of the Pimería Alta began making plans of their own. Father Garcés and his fellows saw the design for California as complementing their own ambitions to expand their missionary efforts. The success of Garcés's visits to the Papagos, the Gila River Pimas, and the Maricopas provided the catalyst. The padre declared a huge harvest of souls awaited; they needed only missions and missionaries. To Garcés and his superiors, both in the Pimería Alta and at the College of Santa Cruz de Querétaro, the opportunity seemed heaven-sent: they would be able to establish their own chain of missions, as well as administer the vacant Jesuits posts.[18]

They were quick to add that the expansion of "the rim of Christendom" also held benefits for the Spanish crown. Missions along the Gila River would bring the Pimas and Spaniards into closer alliance against their common enemy the Apaches, perhaps forcing the latter to go on the defensive. The new missions also offered the opportunity to establish contact with the Hopi pueblos and beyond to the colony of New Mexico. Finally, missions along the Gila would secure any road from Sonora into California on its approach to the Colorado River. Pushing the mission frontier to the north would fulfill the ambitions of José de Gálvez while enriching both the crown and the faith.[19]

However, to take advantage of this opportunity, the Franciscans would need support in the Spanish government. They began to cultivate it when the father-president of the Franciscan missions in the Pimería Alta personally attended Gálvez for more than two months during his mental breakdown. As he nursed the visitador back to health, Father Mariano Antonio Buena y Alcalde told his patient about Father Garcés's journeys. He painted in glowing terms the opportunities that Garcés had opened up; the Spaniards could push the frontier north to the Gila and Colorado Rivers, strike at the Apaches, and secure the links between Sonora and California. Gálvez eagerly leaped at the suggestions of the father-president; he assured him of his support for the effort and declared that he would personally visit the areas explored by Father Garcés. Though Gálvez's illness prevented him from inspecting the frontier first hand, the Franciscans of the Pimería Alta felt that they had received, more or less, official approval for expanding their missionary efforts. When Gálvez returned to Spain in 1771 to become the newest member of the Council of the Indies, he again expressed his assurance to the Franciscans that he still strongly supported the expansion effort.[20] After Gálvez's departure, the friars remained undeterred. They now pressed their point of view just as strongly to the newly arrived viceroy, Antonio María de Bucareli. However, Bucareli was not a man to act precipitously. He listened to the Franciscans and then set about to examine thoroughly the entire situation before he would undertake any action.[21]

Once again, far removed from the corridors of power, Father Garcés pushed events forward. Convinced that the plans to build new missions on the frontier were as good as done, he undertook another expedition. On August 8, 1771, he departed from San Xavier, ostensibly to locate sites for new mission establishments on the Gila River. "I went," he later wrote, "with the determination that if divine providence should open a way to me I should do something more for the greater glory of God and acquire more information in order to put into practice the decree so important to the service of both Majesties."[22]

He disappeared into the unknown for three months. In his wanderlust, Garcés fulfilled his wish, acquiring crucial information to help implement his plans. The Franciscan pressed all the way down the Gila River to its junction with the Colorado; there, his historic encounter with the Quechans took place, and he had made many friends, among them, especially, his erstwhile guide Olleyquotequiebe. In addition, after crossing the Colorado River, he came within several days' journey of the new settlements of California. On October 31, Garcés showed up at the Mission of Tubutama, some one hundred miles southwest of his station at San Xavier. The resident missionary, Father Esteban de Salazar, undoubtedly relieved to see his long-missing fellow Franciscan, described Garcés as "appearing in good condition, fat, happy, and contented."[23]

As on his previous *entrada*, Father Garcés shared the details with Captain Anza, commander of the presidio of Tubac. Anza thought the padre a fool to have undertaken such a journey in the first place; however, despite his feelings, he interested himself in the reports of Garcés's latest expedition. Anza saw a chance to capitalize on the priest's explorations. In 1737, Anza's father, also a frontier military captain, proposed to the Spanish crown to lead an expedition to find an overland route to California; the project had stalled, however. Now, in 1771, the younger Anza began to make plans to lead an expedition from Tubac to California. His idea held an element of opportunism as well as family pride.[24]

Anza's first step was to discuss with Father Garcés the details of the priest's wanderings. For several months they talked about the region beyond the Colorado River, especially the location of watering holes and mountain ranges and the disposition of the region's Indian tribes. The two men came to the conclusion that the desert west of the Colorado was not impassable and that the distance between Sonora and Monterey was not as great as supposed. As a result of these discussions, on May 2, 1772, Anza wrote to Viceroy Bucareli, formally requesting authorization to open a road between Sonora and California. He also petitioned that Father Garcés be allowed to accompany the expedition as guide.[25]

For several months, Viceroy Bucareli considered Captain Anza's request. With characteristic thoroughness, Bucareli consulted numerous experts and officials and requested detailed reports from both Anza and Garcés. As he assembled this data, the viceroy also received pressure from Spain. José de Gálvez, now a member of the Council of the Indies, urged the approval of Anza's request. Potential Russian and English expansion into the Pacific Ocean continued to worry the Spanish government; therefore, Gálvez argued that the road's opening would benefit Spain by securing the California coast against other European powers. Furthermore, Gálvez maintained that the road would help push the mission frontier northward from Sonora and eventually link it with California and New Mexico.[26]

On September 9, 1773, nearly two years after Father Garcés returned, Viceroy Bucareli called a *junta de guerra* (war council) to deliberate on the defenses of the northern frontier, especially Alta California. The council saw Anza's proposal for opening up a road from Sonora to Monterey as part of a larger plan to guard against the Russians. After reviewing all the assembled data, the council recommended that Anza proceed with the expedition, with Father Garcés accompanying him as adviser. The entire weight of Spain's northern expansion would rest upon this expedition. The defenses of Alta California, the establishment of missions along the Gila and Colorado Rivers, and the linking together of Sonora, California, and New Mexico depended on the results.[27]

Captain Anza received the approval of Viceroy Bucareli and the junta de guerra in the fall of 1773 and at once began to make preparations. Anza's task was eased considerably when in December he received an unexpected asset. At the presidio of Altar, a California Indian, Sebastián Tarabal, appeared. He had fled the Mission of San Gabriel with several companions, crossing the desert toward the Colorado River. All of Tarabal's companions had died of exposure, but he had managed to reach the river where the Quechan leader Olleyquotequiebe rescued him. "The one who wheezes" then delivered Tarabal to Altar, the closest Spanish settlement. The California Indian expected to be punished by the Spaniards for deserting the mission, but instead Anza enlisted him as a guide for his upcoming expedition. Anza realized that with the combined experiences of Tarabal, who had made it from the California coast to the Colorado River, and Father Garcés, who had traveled from Sonora to west of the Colorado, he should be able to trace the route into California.[28]

Anza also saw that the Quechans would have to be handled skillfully if the expedition was to be successful. Both Tarabal's and Garcés's journeys had intersected at the junction of the Gila and Colorado Rivers, the heart of Quechan territory. For the Spaniards to cross the Colorado, the friendship of the Quechans was essential. If they proved hostile, it would be next to impossible to continue to Alta California. To both Anza and Father Garcés, the key to winning the Quechans over was obvious—"the one who wheezes," Olleyquotequiebe.[29]

Years prior to meeting Garcés along the Colorado River in 1771, Olleyquotequiebe had established links with the Spaniards. He had traveled several times to the Spanish mission of Caborca and there developed a friendship with the mission's mayordomo, a man named Palma. Soon, "the one who wheezes" adopted the name of his friend, and the Spaniards called *him*, too, Palma. The Quechan had also visited Altar on an annual basis, possibly to trade slaves for European goods. When Olleyquote-quiebe rescued the runaway California Indian, Tarabal labeled his Quechan benefactor as Salvador (savior). This name, too, stuck, and from then on the Spaniards knew Olleyquotequiebe as Salvador Palma.[30]

When Palma delivered Tarabal to Altar, Captain Anza took advantage of the opportunity to interview the Quechan. Anza informed Palma of the upcoming expedition to California and asked his assistance in maintaining order when the Spanish passed through Quechan territory. Palma assured the captain that his people would welcome the white men. To Anza, Palma clearly possessed a certain amount of leadership among the Quechan tribe, but the extent of his power was unknown. However, Anza reasoned that he could secure the support of both Palma and his people by showering the leader with favors and liberally dispensing goods to the other Quechans.[31]

On January 8, 1774, armed with an abundance of presents for the Quechans and the unexpected guide Sebastián Tarabal, Anza's expedition departed the presidio of Tubac to open the road to California. The party consisted of Anza and twenty of his troopers, five Indian muleteers, four Indian laborers and interpreters, one soldier from California to show the way from San Diego to Monterey, Father Garcés, and another Franciscan, Juan Marcelo Díaz. Ultimately, thirty-four men, sixty-five cattle, and one-hundred-forty horses headed for California.[32]

Anza stopped and gathered last-minute supplies at the presidio of Altar and then, on January 18, headed northwest through the land of the Papagos. Father Garcés described this route—what later travelers would call El Camino del Diablo—as "that terrible road." But Anza was determined to take the most direct path to the Gila River. They reached the river on February 7, several miles upstream from its junction with the Colorado. From the nearby Quechan villages, Salvador Palma and a large following of his tribesmen came out to meet them in a show of respectful hospitality. Anza liberally reciprocated, regaling Palma with symbols of authority and to "confirm" him as leader of his people. He then dispersed beads and other trinkets among the Quechans, winning over many of the tribe.[33]

Unknown to the Spaniards at the time, Palma had more than earned the gifts they gave him. As Anza's party approached their lands, many Quechans saw the Europeans as invaders and prepared to attack them.

Palma dissuaded those tribesmen who favored war by arguing that the Spaniards had never done the Quechans any harm; he also pointed out that the white men were friendly with the Papagos, close allies of the Quechan. When his arguments failed to persuade all the people, Palma declared that he would take up arms in the Spaniards' defense, even if he stood alone. His threat worked, and the tribe decided to let the white men come in peace.[34]

Salvador Palma's authority among the Quechan tribe was not clear to the Spaniards. They realized that he was a chieftain of some import and would later ascribe to him the leadership of the whole nation on terms approaching absolutism. However, this perception was far from the truth. Leadership among the Quechan was extremely fluid: an individual exercised authority based upon *icama* (dream power). The Quechans believed that the conscious and the subconscious were a continuum; therefore, a person's dreams determined success or failure in the conscious realm. If one dreamed well, power would be manifested in the physical world; if one dreamed poorly, failure would follow.[35]

In terms of tribal leadership, dream power came in two primary forms: military and political. War leaders, called *kwanami*, emerged when a man showed prowess in battle. What might be termed civil leaders, known as *pipa taxan* (for the good of the people) were also present. Each extended family or village usually had several. Sometimes, a unique individual would be felt to possess such strong dream power that the people recognized him as the leader of the whole nation. He gained the title of *kwoxot*, meaning simply, "the good."[36]

The kwoxot exercised both civil and military authority over the tribe, but the position was not permanent. If his dream power waned, he could be replaced. Also, even if he maintained his authority, the dreams of individual Quechans might not be in harmony with the wishes of the kwoxot, and his power over them remained limited. The individualism of Quechan society, coupled with the fact that leadership was based on the performance of the leader, could bring about constant shifts among those persons exercising military and political power. The failure of the Spaniards to understand this facet of Quechan society led them to assume that Salvador Palma would and could control his people in an absolutist fashion and that he spoke for the entire tribe, always and everywhere.[37]

Palma himself was not about to disabuse the Spaniards of their opinion of him. Among his people, he had attained the reputation of a great and successful warrior and was undoubtedly a kwanami of some standing. In his youth he had probably witnessed the 1744 visit to the Quechans of the Jesuit Father Sedelmayr and his military escort, and like his fellows he probably had been impressed with the horses and guns of the white men. Palma's visits to the Mission of Caborca and the presidio of Altar had reinforced his opinion of the Spaniards, and he had the wisdom to see that they could be a great force for his people. The meeting with Father Garcés in 1771 and now the arrival of Captain Anza reinforced his desire to obtain Spanish support. To this end, he now bent his will and his dreams.[38]

Palma's threat to protect Anza and his party from any attacks had increased his stature among the Quechans. After Anza bestowed beads and other trade goods on the tribe, Palma's stock rose higher. Many Quechans obviously felt that Palma's icama—his dream power—about the benefits of welcoming the white men was true. When Anza asked for help in crossing first the Gila and then the Colorado Rivers, the Quechans, under Palma's leadership, constructed rafts to ferry the Spaniards across both rivers. Once the crossing had been made without loss, Anza gave more gifts to the Quechans, again proving Palma's icama. The doubts the Quechans might have had about the Spaniards evaporated amid the glass beads and bolts of cloth the white men spread among the tribe.[39]

Having established friendly relations with the Quechans, Anza headed his expedition westward; however, the sand dunes immediately west of the Yuma Crossing proved to be too much. The captain decided to abandon much of his impedimenta and exhausted animals and set out for the California Mission of San Gabriel with a reduced force. He left the majority of his animals and most of his supplies, along with three soldiers and four muleteers, under Palma's protection. With Father Garcés and Sebastián Tarabal serving as guides, Anza departed the Colorado River on March 2, 1774. The Spaniards successfully negotiated what is today the Imperial Valley and the San Jacinto Mountains, reaching Mission San Gabriel twenty days later. A route linking Sonora and California had been established. Anza and Garcés had finally accomplished what José de Gálvez and other Spanish leaders had dreamed of for so many years.[40]

Meanwhile, at Yuma, Salvador Palma scrupulously protected the Spanish goods and animals left in his care. Not long after the Spaniards' departure, the Quechans picked up a rumor that Anza and his party had been ambushed and destroyed by hostile Indians. Despite Palma's promises of continued protection, the seven soldiers and muleteers left at Yuma fled back to Altar with many of the horses. Undeterred, Palma continued to guard the remaining animals and equipment that Anza had entrusted to his care. His constancy was rewarded when Father Garcés and twelve others returned to the Colorado on April 25. Captain Anza and the remainder of the expedition arrived soon after, on May 10.[41]

Garcés and Anza both praised Palma's behavior and promised him great rewards for his assistance. Despite the success of the expedition in opening a road from Sonora to California, the Franciscan and the captain were realistic about the fragile nature of the new route. Clearly, the Quechans could close the new road any time they chose. Crossing the Colorado was difficult, and Anza and his men had successfully done so only with considerable aid from the Quechans. Anza summed up the situation succinctly when he later wrote to Viceroy Bucareli: "If the peoples who dwell along this great river are attached to us, we will effect its passage. . . . [I]f they are not, it will be almost impossible to do so."[42]

To insure the support of the Quechans, the Spaniards needed the cooperation of Salvador Palma, and they now set about to woo him. To reinforce Anza's earlier public "confirmation" of Palma's authority as "governor" of the Quechans, the Spanish captain again publicly renewed his support for Palma: Anza made it clear that Palma's position was backed by the power of the white men. If Palma had not been kwoxot—"the good"—before this, Anza's declaration probably firmly established Palma's leadership of the Quechan nation.[43]

For his part, the Quechan leader must also have realized that the Spaniards could give his people more than beads and cloth. An alliance with the white men would increase the power of the Quechans in comparison with their neighbors. The possibility of a permanent peace between the rival Quechan and Maricopa–Gila Pima Leagues appeared; should the enemies of the Quechans spurn an end to hostilities, the military power of the Spaniards could then be turned against them. Palma's plans had already achieved some notable success. Probably stimulated by Father Garcés's visit during his journey in 1771, the Quechans, led by Palma, in the intervening three years had concluded peace with several of their fiercest enemies. These included the Halykwamais and Kohuanas to the south on the Colorado River and some of the Maricopas along the Gila. However, enmity still existed between the Quechans and many other peoples.[44]

Captain Anza, Father Garcés, and their companions left the Colorado River on May 15, 1774. Anza urged Palma to maintain peace with the neighboring tribes and to bring to Sonora any Spaniards that might come among the Quechans. The captain then presented Palma with a staff of office and rewarded him with several cattle and bolts of cloth. Anza concluded the ceremony by admonishing the Quechans to obey the commands of Palma. The captain later reported that he wished he could have given Palma more presents, "for his equal is not to be found amongst his kind." When Anza and his party left Quechan territory, a milestone was reached for both peoples. Quechans and Spaniards had taken the measure of the other and both had developed ulterior motives for assisting each other.[45]

3

The Gospel on the River

Franciscans Preach to the Quechans,
1775 to 1776

VICEROY BUCARELI in Mexico City received news of the success of Anza's expedition in June, 1774. He soon started preparing to send colonists and soldiers over the new route to strengthen the settlements in Alta California. He also seriously considered advancing the Spanish frontier in Sonora by establishing missions and presidios along the Gila and Colorado Rivers. For several months, he gathered information on the best locations for these establishments and their potential costs and benefits. Captain Anza and Fathers Díaz and Garcés compiled reports on their experiences for the viceroy to review.[1]

As part of his fact-finding investigations, Bucareli requested that both Anza and Garcés travel to Mexico City to deliver their accounts of the expedition in person. However, an illness prevented Father Garcés from complying with the command; instead, his fellow Franciscans began assembling a series of Garcés's written recollections and recommendations to forward to Bucareli. Meanwhile, Anza proceeded to the viceregal court in November, 1774, where after delivering his report he was regaled and rewarded by Bucareli, and promoted to lieutenant colonel.[2]

For more than two months, the viceroy discussed with Anza the prospect of outfitting a second expedition to Alta California. This time Anza would shepherd a large number of colonists across the new road, and Bucareli was determined that the expedition be planned thoroughly. Simultaneously, the viceroy questioned Anza on the placement of missions and presidios on the Gila and Colorado Rivers. Anza declared that the major emphasis should be on placing missions among the Quechans to secure the new route. Though he felt that Salvador Palma could be used to maintain the friendship of the Quechans, Anza still recommended that in addition a large military garrison be set up along the Colorado.[3]

Soon after, Bucareli received Father Garcés's written reports concerning the new road to California. To his surprise, he found that they were somewhat at odds with Anza's recommendations. When Anza and his party left the Yuma Crossing to return to Sonora in May of 1774, Garcés separated from the main party to head north. The wandering Franciscan spent several months visiting and preaching to the Halchidoma Indians who lived along the Colorado River. Father Garcés became convinced that a road from Sonora through the Halchidomas' lands would be easier and more direct to the Spanish settlements at Monterey. As a result, Garcés advised the viceroy to establish missions among the Halchidoma as well as the Quechans and to give a more northerly road from Sonora to Monterey preference over Anza's Yuma route.[4]

Despite the differing opinions between Anza and Garcés, the reports of both men reassured Viceroy Bucareli of the feasibility of the Yuma route. Realizing that the selection of mission and presidial sites would need further discussion, Bucareli decided in the meantime to dispatch the second expedition, commanded by Anza, of colonists and soldiers to travel over the new road to Alta California. As for the Quechans, the viceroy ordered that the Spaniards liberally give gifts to them and continue cultivating Salvador Palma so that he would lead his people into a closer association with the white men. To this end, Bucareli ordered Father Garcés and another Franciscan to accompany Anza on this new journey as far as Yuma. Once there, the priests were to live among the Quechans to prepare them for missions. Exactly how many missions and when they would be established Bucareli did not specify, saving the exact details for the future.[5]

On October 24, 1775, Lieutenant Colonel Anza departed from Tubac on his second expedition to California, having assembled a party of 240 men, women, and children. Anza and three other officers, along with Father Garcés, Father Pedro Font, and Father Thomas Eixarch, led the group. Twenty recruits with 165 dependents were to garrison and colonize the new settlements in Alta California. Eighteen soldiers from Sonora, including ten veterans of Anza's first California trek, acted as escort. Thirty cowboys, mule packers, interpreters, and servants completed the roster.[6]

After reaching the Gila River, Anza led his party downstream and approached the Colorado junction on November 27. Salvador Palma, another chieftain whom the Spaniards named Pablo, and a large number of Quechans greeted the travelers on their arrival. Palma showed great delight at the Spaniards' coming and, according to Font, "went about saluting everybody, giving an embrace to each, men, women, and children alike." Despite this warm welcome, Father Pedro Font was skeptical of Palma's authority over the Quechans. Font confided to his diary that the basis of Palma's leadership was his "intrepidity and verbosity," and especially "the esteem the Spaniards have shown him recently."[7]

The next day, Palma escorted the Spaniards to a village where the Quechans had constructed a large *ramada* to shelter the expedition. The troopers delighted the Indians by firing a salute with their muskets, and a festive mood permeated the camp. Soon after, a leader of one of the Maricopa groups, named Carlos, appeared with an entourage and ostentatiously concluded a peace treaty with Salvador Palma. Father Font remarked that this peace had been urged upon the tribes by Father Garcés and Lieutenant Colonel Anza during their previous visit, especially after Anza had warned them "that the king did not wish them to have wars, and that if any tribe injured another, Spaniards would come to avenge the wrong."[8]

When the expedition first arrived, Palma asked Anza if the colonists had come to live among the Quechans. The commander answered that they were going elsewhere, but that Spaniards would come to settle among Palma's people "in due time." That evening, Father Font, through an interpreter, talked with Palma at great length. He asked the Quechan if he wished that "fathers should come to live there with his people." When

Palma assured the Franciscan that this would please him greatly, Font explained that the Quechans would need to learn Christian doctrine as well as masonry and carpentry and to "live together in a pueblo . . . and not scattered out as now, and that they would have to make a house for the father and a church." Palma agreed, declaring that "he and his people wished to be Christians, and friends with the Spaniards." To this end Font informed Palma that Fathers Garcés and Eixarch would stay among the Quechans while Anza escorted the colonists on to California.[9]

On the following day, Palma demonstrated his goodwill toward the Spaniards by having his people aid the expedition in the difficult task of fording the Colorado. After crossing without loss, Anza proceeded to Palma's village, where it was agreed that the Quechans would build a home for Fathers Garcés and Eixarch. Then Anza presented the Quechan leader with a set of clothes, a "shirt, trousers, a jacket with a yellow front and some decorations, a cape . . . of blue cloth decorated with gold braid, and a cap of black velvet adorned with imitation jewels and a crest like a palm." The commander then gave the rest of the people in the village presents of glass beads, cloth, and tobacco.[10]

With his European suit of clothes and the gifts from the Spaniards still in hand, Palma's prestige among his people must have soared. The material benefits of friendship with the white men were further enhanced by the promise of peaceful relations between the Quechans and their neighbors. Not only had the Maricopas led by Chief Carlos made peace, but some Halchidoma Indians from the north had also appeared and shown a friendly disposition. The promise of a Spanish alliance would clearly tilt the balance of power in the region in favor of the Quechan League.[11]

On December 4, Anza and the bulk of his party set out from the Yuma Crossing. They successfully reached their destination and established the settlement of San Francisco in Alta California. In the meantime, Fathers Garcés and Eixarch remained at the river, along with three Indian interpreters, two muleteers, and two servants. For the first time, Spanish priests had come to live among the Quechans for an extended period. The impact of this initial encounter would go far in determining future relationships.[12]

Father Thomas Eixarch had been sent on the expedition for the express purpose of catechizing the Quechans. The day after Anza's departure, he found himself virtually alone among his new charges, when Father Garcés set out on yet another journey. Viceroy Bucareli had given Garcés permission to gauge the attitudes of the surrounding tribes regarding Spanish settlements in the region. On December 5, Garcés headed down the Colorado to visit the tribes there, taking with him two interpreters and the California mission Indian, Sebastián Tarabal, who was serving as a muleteer.[13]

Padre Eixarch immediately set about organizing himself to preach to the Quechans. Salvador Palma proved foremost among his tribe in attempting to learn the Christian faith and, along with Chief Pablo, waited constantly upon Eixarch. "These two captains do not leave me alone at all during the entire day," Eixarch wrote in his diary. "They are so prompt with everything I request of them that it is a matter to marvel at."[14]

For several days, the padre slowly began to indoctrinate Palma, Pablo, and other Quechans in the rudiments of the Christian faith. They had long discussions on the nature of God, attended mass, and recited the rosary. When Palma expressed regret that all the good things he was learning would be forgotten after Father Eixarch departed "because there would be no one to teach him," the Franciscan replied that he "would soon return and remain there always, but that it would be necessary to go and speak with the king in order that he might send soldiers and Spaniards" to live among the Quechans. Palma was content with this answer, but Father Eixarch was concerned that the mission project among the Quechans might stall. "The stage is well set," he wrote prophetically, "and if the superiors do not devote themselves to bringing the matter through, I believe that they will be responsible in this affair."[15]

Despite his fears, Eixarch continued his spiritual ministry. He soon discovered that the wine he used for mass was putrid and on December 11 dispatched one of his Indian servants along with Chief Pablo to the Mission of Caborca to bring back fresh wine, as well as more candles and sacred hosts. As they were about to depart, an Indian courier arrived with letters from Captain Anza, and Father Eixarch forwarded these as well. The priest continued to hold discussions with Palma and other Quechans about spiritual matters, often giving gifts of beads and tobacco to the listeners. Eixarch noted that Palma "greatly pleased me, for he is now learning the essentials."[16]

Besides the spiritual welfare of the Quechans, the Franciscan discovered other matters that concerned him. He soon confronted the intertribal slave trade, wherein the Indians often sold war captives to the Spaniards. One day, an elderly Quechan offered to sell to the padre a captive Apache boy, about six years old, in exchange for a horse. After the trade, Eixarch bitterly wrote, "There are many half-breed gentlemen who pride themselves on having Indian captives in practical slavery, ignorant . . . of the fact that the Indians were born free, and that doubtless they have . . . purer blood than their half-breed Spanish lordships."[17]

On January 3, 1776, Eixarch was delighted when Father Garcés returned from his wanderings. The following day, Chief Pablo came back from Caborca with the wine and other supplies. For his part, Father Garcés felt he had made remarkable progress among the tribes south of the Quechans. On his previous journey of 1771, he had urged the tribes to cease their constant wars. Garcés reported to Eixarch that many of the Indians had followed his warnings and made peace with one another and that prosperity had been the result.

Buoyed by these successes, Garcés and Eixarch began to redouble their efforts to spread Christian modes of behavior among the Quechans. They soon convinced Palma to abandon the widespread practice of polygamy and set aside his many wives. Palma complied and announced that he would now consort only with the mother of his six children. He also harangued his tribesmen to follow his example, but with little visible result.[18]

More successfully, the two priests convinced the Quechans to continue peaceful relations with their neighbors. Several groups of Halchidomas, Cocomaricopas, and Yavapais all came to visit the Spanish holy men. Father Garcés showed these visitors special attention, giving them presents and urging them to stop making war. Not to be outdone, Palma made several appearances, wearing his European uniform and brandishing his baton of office. He declared that he desired peace with all his neighbors, not out of fear but because "the king who ruled the Spaniards had given him the cane in order that now he might not fight with anybody." When a few of the Halchidomas said that they may not want peace, Palma replied that if they wanted war, he and his Spanish allies would teach them the error of their ways.[19]

Amid these peace negotiations, Father Eixarch decided to move his and Garcés's lodging to the top of a small hill, about two miles downstream, where the muddy Colorado cut a path between two large prominences. "With propriety they call this place a pass," Father Eixarch noted, "for there are two very high hills between which flows the great Colorado River." Father Garcés on his earlier journeys had christened this natural pass lying at the junction of the Gila and Colorado Rivers as Puerto de la Concepción. Eixarch chose to lodge on the hill on the north bank, observing that this would be a good place to settle Spaniards, "for they will have everything that could be desired for human existence." Eixarch's words were again prophetic, for this would be the exact spot that the Spaniards would choose to settle in the near future.[20]

Assisted by Palma and Chief Pablo, the priests soon had a spacious wattle-and-daub house atop the hill of La Concepción. When they moved into their new lodgings on February 5, the padres were surprised to find that Palma and Pablo had moved their homes to the foot of the hill to be closer to the gray robes. "Other families have done the same," Eixarch wrote, "so that from the daily assemblage of men and women it already looks like an established pueblo."[21]

Not all of the Quechans were so taken with the Spaniards living among them. When Lieutenant Colonel Anza had departed for California, he had again left in the care of the Quechans a number of animals, some for the Franciscans to use and others too exhausted to continue. A few days before moving to La Concepción, the priests found Father Garcés's horse wounded in the belly. Afterwards, Eixarch noted that the Spaniards' horses, mules, and cattle "have destroyed the wheat of the Yumas by eating it and trampling it down." The Quechans blamed the wounding on some Halchidomas, but, Eixarch concluded, "I think it was the Yumas."[22]

The Christian faith the priests were preaching had also lost its appeal to some Quechans. "We have noticed that some old Indians entertain the foolish notion that those who are baptized immediately die," Eixarch wrote. Father Garcés had baptized three adult Indians and one infant, all of whom were sick and near death. Official Franciscan policy stipulated that the missionaries not administer baptism to Indians until they sufficiently understood the nuances of the sacrament. The priests would baptize unconverted natives only when they were near death and, therefore, from the Christian point of view, in danger of losing their soul. This policy worked against the Franciscans. "Father Garcés and I," Eixarch noted, "are disabusing them of their error and . . . they are becoming convinced."[23]

On February 14, Garcés again left Eixarch alone with the Quechans, this time to visit the tribes to the north. Father Eixarch continued with varying success to preach Christianity to the Indians. On Ash Wednesday, he gave ashes to Palma and several other Quechans, noting that

Palma "is very much attached to the things of the church." However, Chief Pablo had not taken to the new Christian ways. He refused to give up his many wives and had not attended mass or the rosary for many weeks. Padre Eixarch concluded that Pablo "does not believe the doctrine which is taught . . . whereas . . . Palma practices it to the best of his ability."[24]

Despite Pablo's seeming rejection of Christian doctrine, or perhaps because of it, Father Eixarch convinced the recalcitrant Quechan to accompany him on a visit to the presidio of Altar and the surrounding missions. Setting out on March 4, the Quechan and the Franciscan crossed the Camino del Diablo and managed to reach the Papago village of Sonóitac. There, Pablo's horse gave out. Continuing on foot, Pablo accompanied Eixarch as far as the mountains near the Mission of Caborca. At this point the padre uncharitably abandoned Pablo, who apparently returned to Yuma on his own while Eixarch visited the Franciscans at the missions of Caborca, Oquitoa, Atil, and Tubutama. After more than a month with his fellows, the priest returned to the Yuma Crossing on April 15.[25]

Upon the padre's return, he had more trouble with Pablo and other Quechans. The priest dispensed gifts to "numerous men, women and children, who manifested the great joy they felt at my return." Many natives regularly attended Christian religious services, for which Eixarch was thankful. However, others displayed reluctance in accepting his religious teachings. Several instances exemplified Eixarch's failure to strengthen his position. The padre baptized a sick child "out of necessity," but when the youngster died, some Quechans blamed Eixarch. Soon thereafter, more than a hundred Quechans attacked four visiting Halchidomas to whom the priest had given gifts. With great difficulty, Father Eixarch rescued the four visitors from death. Even Palma, although he continued his reverence and attendance at Christian ceremonies, complained to Father Eixarch about the Spaniards' "dilatoriness."[26]

Meanwhile, Chief Pablo increased his resistance to Eixarch's teachings. The priest labeled him "a great wizard" and complained that Pablo had recently practiced traditional Quechan healing ceremonies on a sick man rather than calling on the priest to minister to the patient. Eixarch originally had thought highly of Pablo, but he now felt otherwise. He noted in his diary that even Palma was looking for someone to replace Pablo as chief. The Franciscan claimed that the people of Pablo's own village wanted to kill him and only the intervention of Palma saved him.[27]

Father Eixarch realized that the white men's presence had caused problems for the Quechans. He observed that the Indians had suffered a shortage of wheat, beans, and corn, but they had reaped a surplus of other crops. The padre acknowledged that the Spaniards contributed to the shortage because "the horses, mules, and cattle which the expedition left . . . have eaten up nearly all the wheat." He felt responsible and realized that something should be done. "These damages which these poor people . . . suffer might be in justice . . . made good with some equivalent. On whom does this obligation rest?" His failure to find an answer to this problem again presaged troubles in the relationship between Quechans and Spaniards.[28]

Despite these problems, Palma's leadership, based on his pro-Christian and pro-Spanish policies, was in the ascendant. Pablo represented Quechan traditionalists who opposed the presence of the white men; however, he had not demonstrated the dream power necessary to lead the people. This fact was graphically demonstrated when, on May 11, 1776, Lieutenant Colonel Anza and his troopers returned from California. Again, Anza liberally dispensed gifts among the tribe, and again the power of the white men was plain for all to see. The icama of Salvador Palma had again been proven right. Soon, the kwoxot assured his people, the Spaniards would come to stay.[29]

4

Hopes and Promises

Spanish Plans to Settle at Yuma, 1776 to 1777

SALVADOR PALMA was in a quandary. His leadership role among the tribe, his standing as kwoxot, had been assured by his policy of cooperation and accommodation with the white men. He had enriched the tribe with material possessions and had secured peace with many of the neighboring nations, increasing the stature and power of the Quechans throughout the region. But how could Palma maintain these benefits and, therefore, his authority once the white men had gone?

The answer of course was for them not to leave but to stay and establish a permanent presence. Only then could the Quechans assure themselves of a ready supply of European goods, horses, and tools; of prestige and power among their neighbors; and of the spread of the new teachings of Christianity, already embraced by Palma: only then would the kwoxot's leadership become unquestioned.

Palma had asked Anza many times about the Spaniards coming to live among the Quechans, but the commander only offered vague promises for the future. Father Eixarch, Father Font, and Father Garcés also promised to bring settlers, but the Franciscans said they first needed to speak to the king and the king's viceroy, who was far away in the great city of Mexico. Tired of the delays and excuses, Palma made a momentous decision. If the king of the white men needed to be consulted, the kwoxot of the Quechans would go to see the king.[1]

Anza had spoken to Palma before about taking the Quechan leader to Mexico and was not overly surprised to hear the chieftain raise the subject again. However, the colonel was concerned that if Palma left for Mexico City, Spanish influence among the Quechans might evaporate. He decided to consult with Father Font and Father Eixarch on the matter. "We deliberated whether or not it would be well to take him," Font confided to his diary, "and whether any disturbance might arise among the Yuma tribe or on the river during his absence."[2]

On the night of May 12, Anza, Font, and Eixarch interviewed Palma and several of the Quechan elders, and the kwoxot again pressed his request to go to Mexico. Father Font noted that Palma wanted to tell the viceroy "that he and his Yumas greatly wished and would be very happy if Spaniards and fathers would come to their lands to live with them." Anza warned Palma that he might be gone for more than a year and that he ought to take several of his tribesmen to accompany him. The colonel also stipulated that Palma should consult with his people to ensure the continuation of peaceful relations with their neighbors and the pro-Spanish policy instituted by Palma.[3]

To all this, the kwoxot had already prepared his answers. He responded that he gladly would stay a year among the white men. As for the governance of his people, he had selected new leaders—those elders who came with him to the interview. To one of them, Padre Font recalled, Palma delivered a quiver of arrows "that he might defend the country from its enemies and rule on the river." Palma then chose his own brother and two other Indian youths, one of whom was a son of Chief Pablo, to accompany him to Mexico, in order, Anza stated, "that they may witness to the good treatment which he may receive."[4]

Having satisfied himself that Spanish influence among the Quechans remained secure, Anza prepared to return to Mexico City. Father Garcés, however, had not come back from his northern explorations. Anza heard that the Franciscan was among the Halchidomas, nearly twenty leagues north of the Yuma Crossing. He sent a letter to Garcés by a native runner, telling the priest that he had until May 14 to rendezvous with the main party. When Garcés failed to show, Anza decided he could wait no longer, but would leave supplies for the padre with the Quechans. On May 15, Palma and his entourage, with Anza, Font, Eixarch, and the entire expedition except Garcés, left Yuma.[5]

As they departed, the colonel again noted how vital the goodwill of the Quechans was in the difficult crossing of the Colorado River. "In all this journey," Anza wrote in his diary, "I have not been . . . so tired out . . . as in effecting the crossing." A host of Quechans saw their kwoxot and the Spaniards off. "All urged me to come back bringing fathers and Spaniards," Anza recalled, "and they repeated the same to their captain [Palma]."[6]

Father Garcés returned more than three months later, on August 27, to claim the provisions left him. The Quechans were surprised to see him, having heard rumors that the northern tribes had murdered the wandering Franciscan. Numerous people crowded around to see the Spanish priest, "for they had already mourned me as one dead." When Garcés told his curious hosts that he had to return to his mission of San Xavier, they informed him that the journey would be a waste of time. Lieutenant Colonel Anza and their kwoxot had gone to fetch priests and Spaniards to settle along the river, and they would soon return. The Quechans were so confident of this and that Garcés would be assigned to the new settlements that they invited the priest to stay with them in the interim.[7]

Somewhat surprised by the offer, Father Garcés assured the Quechans that he would indeed return soon and that Spanish settlements were being planned; however, as pressing business at his mission awaited him, he managed to bid his Quechan hosts farewell. Traveling eastward along the Gila, Garcés found the Maricopas and the Gila Pimas also certain that Spanish missions would soon come to their country. By the time he reached San Xavier, he realized that a great moment of opportunity had arrived.[8]

Even before setting out with Anza on his second journey to California, Father Garcés had suggested to his superiors and to Viceroy Bucareli that they establish missions and a presidio among the Gila Pimas in the Spanish thrust northward. Although conceding that settlements among the Quechans were of primary importance, Garcés felt that the Pimas should not be neglected. The priest argued that the Gila Pimas had acculturated more to European ways than the Quechans, and as enemies of the Apaches they would assist the white men against the common foe. Furthermore, Garcés maintained, a road linking Monterey, Sonora, and New Mexico could be established among the Gila Pimas, a route that he felt would be superior to Anza's Yuma trail.[9]

The preceding seven month's wanderings had convinced Father Garcés that his opinions were correct. Before his return to San Xavier on September 17, he had traveled from the Yuma Crossing, north across the great central valley of California to Mission San Gabriel. From there, he headed eastward to the Hopi pueblos, just a few days journey from New Mexico, before returning to the Colorado River. With the single exception of the Hopis, all of the Indian peoples Garcés encountered proved cordial. He felt that many of these tribes would willingly accept Christianity and that missionary efforts should begin among them. More importantly, Garcés proved that communication between Alta California, Sonora, and New Mexico was feasible. The grandiose dreams of José de Gálvez and others to link these three provinces together now seemed within Spain's grasp.[10]

Garcés's belief in a route centered on the Gila River did not preclude him supporting the establishment of a Spanish presence among the Quechans. In correspondence with Viceroy Bucareli prior to leaving on the expedition, Garcés had suggested that Spanish settlers be sent to the Colorado River under the protection of a military presidio. Such a move could be affected, the padre reasoned, by the transfer of the two Sonoran presidios of Horcasitas and Buenavista northward, one to the Gila River and the other to the Colorado. These forts would then not only protect the missions at the Yuma Crossing, but also provide support for Garcés's plans to convert the Gila Pimas.[11]

The priest's suggestion involving the movement of military garrisons was not out of place. The Spanish crown's efforts to strengthen the northern frontier had seen a concerted review of the entire military establishment. The result was the formation of a new military command reporting directly to the viceroy and responsible for the establishment of a defensive line of presidios stretching from California to Texas. The officer charged with this realignment was the first commandant inspector of the Interior Provinces, don Hugo O'Conor, an Irish officer in Spanish service and a loyal supporter of Viceroy Bucareli.[12]

When Garcés suggested moving the presidios of Buenavista and Horcasitas northward, he did so with the knowledge that O'Conor had already decided to close those forts because they did not fit into the defensive barrier he was creating. As a result, the viceroy approved Garcés's idea for moving the presidios. With O'Conor's concurrence, Bucareli ordered the presidios transferred upon the completion of Anza's second expedition. However, when O'Conor wrote on December 15, 1775, informing Father Garcés of the approval for the relocation plan, the priest had already departed for the Colorado.[13]

Lieutenant Colonel Anza, on the other hand, disagreed with Father Garcés about where Spanish power should be applied in the region. Anza opposed placing presidios or missions along the Gila, preferring instead to concentrate on establishing settlements along the Colorado River to protect the route he had opened to California. Knowing that Anza had traveled to Mexico City to see the viceroy, Garcés believed that the colonel might prejudice Bucareli against his own ideas. When he returned to San Xavier in September, the Franciscan immediately set about to press his case.[14]

A week after arriving, Father Garcés wrote to the viceroy; he told him of the success of his travels and promised to send a copy of the detailed diary he had kept during his wanderings. Garcés stressed to Bucareli that the Mohaves and Halchidomas, north of the Yuma Crossing, were better suited for missions than the Quechans and the tribes living lower down the river.[15]

In another letter, addressed to his superiors at the Santa Cruz College in Querétaro, Garcés repeated this sentiment and asked them to intercede with the viceroy on the issue. However, Garcés conceded to his fellow Franciscans the strategic necessity in securing the Yuma Crossing and the inevitability that the Spaniards would begin their efforts there. In that case, Garcés suggested, the military should set up a large garrison at Yuma to support two missions; he believed eight to ten guards would be needed to protect each mission, and he also warned that Salvador Palma was the only Quechan able to control the tribe.[16]

Although he made this concession, Father Garcés stressed that the plan for missions among the Gila River Pimas should not be abandoned. Given Commandant Inspector Hugo O'Conor's promise to move the presidios of Buenavista and Horcasitas to the Gila and the Colorado, the padre believed that missions should be established along both rivers, not just the Colorado. Playing the political game to the hilt, Garcés offered to go to Mexico City himself and plead his cause to the viceroy. He also shrewdly noted that no less a power than José de Gálvez, now chief minister of the Council of the Indies, agreed with his plans.[17]

In the meantime, Lieutenant Colonel Anza personally presented his opinions to the viceroy. On October 26, Bucareli received Anza, Salvador Palma, and his three tribesmen in the viceregal court. Amid the pomp and circumstance of the viceroy's retinue, Palma appeared dressed in a cape "in the style of the province of Sonora," over the suit that Anza had given him previously, and holding his cane of office. Speaking through Anza and an interpreter, the Quechan kwoxot announced that he and his kinsmen had come to Mexico City "for the purpose of having a presidio and a mission placed in the center of their country." Bucareli noted that "Anza disclosed this idea at once, promising us exceptional advantages."[18]

Favorably impressed, the viceroy determined to show the Indians the power and magnificence of the white men. First, he had new suits of clothing made for all of them. Then on November 4 he presented them at the viceregal palace at a formal reception in celebration of the king's birthday. Palma cut a particularly fine figure, appearing in a smart military uniform of a blue coat and trousers over a scarlet vest, all trimmed in gold braid. With his own hand, the viceroy presented Palma with another cane of authority. Overwhelmed, the kwoxot could not help but revel in the spectacle presented "by the brilliant concourse of people who were present that day in the palace."[19]

A week later, Anza presented to the viceroy a formal document entitled "Petition of Salvador Palma, Captain of the Yuma tribe requesting that missions be established in his territory." Although composed and written by Anza, Palma purportedly dictated the document. After sketching the story of his life, the kwoxot requested baptism for himself and his people. To prove that he spoke for the whole nation, he claimed to exercise "supreme rule, . . . by right of primogeniture inherited from my fathers . . . from time immemorial." The petition continued, stating that Palma considered witchcraft "as the greatest of crimes" and that he "regarded polygamy with horror." Next, he declared that the Quechans had waged constant war on all their neighbors until Anza and the Spaniards came to Yuma. Then, at Anza's insistence, Palma had made peace with their enemies and convinced his people to "obey the king."[20]

After recounting all the services performed for the Spaniards during the two California expeditions, Palma declared that he had regularly asked that missions be set up among his people. He now formally repeated that request to Bucareli. In exchange, Palma promised to "defend the missionaries and Spaniards from every insult" and to protect the new-found route from Sonora to California. He also promised to forge a pro-Spanish alliance among the neighboring tribes, which would result not only in a great conversion to Christianity, but also in a powerful new military force against the Apaches.[21]

Salvador Palma's petition showed the kwoxot and the Quechans in the most favorable light. It also told the viceroy those things he most wished to hear. The report grossly exaggerated Palma's authority among his tribe, the Quechans' desire for Christianity, and the accomplishments of Anza. How much, if any, of the petition reflected Palma's ideas is difficult to determine, but more than likely the kwoxot was aware of Anza's distortions and embellishments and agreed with them. As for Anza himself, he likely hoped to be named the commander of any new expansion project; as a result, he cast himself as virtually indispensable. Nevertheless, the viceroy was not so simple as to swallow Palma's petition without reflection; Bucareli, therefore, forwarded the document to the viceregal counsel, or *fiscal*, Domingo Arangoyte, for his opinion.[22]

On November 18, Arangoyte responded. The fiscal questioned not only the cost of the project but Palma's motives in asking for missions, and he recommended that Bucareli obtain a detailed report from Anza on the entire matter. Personally, Arangoyte felt that, despite the favorable reports from Anza, Father Díaz, and Father Garcés, the entire project was not as promising as it had been presented. "The present writer is persuaded to the contrary," Arangoyte stated, "and thinks that the measures which may be taken will be a gamble, and that the ministers may be exposed, since they will lack protection, and that the outlay may prove useless."[23]

Following up on Arangoyte's recommendations, two days later Anza presented a lengthy report containing his views on expanding the northern frontier in Sonora. Unbeknown to Father Garcés, Anza actually supported many of the Franciscan's concepts, including establishing missions among the Gila River Pimas and the Maricopas. He also agreed with the plan to relocate the presidios of Horcasitas and Buenavista along the Gila and Colorado to support the missionary endeavor.[24]

Still, Anza felt that the major effort should take place at the confluence of the Gila and Colorado Rivers by placing a presidio and mission among the Quechans. He believed that the assistance of Palma and his people during the two previous Spanish expeditions to California had proven the Indians' loyalty. "I have no doubt we shall obtain the advantages . . . which Captain Palma promises," Anza wrote. "His good faith and that of his tribe appear to me to be sufficiently established." Whether or not Anza actually believed Palma could control the Quechans to the extent he implied was impossible to tell; however, his endorsement of Palma clearly indicated that he saw the kwoxot as the base on which Spanish plans rested.[25]

On the other hand, Anza realized the heavy impact that missions would have upon the natives. He cautioned that the Spaniards must treat the Quechans with respect and special care, "foregoing the severity and force which has been used in other reductions." He advised that the Indians not be subjected to forced labor, but instead be instructed by Spanish workers from Sonora, who could bring their families with them. To ensure just treatment of the Quechans, Anza further recommended that only individuals skilled in dealing with Indians be selected for the operation. The missionaries especially "should be chosen by the superior who governs them, and that in this appointment the [military] commander to whom the new establishments is to be entrusted may not intervene."[26]

Anza continued by warning that the Spaniards should not expect to find the Yuma Crossing brimming with abundance. The Quechans raised only enough crops for their own subsistence, "but with the addition of our people," he noted, "they will suddenly become inadequate." To prevent shortages, he advised that any Spaniards sent to Yuma carry a reserve food supply and that they set about planting new crops immediately. He then observed that the distance of the new settlements from Sonora would require that "clothing, tools for building, seed grain, and other things useful" be sent with the settlers. The pay of the presidial garrisons would also have to be sent annually, either overland or by sea.[27]

In conclusion, Anza again reiterated the central position Salvador Palma would play. The commander reported that the kwoxot and his three kinsmen were advancing in their religious education and were well disposed to receive baptism. He believed Palma's baptism would aid in the conversion of the Quechans and lead to their receiving from the Spaniards "the benefits which with less merit are enjoyed by other tribes who have not given such proof of their docility and affection." Overall, Anza's recommendations were insightful and practical; unfortunately, his calls for detailed planning and careful implementation for the project would, in the end, be forgotten and ignored.[28]

As Anza pled the cause of Salvador Palma before the viceroy, Father Garcés and his fellow Franciscans continued pressing their own views. Father Juan Díaz, who accompanied Garcés on the first expedition to California in 1774, now joined him in his efforts. Díaz, the acting president for the missions of the Pimería Baja of southern and central Sonora, was preparing to travel to Querétaro to make a report on these missions. The Santa Cruz College hoped to transfer its operations in the Pimería Baja to the Franciscan province of Santiago de Jalisco, allowing the college to concentrate on the expansion of missions to the Colorado and Gila. Realizing that Father Garcés's opinions would hold weight, Díaz ordered him to bring his unfinished diary to Mission San Ignacio, nearly one hundred miles south of San Xavier. Confounded by Garcés's atrocious penmanship, Díaz set several Franciscans to copying and arranging the papers into a usable form for presentation to the viceroy.[29]

As Garcés's diary was being transcribed, his superiors in Querétaro formally petitioned the crown to transfer the jurisdiction of the Pimería Baja missions to the Franciscans of Jalisco. After the successful completion of Anza's California expeditions and Father Garcés's other explorations, Viceroy Bucareli finally approved the transfer. Eight more Franciscan friars from the Querétaran college were now available for the northern expansion.[30]

During the transcription of his diary, Garcés continued his own individual efforts on December 25 by writing to Father Diego Ximenes Pérez, the guardian of the Santa Cruz College, about the entire missionization project. Earlier, the guardian had inquired if Garcés would join any future establishments along the Gila and Colorado. Garcés replied modestly, "I will advise that which I can in order to influence by work and by letter in the new foundations." Still, he felt he lacked the talent for leadership and suggested that Father Díaz be named as president of the new missions. Garcés then confided that despite his earlier calls for numerous missions along the Gila and Colorado, he now believed that a smaller effort, if properly provisioned and planned, would have to suffice for the present.[31]

Garcés's acceptance of a scaled-down effort came in part from a sweeping governmental reform initiated by the Spanish crown. The previous

May, José de Gálvez had convinced King Charles III to appoint a new military commander for the entire northern frontier of New Spain. This new officer, the commandant-general of the Interior Provinces, would control all military and civil actions in an area stretching from California through Sonora, all the way to Louisiana. Most importantly, the new commandant would have vast powers independent of the viceroy in Mexico City. In many respects, the position amounted to the creation of a separate viceroyalty.[32]

The Franciscans realized that the creation of the position of commandant-general might result in delays. Viceroy Bucareli, who supported Father Garcés's plans, would no longer have responsibility for the northern frontier, and the padre feared the new commandant-general would not be familiar with him or his ideas and might shelve the project. Hoping to avoid just such an event, Garcés pled that Father Ximenes Pérez, in his position as guardian of the Santa Cruz College, seek an immediate interview with the new commandant-general upon his arrival in Mexico City. The guardian was to impress upon the new official the importance of completing the mission expansion.[33]

For his part, Father Garcés determined to press ahead on his own. By January 3, 1777, the Franciscan scribes at San Ignacio completed the transcription of the diary of his explorations to California and New Mexico, along with a map prepared by Father Pedro Font. To these, Garcés appended a series of "Reflections," in which he forcefully argued in great detail for a massive missionary effort along the Gila and Colorado Rivers. With future administrative changes likely to occur, in many ways the reflections were Father Garcés's last best hope for having his dreams fulfilled.[34]

His work contained eight sections. In the first two, Garcés summarized the numbers and locations of the Indian tribes he had encountered and the elaborate system of alliances and enmities that characterized the Quechan and the Maricopa leagues. As the power of these Indian confederations extended to peoples all the way to Alta California, he emphasized the necessity "for the arms of our King . . . to subdue and rule over the Río Colorado in order to render permanent the establishments of Monterey and elsewhere."[35]

To that end, Garcés recommended a total of fifteen missions among the peoples of the Colorado and Gila Rivers. Along the Colorado northward from its mouth, the Franciscan called for two missions among the Coco-

pas, one for the Halykwamais, two for the Quechans, two for the Halchidomas, and two for the Mohaves. On the Gila, he wanted two missions
each for the Gila Pimas and the Maricopas; the Papagos, who inhabited the
deserts between the Gila and the Colorado, were to receive another pair.[36]

To protect the new missions, Garcés continued, two presidios of fifty
men each should be established, one along the Colorado and one along
the Gila. Each presidio initially would be responsible for guarding two
missions, but if more were set up, the number of troops would have to be
increased. The padre counseled that each mission should have a guard of
at least ten men, that the soldiers ought to be married, and that the
Spaniards on the Colorado place their establishments on the west bank of
the river as a defense against the Apaches. Garcés stressed the vital necessity of a large military presence along the Colorado: "All these nations are
numerous, powerful, and very warlike . . . and if we have to secure this
river properly, this must be done with an adequate force."[37]

In dealing with the Apaches, Garcés suggested that if a greater number
of troopers could be gathered, the presidio destined for the Gila River
might be placed farther to the north along the Río de la Asunción, the
present-day Verde River. A strong garrison at that point would separate
the Yavapais from the Western and Chiricahua Apaches, forcing the
Yavapais into the Spanish camp, thus isolating the two Apache groups.
Garcés also maintained that a more northerly presidio might intimidate
and subdue the Hopis as well. Perhaps more importantly to the padre, a
presidio along the Río de la Asunción would safeguard the new road he
had opened up between New Mexico and Monterey.[38]

He next turned his attention to the routes between Sonora, Alta California, and New Mexico. Remembering his experiences on "the terrible
road" of the Camino del Diablo between Yuma and Sonora, Garcés argued that only groups of moderate size would be able to utilize the route
opened by Anza's expeditions. In the padre's opinion, "the shortest and
best way" was to travel up the Santa Cruz River to the Gila, in the area of
today's Gila Bend, and then head northwest to cross the Colorado at a
point south of the present-day Bill Williams River, in the land of the
Halchidomas, and proceed thence to Mission San Gabriel in California.[39]

As for reaching New Mexico, Garcés believed that the path he had
opened from San Gabriel eastward to the Hopi pueblos would suffice
until further explorations were undertaken. After reading recent reports
on the expedition Fathers Silvester Vélez de Escalante and Francisco

Atanasio Domínguez made from New Mexico westward into the Great Basin, Garcés speculated that some of the rivers they encountered might form a waterway stretching toward the California coast; if so, he dreamed that trading routes between China and New Mexico might possibly be opened. Perhaps even goods from Spain might be shipped to the orient via the Mississippi.[40]

Putting aside the fanciful for the practical, Father Garcés next discussed the issue of how best to equip and supply the missions along the Colorado. Overland supplies might come from Chihuahua City, north to the Gila River, and then to the Yuma Crossing, but the padre believed this route too long and vulnerable to Indian attack; sending supplies by sea might be a more practical solution. Ships could carry the cargo from Sonora to the mouth of the Colorado, and then, in small boats "with oars and sails," continue on up the river to the settlements. "If it were found possible to take the vessel upriver to the Yumas," Garcés wrote, "she could unload at the very presidio and missions . . . and when this should not be practicable . . . unload the bark in some one of the creeks or coves of that shore [i.e., the head of the Gulf of California] and thence take all the cargo on pack animals up to the presidio and missions." With this statement, the good father anticipated by eighty years the advent of river traffic along the Colorado.[41]

Father Garcés also suggested a third possible route. Supplies could be sent overland from the Pacific Coast, especially from San Diego. He believed that this route might prove more advantageous than the others, since it would avoid the necessity of overland travel through regions where, "in case of insurrection," natives could cut the lifeline to the new missions. "They could not obstruct" supplies sent to San Diego, Garcés observed, "conveyance being by sea." Should this route be established, the padre recommended the soldiers at San Diego presidio be placed under the control of the commander of Yuma rather than the one of Monterey. Since the San Diego troops were nearer to the Colorado than to Monterey, they "would be able to give aid more promptly in case of necessity."[42]

In conclusion, Father Garcés summoned all his eloquence in one final burst of pleading. He argued that the failure of the Spaniards to press ahead earlier with missions had resulted in God unleashing the Apaches upon the white men for their laxness, "an instrument to punish our sins." He asked rhetorically, "if that which has been expended in contending with the Apache . . . had been employed in new establishments, where would not now be raised the standard of the holy cross?" The priest maintained that his missionary project offered the opportunity to restore the blessings of the Almighty and to revive "that antique Spanish spirit . . . for the acquisition of the precious pearls that are souls."[43]

Lest any bureaucrat object to the cost of his plans, Garcés noted that King Charles III had manifested a special desire to make new conversions to Christianity. "All of us who have the good fortune to be vassals of such a great king have learned his royal disposition to desire rather souls for God than moneys for his exchequer . . . opening the gates of heaven to so many souls even though there remain [but] few millions in the royal coffers." Garcés concluded his oration on a note of hope mixed with foreboding. "Soon the king our lord will do that which is at once so sacred and suitable a thing . . . the way is open to be able to enter [and] to reap the harvest, and that if it be not gathered now, it will be simply because no laborers are sent."[44]

As Father Garcés sent off his finally completed diary and reflections, the bureaucratic entanglements that he had dreaded seemed to be gathering. In his cover letter to Father Ximenes Pérez, guardian of the Santa Cruz College, Garcés complained about the lack of response from Commandant Inspector Hugo O'Conor. He had written to O'Conor three times about the transfer of garrisons of Horcasitas and Buenavista to the Gila and Colorado Rivers, but had not received a single reply. In response, he again asked Father Ximenes Pérez to intervene with the secular authorities on behalf of the mission project.[45]

Padre Garcés's fears of bureaucratic delay were well justified. In December 1776, Teodoro de Croix, known as the Caballero de Croix, arrived in Mexico City to assume his duties as the first commandant-general of the Interior Provinces. No stranger to Mexico, the caballero had been employed in several governmental posts when his uncle, the Marqués de Croix, served as viceroy of New Spain between 1765 and 1771. Yet his command experience was limited, and his knowledge of the northern frontier virtually nonexistent. Despite this, the caballero possessed an arrogant and imperious assurance of his own abilities and importance.[46]

Soon after his arrival, tensions developed between the new commandant-general and Viceroy Bucareli. Despite assurances from Madrid to the contrary, Bucareli naturally felt that the establishment of a new government for the Interior Provinces was a reflection on his own abilities.

His suspicions were no doubt reinforced when Croix publicly and repeatedly condemned the existing state of affairs along the northern frontier. Croix especially criticized the tenure and achievements of Commandant Inspector Hugo O'Conor, an appointee and loyal supporter of Bucareli. As Croix issued these grand pronouncements about the Interior Provinces, it did not seem to matter that he had never come closer than two thousand miles to the frontier; his assertions galled Viceroy Bucareli. Tensions between the two continued to escalate.[47]

Aggravating this animosity, the Spanish crown had deliberately left the precise jurisdictions of both men vague, and their responsibilities often overlapped. The inevitable result was, as Father Garcés had predicted, a bureaucratic reshuffling that stalled the momentum of his mission project.[48] The king himself revealed the inherent problems caused by the confusion of authority. Once informed of Salvador Palma's petition to receive baptism and to have Spaniards come and live among his people, Charles III endorsed the idea "with particular pleasure." In February 1777, the king, through Chief Minister of the Council of the Indies José de Gálvez, issued a series of orders granting the Quechans "missionaries and the protection of presidial troops which they need." Gálvez sent the orders, written in almost exactly the same form, to both Viceroy Bucareli and Commandant-General Croix. Croix's orders read that the king had instructed Bucareli to give the Quechans missionaries and troops, but concluded, "to your Lordship . . . I hereby communicate a like order, that you may fulfill the part that belongs to you"—all the while holding little indication of just what Croix's or Bucareli's "part" was to be. To further complicate the situation, the royal orders contained no specific time frame for completing the assignment. They stated only that Palma and his three tribesmen should be baptized and that the Spaniards "in good time" provide the requested missions and presidios. The vagueness of the royal orders, combined with the jurisdictional battle between Croix and Bucareli, brought Father Garcés's fears of delay to the forefront.[49]

In the meantime, Salvador Palma continued his visit with the Spaniards, seemingly fulfilling the promise of his life's role as kwoxot of the Quechan nation. On February 13, he was baptized into the Roman Catholic faith in the great cathedral of Mexico, with Lieutenant Colonel Anza standing as godfather. In honor of the king and of Viceroy Bucareli, he was given the names Salvador Carlos Antonio. At the same time, Palma's brother was baptized and given the name Ygnacio Joseph, with Don

Pedro de Anza standing as godfather. Palma's other companions, also anointed, were named Joseph Antonio Marcelo and Pedro, with other kinsmen and friends of Anza's acting as their sponsors. For the ceremony, the viceroy gave all four Indians new suits of clothing. The spectacle provided yet another opportunity for the Spaniards to impress their power and splendor upon the Indians.[50]

As he knelt before the altar of the cathedral, Palma's icama, his dream power, must have seemed crystal clear to both himself and his three companions. His path seemed irrevocable. By inviting the white men to come and stay among his people, he would gain power and renown for himself and for the Quechans. An alliance with the Spaniards would guarantee his own position as kwoxot and assure his nation of a steady supply of European goods, weapons, and horses.[51]

Accompanied by Lieutenant Colonel Anza, Palma and the other Indians headed home in the first week of March after spending more than four months in the capital. Viceroy Bucareli and Anza continued to assure Palma that Spaniards and priests would soon come to live among his people. Although the four Indians may not have understood their new role as "vassals" of the crown, they more than understood the potential benefits of supporting the Spaniards—benefits made all the more apparent by the trunkload of clothes and other presents they carried home with them.[52]

On the journey northward, the Spaniards continued to teach Palma and his companions about Christian spirituality. When they reached the city of Durango, Palma, who no doubt had already received the sacraments of the Eucharist and penance, took part in yet another ceremony. On April 3, he was anointed with holy oil and confirmed in the city's cathedral; again, Juan Bautista de Anza stood as his sponsor. With his confirmation, Palma had completed all of the necessary requisites to become a fully participating Christian.[53]

By the middle of May, Anza, Palma, and their cavalcade reached the Sonoran presidio of San Miguel de Horcasitas. Realizing the anxiety of the Indians to return to their people, Anza ordered Capt. Pedro Tueros, commander of the presidio of Altar, to escort Palma and his companions the sixty leagues between Horcasitas and Altar. In July, as the kwoxot and a small escort of a corporal and three soldiers started on the last leg of their journey to the Yuma Crossing, Tueros once again impressed upon the Indians the friendship and power of the Spaniards.[54]

Though the nature of Palma's reception at Yuma was not recorded, the Quechans must have been pleased by his return after an absence of fourteen months. The kwoxot immediately opened the large trunk to show the "shirts, richly garnished coats, capes of deep red and of lace gallooned blue, tricorn hats, a cane, and other showy jewels" the Spaniards had given him. The ostentatious clothing and other gifts made a great impression upon the people, especially after Palma promised that all members of the tribe would receive similar presents as soon as the Spaniards arrived to live among them. By welcoming the white men into their land, Palma assured the Quechans that they would all become rich and gain power over their enemies. He had seen the awesome might of the Spaniards, their cities, and their great numbers. Prosperity, perhaps even survival itself, could only be achieved if the Quechan allied with the Spaniards. Again, the people saw that Palma's icama was true, and they heeded his words. They would wait for the coming of the Spaniards, as the kwoxot asked, and they would welcome the white men. However, amid the clothing, glass baubles, and the hope for the future, neither the Quechans nor their chieftain could foresee how long their wait was to be.[55]

5

Voices Crying in the Wilderness

The First Mission to the Quechans, 1778 to 1779

APPARENTLY, the Caballero de Croix was reluctant to leave Mexico City. The primitive backwaters of the northern frontier—Croix's new command—did not equal the diversions and polite society offered by the capital. As the first commandant-general of the Interior Provinces, Croix's responsibilities included all civil and military operations in the provinces of Texas, Coahuila, Nueva Vizcaya, New Mexico, Sonora, Sinaloa, and Alta and Baja California. His powers rivaled those of the viceroy, and he had the ear of one of the king's most powerful and trusted advisers, José de Gálvez. Therefore, the fate of Father Garcés's plans and Salvador Palma's hopes rested in Croix's hands.

Though he had a formidable task ahead of him, after his arrival in December 1776 the caballero remained in the capital for more than seven months rather than proceed north to the Interior Provinces. Whatever reasons he had for lingering, he diligently gathered information on the state of his new command. Croix requested reports from a variety of sources, including Viceroy Bucareli, Commandant-Inspector Hugo O'Conor, and many of the provincial governors. Much of the information Croix received, however, was contradictory. Commandant-Inspector O'Conor assured the caballero that the northern frontier was in good shape militarily; some of the governors, however, declared that Indian attacks had brought their provinces to the verge of ruin. Instead of waiting to investigate the situation for himself, the caballero judged the gubernatorial reports to be the most accurate, and he chose to believe the worst. He subsequently declared that the Interior Provinces were in a "deplorable, ruinous state" and accused O'Conor, an appointee and supporter of Bucareli, of lying about frontier conditions. Not surprisingly, the Caballero de Croix soon found himself at odds with Viceroy Bucareli.[1]

In the midst of all of his information gathering and jockeying for power with the viceroy, the caballero acquainted himself with Father Garcés and his plans for missionary expansion. In March 1777, the caballero wrote a letter to the priest to assure him that he supported the Franciscan's initiatives. Croix approved the transfer of the presidios of Horcasitas and Buenavista to the Gila and Colorado Rivers in support of new missions. He even went so far as to declare that he intended to supervise the project himself, when he visited Sonora during an inspection tour of the entire northern frontier.[2]

Croix finally left Mexico City on August 4, reaching the Interior Provinces two months later. Upon his arrival at his headquarters in the city of Chihuahua, he found himself beset by a complex series of military problems that pushed Father Garcés and his plans far to the rear of the commandant-general's concerns. The king's orders to Croix stated that "the defense and extension of the great territories included in your command" were his primary duty. However, his orders also bid him to undertake "the conversion of the numerous nations of heathen Indians who live in the north of western America." The caballero quickly realized the impossibility of converting the Indians without first subduing those nations hostile to the Spaniards, especially the Apaches and Comanches.[3]

He attempted to address the situation on his journey north and on August 22 wrote a letter in which he argued and then begged Viceroy Bucareli to dispatch immediately two thousand troops to reinforce the Interior Provinces. The commandant-general also asked Bucareli to continue overseeing events in the new California establishments because he lacked information to deal with the situation there. The viceroy, however, refused the caballero's request for reinforcements; Spain's impending war with Britain made it an impossibility. Bucareli could only offer guidance and counsel to Croix on how to deal with events in California.[4]

Unable to acquire more troops for the northern frontier, Croix decided to reorganize and retrench his forces as best he could. First, he inspected the garrisons of Nueva Vizcaya, Coahuila, and Texas, ensuring that they were properly armed and supplied. Next, in the spring of 1778 he convened three juntas de guerra, and by July they had drawn up detailed plans for dealing with the Indians in the eastern and central Interior Provinces.[5]

While Croix dealt with the defensive problems of his command, the hopes of Father Garcés and Salvador Palma for missionary expansion to the Gila and Colorado Rivers, so bright in the spring of 1777, now seemed forgotten. Garcés expressed his concerns over the delay on February 18, 1778, in a letter to Father Diego Ximenes Pérez, the guardian of the Santa Cruz College in Querétaro. He assured the guardian that he still wished to work on the project, and he still expected Croix to visit Sonora in the very near future as the caballero had assured him. He then confided in the guardian that he was anxious to see what type of man Croix really was. Conceding that the preparations for the missions were still inadequate, Garcés believed that the Franciscans could prepare at least those aspects of the project that they had control over, such as selecting priests to man the missions. Specifically, he asked the college to choose older, mature men as they would be most suited for the rigors of the new conversions. Though he continued pressing for adequate planning, Garcés must have wondered if any part of his grand endeavor would ever come to fruition.[6]

Salvador Palma, too, had similar worries. When he had returned to the Yuma Crossing in July 1777, Palma had assured the Quechans that the white men would soon come to live among them, bringing loads of presents and gifts. As the summer turned to fall and the fall to winter, no sign of the Spaniards and the promised bonanza of goods appeared. To many Quechans, Palma's icama had clearly waned; his dreams no longer showed the right path. As his dream power diminished, so did Palma's authority among his people.[7]

In March 1778, Palma decided to travel to the presidio of Altar to discover if what many of his people were saying was true—that the Spaniards had deceived and used him. The commandant of Altar, Capt. Pedro Tueros, somewhat taken aback by the arrival of Palma, had the good sense to realize that the Quechan represented the cornerstone of the entire Colorado River mission project; therefore, Tueros regaled Palma to the best of his ability and assured the chieftain that the great lord of the white men, the Caballero de Croix, would soon come to visit the Quechans. The captain informed the kwoxot that having to deal with enemies far to the east had delayed the caballero, but once they had been vanquished Palma could be assured that priests and Spaniards would come to live with his people. The white men would bring gifts of horses and clothing, and they would teach all of Palma's tribe the ways of Christianity. Tueros's words restored Palma's faith. After receiving what meager gifts Altar could offer, Palma returned to Yuma, again convinced that the Spaniards would soon follow.[8]

However, as weeks turned into months and another harvest was gathered, still the white men did not arrive. The people refused to listen to anything Palma told them, mocking his words. "His *paisanos* were menacing him," the Spaniards later reported, "judging as lies that which he had so many times promised them." Clearly, Palma's position as kwoxot was in danger, and may have already been lost. Given the tone of some of his tribesmen, he may also have been in danger of losing his life as well.[9]

In desperation, in January 1779 Salvador Palma and several companions again traveled to Altar to seek the aid of Captain Tueros. However, Tueros, who had been named military commandant of Sonora, was now at the presidio of San Miguel de Horcasitas to the south. More determined than ever, Palma resolutely continued his journey and caught up with Tueros on January 19. Palma demanded to know why the Spaniards had not come; it had been almost two years since he had returned from Mexico City filled with Spanish promises, and he informed Tueros that the Quechans were losing faith in the word of the white men. Palma went on to present, in no uncertain terms, his precarious position, recounting to the captain "the motives that obliged him to repeat his demands."[10]

The Quechan leader then changed his tactics. If the subsistence of the priests concerned Tueros and the others, they should not worry; he assured the captain that the Quechan villages were well provided with food and other essentials and any Spaniards sent would lack for nothing. He then played the religious card, lamenting that his son had not been baptized and did not have anyone to teach him the ways of Christianity. An elderly Quechan, who had accompanied Palma, chimed in, telling Tueros that all the Quechans wished for baptism.[11]

Captain Tueros realized that a crisis was brewing and did his best to mollify Salvador Palma. The officer explained to the Quechans that Commandant-General Croix had been delayed visiting Palma and his people because he had been taken ill and was recuperating in the city of Chihuahua. Tueros again promised that Spaniards would settle among the Quechans and assured Palma that he would soon be "consoled, dressed, and comforted." Tueros then had his soldiers escort the Quechan leader and his fellows back to Yuma.[12]

However, a week later, on January 27, Palma again showed up at Horcasitas, this time accompanied by representatives from the nations bordering the Quechans, including the Halykwamais, Halchidomas, Mohaves, Kohuanas, and even one from the Maricopas. Palma informed Captain Tueros that all the neighboring tribes were asking for missionaries, especially Father Garcés, to come their lands. Palma complained that visitors from the surrounding nations came almost daily to his village to see if the Spaniards had arrived. They pestered Palma so much that "he could neither eat nor sleep." The other Indians then spoke up on behalf of the Quechan leader; they said they were friends of Palma and assured Tueros that he would treat the missionaries well because "he had a good heart." Palma even offered to leave an interpreter, "who had been in Mexico" to see the viceroy, to wait at Horcasitas for Croix and request missions from the caballero directly.[13]

Captain Tueros told Palma and the other Indians that he had heard their words and all that they said was good. The captain then promised that he would send a report of the conference to the chief of the white men and that he would personally relay Palma's complaints to the caballero. Realizing that he had done all that he could, Palma on February 2 began the long journey back to the Yuma Crossing.[14]

By the end of that month, Captain Tueros had dispatched a series of letters to Croix, noting the urgency of Palma's requests and indicating the dangerousness of the situation. In response to the reports, the caballero immediately began to scramble for a solution. Croix's duties had prevented him from giving any serious attention toward establishing missions at Yuma, but he could no longer put off dealing with them. Although undoubtedly he wished he could scrap the entire project, the royal order of February 14, 1777, specifically commanded him to make the effort. Palma's visits to Horcasitas forced the issue.[15]

To control operations in the western sector of his command better, Croix planned to establish his capital at Arizpe, Sonora. However, until he arrived to supervise the complexities of the Yuma project personally, he decided to rely on temporary measures. On February 5, he wrote letters to Father Francisco Antonio de Barbastro, the Franciscan president of the missions in Pimería Alta, to Don Pedro Corbalán, intendant-governor of Sonora, and to Father Garcés. The commandant-general informed all three men that the long-awaited Yuma mission project finally would be undertaken. However, Croix maintained that for now he could support only two missionaries, including Garcés, and a military escort; Captain Tueros would provide the soldiers and would work out the final details with Garcés. For his part, Croix specifically charged the padre to "console the Yumas and begin the catechizing and baptism of those infidels" until such time as Croix himself arrived to oversee the final disposition of the new establishments.[16]

To send only two priests and a small group of soldiers into the midst of three thousand Quechans of unknown disposition was an extremely dangerous move, flying in the face of all the information compiled over the last four years. Commander Anza had urged the establishment of a presidio with a larger than normal garrison of at least eighty men to support missionary efforts among the Quechans. Viceroy Bucareli and Commandant-Inspector Hugo O'Conor both had envisioned moving the presidios of Horcasitas and Buenavista, with a combined force of more than one hundred men, to the Gila and Colorado Rivers to support the new missions. Father Garcés had previously stated that the project required an essential minimum of a presidio of fifty soldiers, with ten extra troopers at each mission site.[17]

Why Croix chose such a risky operation is easily understood. Since 1777, rebellious Seri and Piato Indians in western Sonora had joined Apaches in raiding Spanish settlements throughout the province. These new attacks forced Croix to abandon the idea of moving the presidios of Horcasitas and Buenavista northward, since he needed to control both the Seris and their allies. Furthermore, as Spain drifted closer to war with Great Britain over the rebellious American colonies, Croix received orders to adopt a defensive posture in the Interior Provinces, curtailing his plans for a general offensive against the Apaches. In the light of these new developments, the caballero obviously believed that a smaller, limited effort was all he could afford to expend on the Yuma project.[18]

Though Father Garcés and his fellow Franciscans were acutely aware of the dangers presented by Croix's limited enterprise, they began making plans. Garcés specifically requested that the college appoint Father Juan Díaz to accompany him to the Yuma Crossing. Padre Díaz was one of the most respected and experienced Querétaran missionaries and had served more than ten years on the northern frontier.[19]

Díaz was born in 1736 in the Villa de Alaxar in the archbishopric of Seville, the son of Juan Marcelo Díaz and Feliciana Vásquez of Badajoz. He had entered the Franciscan order on February 23, 1754, at age eighteen at the Convento de San Ildefonso de la Villa de Hornachos. He set out for missionary service in Mexico and joined the Santa Cruz College in Querétaro in 1763. Five years later, he was one of the first group of Franciscan friars sent to Sonora.[20]

Assigned as minister to the Mission of Caborca, for the next seven years Father Díaz gained firsthand knowledge of the many Indian nations of the province. In 1775/1776, he accompanied the Anza expedition to California and as president of the Pimería Baja missions had successfully overseen the transfer of those establishments to the Franciscan province of Santiago de Jalisco. A vigorous supporter of missionary expansion to the Colorado and Gila Rivers, he was, after Garcés, the project's most vocal advocate. During his many assignments, Father Díaz had demonstrated organizational and leadership ability, cartographical skills, and a certain erudition, all of which Father Garcés felt he lacked. Together, they would complement each other.[21]

Despite this, Díaz's and Garcés's superiors were acutely aware of the dangers presented by the caballero's limited missionary enterprise for Yuma. Out of concern, Father Francisco Antonio de Barbastro, president of the Pimería Alta missions, called a conference with Garcés and Díaz to discuss the situation. The two padres had no illusions about the hazards of Croix's reduced missionary proposal. They informed Father President Barbastro that Salvador Palma's actual authority over the Quechans was not as great as had been reported, and that, even if Palma fully cooperated with the missionaries, his ability to control individual members of the tribe was fluid at best. Added to this, the Franciscans remembered terrible proof that missions with only a small military escort invited disaster. In 1773, Father Juan Crisóstomo Gil de Bernabé had established a small mission among the Seris at a place called Carrizal, isolated and many miles away from the nearest presidio. Although the mission had a guard of fifteen men assigned to it, the troopers were often sent on detached duty and were scarcely ever present. As a result, a group of Seris rebelled when the soldiers were absent, murdering Father Gil. These circumstances were remarkably similar to those that the caballero now ordered Fathers Garcés and Díaz to undertake.[22]

With the death of Father Gil haunting Garcés and his companions, they discussed the Yuma situation. The father president stressed to both priests that they were free to refuse to go and there would be no aspersions on either of them. Despite this face-saving opportunity, Garcés and Díaz declared their willingness to undertake the mission; they had given their word to the Quechans, and if they did not go now, the opportunity might never come again. Father Garcés declared, "We ought to put confidence in God in whose cause we go. . . . This is the desire of the Commandant-General and the first project that offers itself to him, and his honor is at stake. It is especially recommended by the court, and I am convinced that the establishment of a presidio on the Río Colorado is to take place soon." Although Garcés's faith in the Almighty was unquestioned, his faith in the Caballero de Croix remained unproven.[23]

Determined to press ahead regardless of the risks, on March 23, 1779, Father Garcés wrote to Capt. Pedro Tueros at Altar presidio to request the military escort. Fearing that Tueros would balk if he asked for a large number of troops, the padre requested an escort of fifteen men, six from the presidio of Tucson and nine from Altar. He recommended that Don José Dario Arguello, second sergeant of Altar, be named military commandant and that at least one of the soldiers have carpentry skills to aid in the building of shelters and other necessary items.[24]

Drawing on "the great experience I have of the Yuma nation" and on his observations of the new missions in Monterey, Father Garcés believed escort soldiers without wives would be "very prejudicial" to the operation; therefore, he recommended that the soldiers' families be allowed to accompany them. The women would be invaluable in establishing the settlements and would also insure the "complacency" of their husbands, no doubt keeping them away from the Quechan women. The Franciscan declared that without the soldiers' wives, "the future of these establishments will be impossible."[25]

Recalling from his previous visits the scarcity of food on the Colorado

River, Garcés suggested that Tueros have the quartermaster at Altar give the troopers provisions for at least three months, insure they were well clothed and armed, and include a large amount of gifts for the Indians in the supplies. The padre also asked that the sergeant keep strict supervision over the soldiers to prevent them from hindering the conversion of the Quechans. Garcés requested that the captain make the detachment aware of two things: first, that in all matters but defense, the missionaries were in command; second, that the soldiers played a crucial role in converting the Indians as "the greatest Christians need to be observed in a new conversion." By assisting in the indoctrination of the natives, the priest declared that the troopers would secure the "peace and good harmony necessary for stability" at the new mission.[26]

Father Garcés next addressed the dangers of being isolated among the Quechans and surrounding tribes with such a small escort. For greater security, the Franciscan suggested the inclusion of several civilian settlers, preferably retired or invalided soldiers, "in the same mission, with the right to sow and hold some pieces of land of their own, without injury to the natives." Obviously, Garcés hoped that veterans who settled at Yuma could in turn augment the military force of the new mission.[27]

Finally, the padre asked that the escort include several *niforas,* or Indian war-captives who had been sold, by various tribes, to the Spaniards at an early age. He believed the niforas would prove invaluable as interpreters and as assistants in the daily operations of the mission; more importantly, they would serve as examples to the Quechans of Indians who had been successfully acculturated.[28]

On the same day that he wrote to Captain Tueros, Garcés also sent a letter to the caballero, both thanking the commandant-general for initiating the Yuma project and simultaneously asking that it be enlarged. Garcés assured Croix that his decision "would be celebrated in heaven" and that God would favor the caballero's military operations with success. The padre then self-effacingly stated that although "the love I have for the Yumas and the other nations is well known, I was not given all the aptitude necessary for such a formidable enterprise." Still, the Franciscan believed that with the guidance of Divine Providence and obedience to Croix's orders, he could contribute in some small way.[29]

With the blandishments out of the way, Father Garcés pressed Croix to expand support for the Yuma missions. The priest suggested setting up a detachment, independent of the planned presidio for the Colorado, of twenty-nine or thirty men, supplied by the quartermaster at Altar. With this force Garcés believed "they would ultimately be able to found at least three missions." To attract civilian settlers to Yuma, the caballero might supply one hundred pesos to pay the expenses of conducting each family there; should this prove too expensive, the soldiers alone would have to suffice. Garcés concluded by proclaiming the conviction of he and his *compañero*, Father Díaz, that the detachment was the minimum force necessary to fulfill Croix's orders "in the spirit with which they had been dictated."[30]

The Franciscan's hopes for more soldiers were soon dashed. On April 14, Captain Tueros responded that he could afford to send only Sergeant Arguello and eleven *soldados de cueras,* or leather-jacketed soldiers, as the military support for the Yuma mission. Eight were from Altar, and four were from the presidio of Tucson; continuing Indian problems in Sonora prevented Tueros from providing more. The captain also informed the priests that, after a great deal of soul-searching, he had decided not to allow the wives of the soldiers to accompany them. As the escort was small, the soldiers would often be absent from Yuma on detached duty to deliver mail and get supplies from Sonora; therefore, the Spanish women would often be left alone, and Tueros feared the Quechans might molest or kidnap them while their husbands were away.[31]

Tueros continued his litany of negatives. He declared he did not have the authority to allow civilian settlers to be enrolled for the Yuma expedition, but he would refer the matter to the caballero. The captain also reported that no "educated niforas" to act as interpreters were available in the area. He did agree, however, to supply the Franciscans with mules and cattle for breeding, and he would order the soldiers of the escort to help construct the buildings for the mission and to obey Garcés and Díaz in all but military matters.[32]

Undoubtedly disappointed by the lack of support, Fathers Garcés and Díaz determined to press ahead with the project. In May, Díaz traveled to the city of Alamos in southern Sonora to get the money for supplies. As ordered by Croix, Intendant-Governor Pedro Corbalán drew up a draft for two thousand pesos to cover the expenses for the new mission. Díaz then retraced his steps northward to the mining boomtown of La Cieneguilla and met with Don Antonio Enriques de Castro, a wealthy merchant who served as the Franciscan's *síndico,* or factor. With Castro's help,

Father Díaz spent the next several weeks traveling throughout the region gathering supplies.[33]

The two thousand pesos evaporated quickly. Díaz spent nearly 600 on religious objects "to celebrate the Divine Offices and administer the Holy Sacraments"; another 480 went on four mules with trappings and "gifts and utensils" for the Quechans. Knowing the fondness of the Indians for tobacco, he had a large crate constructed and filled with the weed, and he acquired another mule to carry it, all for the price of more than 350 pesos. For himself and Father Garcés, Díaz spent only 231 pesos "for our own fitting out," and from the church at Caborca he obtained 150 pesos' worth of "things for the mission." He laid the remaining money out "to pay some youths" who had loaded the freight and for "supplies for the road."[34]

The summer of 1779 was well underway by the time Fathers Garcés and Díaz, with their newly purchased goods, were ready to journey to Yuma. In late July, they arrived at the presidio of Altar and met the commander of their military escort, twenty-five-year-old Sergeant José Dario Arguello. A native of the city of Querétaro, Arguello had served in the regular army regiment of the Dragoons of Mexico and had seen action against the Apaches in both Chihuahua and Sonora. Promoted to sergeant, he had transferred to the Altar garrison only the previous year. His assignment to Yuma was his first independent command. No doubt, leaving his wife behind at Altar, as would all the military escort, increased the pressures on Sergeant Arguello.[35]

Regardless, Arguello, his command of ten troopers, and one Opata Indian scout set out with Garcés and Díaz on August 1. In the painfully intense heat of the summer, the little party headed northwest along Garcés's "terrible road," El Camino del Diablo. After several days, they reached the Papago village of Sonóitac, the halfway point to the Yuma Crossing.[36]

On August 10, they hit the trail again, but as their water began to give out they were forced to return to Sonóitac. Arguello and the soldiers wanted to abort the mission and return to Altar, but the two Franciscans would not hear of it. Garcés and Díaz realized that a delay at this point would probably result in the abandonment of the entire project, and they were not going to risk that happening. Later, writing about the trek in Yuma, Garcés said he had decided to march to Quechan territory "swiftly with two soldiers, and to stay here with one scout, without my compañero, without anything to say mass, and little to eat." Only in that way could he obey Croix's orders to complete this "great service to God"; Father Díaz, Sergeant Arguello, and the rest were to stay at Sonóitac to await the monsoon rains, which would refill the water holes along the trail, planning to rejoin the advanced party as soon as possible.[37]

Showing remarkable endurance, Father Garcés and his three companions crossed the remainder of the Camino del Diablo. When they reached the Quechan villages at the Yuma Crossing on August 31, a host of people, all eager for gifts, almost immediately surrounded the four riders. Salvador Palma waded in among the crowd and greeted Garcés and the others warmly. Finally, the Spaniards had come.[38]

During the next few days, Garcés met with the Quechans, giving them gifts, and he dined on some roast lamb especially prepared by Palma. He regaled the Quechan "captains," visitors from other Indian nations, and several tribesmen who acted as interpreters. In talking with everyone, Garcés discovered that all was not well at Yuma. The Halchidoma tribe had recently attacked the Quechans "and had caused some loss." Always the peacemaker, the Franciscan calmed the outraged Quechans with difficulty. He also sent a message to the Halchidomas, admonishing them to cease their aggression.[39]

Overall, events went smoothly for Garcés as he awaited his companions. He baptized several infants and a few adults shortly after his arrival; however, he could not preach effectively as the majority of the tribe was scattered, planting their fields, and could not be gathered together to hear him. Meanwhile, Salvador Palma proved extremely helpful to the padre; the kwoxot even started building a house for the priest at the Puerto de la Concepción on the hill on the western bank. However, after observing the villages, the padre realized Palma had exaggerated the amount of food the Quechans could produce, and upon the arrival of Father Díaz and the detachment of soldiers, there would not be enough to support them all.[40]

On September 2, a few days after reaching Yuma, Father Garcés wrote letters to Intendant-Governor Pedro Corbalán and to Commandant-General Croix. In his missal to Corbalán, the priest begged the intendant immediately to forward another three hundred pesos' worth of "beads, breeches, sayal or bayeta [types of woolen cloth]" as presents for the Quechans. The Franciscan explained that he had used up most of his scant provisions as gifts upon his arrival, and in addition he had found it necessary to barter his supplies for food for himself and his three companions.

Garcés apologized for not being able to give a more precise cost-estimate for the gifts he needed, but he assured the intendant that the request was not superfluous. He noted that although such expenses would be high at the beginning of the project, they would not reoccur after the missions were on a firm footing. To that end, the priest requested that Corbalán allow him to solicit funds from his fellow Franciscans in the Sonoran missions. Furthermore, if Corbalán would send four more Opata scouts, along with a muleteer and a carpenter, the intendant could be assured that the Spaniards would successfully complete what they had started.[41]

In his letter to Corbalán, Father Garcés wrote almost exclusively about his desperate need for supplies, but to the Caballero de Croix the padre was more loquacious. After noting the inevitable delays in gathering supplies before the start of the journey, Garcés related the difficulties the party had encountered along the Camino del Diablo and how he went on ahead to Yuma to insure Croix's orders would be fulfilled.[42] He then reported on his observations of the current situation at the Yuma Crossing, taking every opportunity to press his case for more missions and soldiers. Garcés relayed his view on the apparent future shortage of food, and seizing upon this point appealed to Croix to establish a second mission among the Kohuana tribe, south of the Quechans. The Franciscan wrote that the Kohuanas had "vast fields that promise abundant supplies," which would allow the Spaniards recourse to the crops of both nations. If the caballero sent out ten more soldiers, or eight troopers with four Opata scouts skilled in carpentry, the missionaries could win both the Quechans and the Kohuanas to the faith. The government might then encourage civilian settlers to join the mission enterprise, and Garcés even went so far as to suggest where and how to pasture the settlers' herds of cattle.[43]

Padre Garcés went on to declare that, with further troops and supplies, they could also set up missions among the Cocopas, even though they were the inveterate enemies of the Quechans. Clearly, Garcés hoped that by establishing several missions he could bring peace to the tribes of the Quechan and Maricopa–Gila Pima Leagues. He informed Croix that he had already met with representatives of the Mohaves and their enemies the Halchidomas and believed both people were ready for missions. However, he pointed out that the preferential treatment the Spaniards had shown to the Quechans was alienating the Gila Pimas and the Papagos of Sonóitac; these tribes were "greatly scandalized" by what they felt were

Spanish lies, since they had not been sent the promised missions for themselves. Consequently, Garcés shrewdly asked Croix what to say to these people to "give them true hopes."[44]

Knowing of Croix's parsimonious nature, the Franciscan anticipated the commandant-general balking at the cost of several new missions; Garcés therefore offered the caballero a money-saving alternative: if Croix authorized the placement of several more missions among the tribes bordering the Quechans, and if the missions had their own military escorts, Garcés declared that the entire effort "could be effected without a presidio." The priest hedged, however, admitting that such a move would obviously require further consultation and examination.[45]

Returning to what was, rather than what should be, Father Garcés continued by asking for more money and supplies in order to win over the Quechans. The padre contended that the project, though just beginning, would have to act "like a rich establishment" for the time being. They should liberally dispense gifts to the Indians who came to visit and to the interpreters they employed. Garcés also requested canes of office (*bastones*), to bestow upon "the captains of the nations."[46]

To obtain more men to work at the mission immediately, Father Garcés proposed a bargain: he would trade one soldado de cuera for a carpenter, or, more ambitiously, two troopers for four Opata scouts skilled as muleteers and carpenters. The padre believed the Opatas would aid considerably the construction of the new establishments. Indeed, Garcés declared that carpenters, millers, and workmen would prove more useful in "civilizing" the Quechans "than many arms." Furthermore, if these laborers were sent out as settlers, their support would cost half as much as soldiers.[47]

As the Franciscan wound up his letter, he informed Croix that, as they had previously agreed upon, he was naming the new mission at Yuma La Purísima Concepción, taken from the name earlier given to the Yuma Crossing, Puerto de la Concepción. However, he caustically remarked that the caballero was now responsible for proving how "immaculate" the new enterprise would be now that it had finally been conceived. As for himself, the padre declared that he was willing to die rather than see the mission fail. He would "go to that extremity with great pleasure" in order to complete the work that had now begun.[48]

Garcés concluded his letter to Commandant-General Croix with a warning about the heightened tensions among the Indians of the region. Although Salvador Palma appreciated the necessity of peace for his people, he had managed only with difficulty preventing them from going to war. Characterizing the Quechans as "turbulent," the padre stated that "they were wanting to fight with the other nations"; the enmity between the tribes of the Quechan League and the Maricopa-Gila Pima League was simmering just below the surface. Clearly, Garcés felt that the prevention of a general war depended on the success or failure of his "new establishments" at Yuma. After finishing his reports, on September 3, Garcés dispatched the two troopers of his escort to carry them back to Sonóitac, where they would be sent on to Altar. The priest remained alone among the Quechans, the Opata scout his only guardian.[49]

As the soldiers headed back, Father Díaz faced problems of his own. The fears of renewed Indian hostilities that Garcés had expressed to Croix proved to be justified. While waiting at Sonóitac, Father Díaz received alarming news from the natives of the place. Angry that the Spaniards favored the Quechans, Papagos from other villages planned to come to Sonóitac and attack Díaz and his companions "in order to kill them all and get possession of the provisions and horses." Upon hearing this, Sergeant Arguello concluded that discretion was the better part of valor. Four soldiers had returned to Altar on detached duty, leaving Arguello with only four men on hand. The sergeant hastily prepared to flee. "By use of argument and entreaties," Father Díaz prevented the troopers from abandoning him; instead, they sent to Altar for help.[50]

Shortly after this crisis, the two troopers from Yuma arrived. Along with their other dispatches, the soldiers carried a brief letter for Díaz. In this communique, Garcés informed his compañero that "he had found the place much stirred up" as a result of the recent attack of the Halchidomas, and although Palma and his followers were content, other Quechans were "somewhat surly." Garcés stressed his great need for essential supplies and begged Díaz, if he and the detachment could not continue on to Yuma, immediately to send the two soldiers back with barter goods "that they might get something to eat."[51]

Father Díaz, however, had a new problem: in the midst of his concerns for Garcés, the soldiers on detached duty at Altar returned carrying an exasperating letter for him from Captain Tueros, ordering the priests to abandon the Yuma project altogether. The captain had been informed that the Caballero de Croix would soon be in Sonora and believed both Father Díaz and Father Garcés should return and discuss the situation with Croix in person. Díaz refused to comply, telling Tueros in his reply that since Father Garcés was already at the Colorado River, "it was wiser and even necessary to continue what was begun."[52]

With Sergeant Arguello's detachment of ten soldiers reunited, Father Díaz pressed on from Sonóitac despite Captain Tueros's admonitions. On October 2, the Spaniards, accompanied by some Indian interpreters, arrived at Yuma. It was hard to tell who was happier to see them, Father Garcés or the Quechans. "They found themselves surrounded by innumerable Indians, who came for the distribution of clothes, tobacco and other things."[53]

The priests immediately had their hands full with their initial mission to the Quechans. Sergeant Arguello later recalled that "with great joy the natives presented to us . . . more than 200 children so that they could be Christianized, which was carried out the same day, and continued the following, with the same operation; and as many of their fathers and mothers were granted this freedom." The Franciscans also started to evangelize the surrounding villages. Garcés reported, "We have baptized many infants of the nearby *rancherías* and there meet each day some adults for Catechism."[54]

However, the joy of the Quechans proved short-lived. "A few days later," Arguello remembered, "I noticed in the Indians a sort of muttering." Upon asking an interpreter what the problem was, the Indian told Arguello that many Quechans felt Salvador Palma had deceived them concerning the amount of gifts the Spaniards would give out. "This supposed kinglet," as the sergeant contemptuously referred to Palma, "made them a very long harangue in which he made them understand the richness of life in Mexico and that when the Christians were come, the rest of them would be presented [with gifts] like him." Reportedly, Palma made these statements to "persuade all his paisanos so that they would become Christians."[55]

In the sergeant's opinion, the "principal motive" behind the Indians' request for missionaries was their desire for Spanish goods. For his part, Arguello tactlessly informed the Quechans that they would have to work if they wanted to dress and eat as the Spaniards did. Nevertheless, he often gave out gifts of glass beads, realizing that the expectations Palma had created among his people left his small command "exposed."[56]

The Quechans' insatiable desire for presents, especially clothes, also concerned Father Garcés and Father Díaz. "I always believed that it would not be such an easy thing as Palma painted," Garcés later wrote to the caballero. The padre believed the greatest obstacle to converting the Quechans was their constant demands for gifts. Gifts having been lavished upon them since the days of the Anza expeditions to California, "[w]e have been much prejudiced by the disinterested treatment that has been made to these natives in the previous expeditions," Garcés concluded.[57]

Salvador Palma had greatly exacerbated the problem by telling his people that when the white men came "they would bring them many bales of clothing so that all could dress themselves to their satisfaction." However, when Garcés and his companions arrived, the Quechans saw that "there were very few of the provisions relative to their hopes." The Indians were angry and disappointed, and as a result the Spaniards found they had to barter their own supplies in order "to obtain a little maize," and even had to ask for food from the Kohuana tribe.[58]

Yet perhaps more disturbing to all the Spaniards was the actual nature of Salvador Palma's authority among his people. Although it was clear to the Spaniards that Palma was a chieftain of some import, the nature of his authority confused them. "I do not know," Arguello stated, "with what foundation he came to be named, being a particular Indian among the number of the Yuma Nation; that from what I understood and afterwards observed, he has no position of superiority among them."[59] It was perhaps impossible for Sergeant Arguello or any other Spaniard to comprehend the fact that Palma's authority was based on icama; in such a situation, he could hardly ever "command" another Quechan, having instead to convince them of the power of his dreams by demonstrating material and physical success. That this was the basis of all leadership throughout Quechan society, and that each Quechan individually would choose when and whom they would "obey," was a reality never quite grasped by the Spaniards.[60]

However, it was clear to everyone that Salvador Palma's ability to control his tribesmen was marginal at best. Although Father Garcés felt that Palma and some others were sincerely desirous of becoming Christians "because of the greater light they had acquired," he also knew it would be wrong to think that Palma could convince the whole tribe. "Only his own ranchería, which is very small, recognizes him," Garcés noted. Among the Quechans as a whole, the padre saw that "only in matters of war do they give Palma some acknowledgment." With obvious disapproval, Garcés wrote that it was the individuality of Quechan society that limited Palma's authority. "All the subordination of these natives . . . is very voluntary; therefore they obey . . . if they want and [only] on those subjects that conform to their brutal appetites."[61]

To overcome the independent nature of the Quechans, Fathers Garcés and Díaz wanted to gather the Indians in a formal mission, where they could be inculcated and converted to Christianity. Such a "reduction" of Indians had often been accomplished by offering the natives a dependable food supply or through physical compulsion. Among the Quechans, the two Franciscans found themselves without the means of doing either.[62]

Following the Spaniards' arrival, many circumstances proved detrimental to the mission enterprise, especially an escalation of small-scale attacks between tribes of the Colorado River. The hostilities started when some Quechans killed a group of Halchidomas, who were returning from a visit to the Kohuanas, their allies to the south. In retaliation, the Kohuanas slew two Quechans. As a result, the Quechans wanted to launch campaigns against both the Halchidomas and Kohuanas, but "the grace of God," and no doubt Garcés's entreaties, averted war.[63]

Even in the face of these hostilities, the Halchidomas and Kohuanas both asked that missions be set up in their lands. A chieftain of the Halchidomas visited Garcés to say "that they had gathered many crops, and hoped that we would go to their lands." Likewise, the Kohuanas also invited the Spaniards to settle among them, offering abundant crops, and even promising to construct a palisade fort "so that [the Kohuanas] can form our habitation."[64]

Father Garcés no doubt hoped more Spanish missions among the Colorado River tribes might result in a lasting peace. On November 6, he composed a lengthy letter to the Caballero de Croix to inform him of what had been accomplished and what was still necessary to convert the peoples of the region; the isolation of the new mission exacerbated the situation. He reminded Croix that they were far from support, either from Sonora or California, should the need arise, and the roads were difficult to cross, even in the best of times. With another eighteen men, Garcés believed he could establish missions among the Halchidoma and Kohuana tribes, to which he "might have immediate recourse" should any trouble with "some of the nations" arise. At the very least, said the padre, the present detachment should be increased to twenty men.[65]

Besides indicating the need for more men, the priest also reported that the twelve troopers of his escort were in poor condition. Garcés contended that the lack of adequate funding had prevented the soldiers from bringing their families with them. In addition, some of the troopers of the escort rotated back to their presidio each month; for a newly founded mission, said Garcés, this practice was "pernicious." Knowing they would be rotated out, the soldiers "will not bring their families or join with their kinsmen." Indeed, after the soldiers of the escort from Tucson had moved their families to Altar in order to be closer to them, they were ordered to send them back to Tucson. Without their women to support them, the soldiers had no one to make them even a tortilla.[66]

In addition to impoverishing the soldiers of the escort, according to Father Garcés, the lack of family life drove the Spanish men into illicit sexual relations with Quechan women. The Franciscan reminded Croix that similar liaisons had caused great trouble at the California missions. Salvador Palma had registered his disapproval to Father Garcés as well, stating that Quechan women should not serve the troopers "for two or three nights" and then have the Spaniards depart, never realizing "how they had bred their sons." Palma's views no doubt reflected his adopted Christian belief in monogamy, but some Quechan women obviously were not so constrained. For Father Garcés, the whole matter served as "a great sermon for the Yumas to see the shame and manners of the Spaniards."[67]

Limiting his aggrieved morality, Garcés concluded his letter by reiterating to Commandant-General Croix the need for further support for the enterprise. As proof that his requests were valid, the Franciscan asked Croix to refer to his previous reports on what was necessary for missions among the Quechans. Then, turning to flattery, the padre wrote that he hoped to complete "the grand ideas" initiated by Croix. He and Father Díaz awaited the day when they would personally welcome the caballero to the Yuma Crossing.[68]

During the next six weeks, the Spaniards toiled along the Colorado River. Fathers Garcés and Díaz preached the word of God to the Quechans and attempted to restrain those who wanted to attack their neighbors. Sergeant Arguello's small command was constantly busy. Several soldiers attended to the needs of the priests, and the others assisted in constructing living quarters and, most likely, a small chapel. Sometimes Arguello dispatched men to tranport supplies from the presidio of Horcasitas or to accompany dispatch riders to and from Altar. Arguello also took a few troopers on visits to the surrounding nations, assessing the populations and the types of crops grown. All the while, the men had to barter with the Quechans for food, trading their tobacco and other supplies.[69]

On December 27, Father Garcés again sent a letter to the Caballero de Croix. Having been informed of Croix's order of May 14, 1779, to suspend the establishment along the Colorado River, Garcés noted that fortunately the order had arrived too late to delay the project. Otherwise, "Palma would have perished at the hands of his own people, as they imagined he had deceived them." [70] Garcés again reported that all was not going well among the Quechans. He claimed that Croix's original instructions for the missions were "inviolable precepts," but that he simply did not have "the most serious necessities" to tend to those Indians that were sick or old, nor even to conduct catechism properly. Clearly, the lack of money and supplies were hamstringing the Franciscan's efforts to Christianize the Indians.[71]

Pleading for Croix not to compare the Yuma project with more formal (and no doubt more successful) establishments in Sonora and elsewhere, Father Garcés asked the commandant-general to consider the special circumstances of the new mission, along with the methods being used to attract the Quechans. "You cannot measure all foundations with one yardstick," Garcés argued, "perhaps a method that has been good in other parts, will here be impracticable." The priest blamed himself for the mission's difficulties. He declared that he did not have "the sagaciousness of understanding" to find the most effective measures to convert the Quechans. Regardless of the causes, the padre felt that the mission was in "critical circumstances," a fact that Croix must be made aware of. To that end, Father Díaz had asked permission from the Santa Cruz College to travel to Arizpe to discuss the situation personally with the commandant-general.[72]

The pessimistic tone of his letter continued: Garcés complained that Intendant-Governor Corbalán had refused to forward the requested three hundred pesos; this refusal troubled the padre because he "lacked many things for the church" he was building. He warned that without these funds or other supplies that Croix could send, there would be "very bad results." Indeed, as Garcés lacked gifts to give the Quechans, he found it difficult "to baptize the children . . . or the adults" in the villages downriver from the mission, where "the greater part of the people" resided. The Quechans' never-ending demands for gifts, coupled with their lukewarm adherence to Christianity, led to Garcés questioning his own ability. He confided to the Caballero de Croix that in addition to more men and more money to make the mission a success, perhaps he needed "more spirit and talent."[73]

Almost parenthetically, Garcés then informed Croix that a deserter from the California presidio of Monterey, José Hermenigildo Flores, had reached the Colorado River. With a momentary flicker of hope, Garcés asked that Flores, and any other deserters that might be caught, serve at the Yuma mission; if not, the Franciscan wheedled, at least let him keep the mules sent from Altar to carry the prisoner back.[74]

A few days after the feast of the Nativity, in the year of Our Lord 1779, Father Garcés and Díaz watched as a small detachment of soldiers bearing the letter to the commandant-general forded the Colorado River into Sonora. As they stood atop the hill of the Puerto de la Concepción, their breath visible from the cold, the two Franciscans knew that their lifework was carried in the troopers' leather saddlebags. The success or failure of the Spanish mission at Yuma now depended entirely on the will of God and the mercurial temperament of the Caballero de Croix.[75]

The Knight's Gamble

*Two Military Colonies Are Established at
Yuma, 1779 to 1780*

ON NOVEMBER 13, 1779, Teodoro de Croix rode into the Sonoran town
of Arizpe, the capital of the Interior Provinces of New Spain. For the
preceding six months, the caballero had lain ill in the frontier city of
Chihuahua. Believing several times that he was at death's door, he had
asked for the sacraments, but God had spared him; yet new tribulations
tempered the mercy of the Almighty, or so it must have seemed to Croix
as he entered his new capital. Arizpe was a dirty, cramped, hovel of a
place, even compared with Chihuahua. It had a population fewer than a
thousand people, mostly Indians and mestizos, who lived in constant fear
of Apache depredations. For the commandant-general, Arizpe was as far
away from Mexico City as the earth was from the moon.[1]

Still, Croix had a job to do, and he set out to do it. Having been along
the northern frontier for two years, he had experienced the difficulties of

the region for himself and he now tempered his earlier histrionics. He had seen the vast distances, the poor logistics, the corruption of the presidial officers, and, most importantly, the formidable Apache menace. He had attempted, rather successfully he believed, to remedy the military deficiencies along the eastern half of the Interior Provinces. By shifting himself and his command to Arizpe, he hoped to do the same for the western areas, especially Sonora.[2]

For many residents of the province, the arrival of the commandant-general was more than welcome. It happened that, when the Interior Provinces had been placed under a unified military command in 1771, warfare in Sonora had escalated. The Apaches continued their assaults, and other native groups, such as the Seris, had attacked as well. Hopefully, the caballero could implement an effective military solution to Sonora's Indian problems, as he had done elsewhere along the frontier.[3]

However, Croix's plans for curtailing Indian depredations in Sonora were dealt a severe blow. In 1778, the caballero had designed a massive campaign to strike at the Apaches throughout the western half of his command, but in February of the following year he received orders from Madrid to postpone his upcoming offensive. War with Britain was imminent, and the king ordered the commandant-general to stay on the defensive until after Spain had dealt with the English; consolidation rather than expansion was to be the order of the day. For the people of Sonora, the royal order meant a continuation of reacting to Apache attacks rather than preempting them.[4]

As he searched for methods to curtail the Indian raids that sometimes occurred within miles of his residence, there was one area that continued to intrude on Croix's schedule—Padres Garcés and Díaz and their struggling mission among the Quechans. What the commandant-general proposed to do was anything but clear.

Garcés and Díaz themselves were absolutely certain what should be done: to insure the success of the mission of La Purísima Concepción, they needed more supplies and soldiers. In early 1780, the priests received word that Croix had finally arrived in Arizpe. They agreed between themselves that Díaz should personally lay their cause before the commandant-general, relating the situation at the Colorado River mission and the grave necessity for more support.[5]

Before Díaz could go, however, the priests had to secure approval from their superiors at the Santa Cruz College in Querétaro. To insure the presence of two missionaries among the Quechans, as originally ordered by Croix, Garcés and Díaz requested another Franciscan be sent to Yuma during Díaz's absence in Arizpe; the padres did not want to give anyone the opportunity of saying that the Franciscans were not holding up their end of the enterprise. The leaders of the college soon agreed and dispatched a third priest to the Colorado River. In late January 1780, Father Juan Antonio de Barreneche reached La Purísima Concepción after "a great deal of exhausting effort." Within a short time of the newcomer's arrival, Father Díaz set out to confront the Caballero de Croix.[6]

On February 12, 1780, some days after his arrival in the capital, Díaz laid before the commandant-general a five-point report that detailed conditions at the Yuma mission and listed the amount of support both Garcés and Díaz believed essential.[7] First, the peace established by Father Garcés among the region's tribes was coming apart. The Halchidomas had recently stolen a large number of horses from the Quechans, wantonly killing those animals they could not take. Furthermore, Díaz noted the Halchidomas launched this raid despite the presence of the Spanish troops; now the Quechans agitated to attack not only the Halchidomas but the Kohuanas as well. However, the greatest potential problems lay in the fact that those two tribes were allied with the Maricopas, the Gila Pimas, and the Papagos del Norte. An attack by the Quechans could activate the system of alliances between the members of the Quechan League and the Maricopa–Gila Pima League, plunging the entire region into war. The only way to prevent this catastrophe, Father Díaz declared, was for Croix to authorize two more missions along the Colorado River, one for the Halchidomas and the other for the Kohuanas.[8]

To garrison these new establishments, Díaz maintained that another twenty soldiers would be needed to support the twelve troopers already among the Quechans. In addition, Croix should assign to each of the three missions an interpreter, a muleteer, a carpenter, a mason, and a husbandman, each one supported by the government for a period of three years. Two more priests should also be sent to each mission to insure a more effective catechizing of the Indians. Most importantly, Croix should set aside adequate funds for equipping and maintaining the new foundations. Not surprisingly, Father Díaz also argued that the religious should have ultimate control over the military garrisons, as well as over all supplies and funds.[9] If it were not possible for the commandant-general to undertake measures for the conversion of the Halchidomas and Ko-

huanas at this time, Díaz begged that Croix at least immediately authorize another mission, with an escort of ten soldiers, to aid in converting
the Quechans. The Franciscan declared that the addition of this second
mission would restrain the Quechans from attacking their neighbors.[10]

Upon receiving Father Díaz's report, Commandant-General Croix realized that he could no longer postpone dealing directly with the situation. In 1777, he had been ordered by the king to convert the Quechans
and to secure the Yuma Crossing by allying with them. Now, after almost
three years of delay, the fledgling mission of La Purísima Concepción
threatened to be stillborn, despite the best efforts of Father Garcés and
Father Díaz. Croix had either to reinforce the two Franciscans or order
them to abandon the effort and return home. The caballero finally decided that the time had come not only to obey the king's order, but to
comply as well.[11]

In the three years, however, since the king's directive, the military
situation in Sonora had changed dramatically. The cornerstone of the
plans put forth by Father Garcés, Lieutenant Colonel Anza, and others
had been the moving of the two presidios of Horcasitas and Buenavista
northward to the Colorado and Gila Rivers; these presidios represented
the necessary underlying forces for the entire missionization project.
However, as Seri Indians continued their hostilities, coupled with the
Apache menace, in Croix's opinion the circumstances ruled out the presidios' relocation. If the caballero could not move the two forts, he had to
come up with another solution for an adequate military force to protect
the missionaries along the Colorado River.[12]

With the recently written report of Father Díaz in hand, Croix discussed the matter with his *asesor,* Don Pedro Galindo y Navarro. Galindo,
assigned to the caballero's staff in 1777, had accompanied Croix throughout his journeys in the Interior Provinces. He served as a legal adviser for
the commandant-general in all matters respecting Croix's command, and
Croix highly valued Galindo's opinions. It didn't hurt that the adviser's
reputation for frugality matched a similar streak within the caballero.[13]

By February 17, Croix and Galindo had drawn up a rough outline for a
program to secure the Spanish presence along the Colorado River. Two
"pueblos or missions" would be established among the Quechans. Each of
these settlements would be composed of ten soldiers, ten civilian farmers,
and five civilian laborers, all with their families. A total of four Franciscan priests, including Fathers Díaz and Garcés, would serve the spiritual

needs of the communities. Together, these two "military colonies" would provide a force of fifty Spaniards to secure the Yuma Crossing.[14]

To counteract the independence the religious orders had traditionally maintained over missions, Croix and his adviser Galindo decided to appoint a military commandant who would also serve as the *juez político* (civil judge). This would combine military and civil authority in a single individual directly responsible to the commandant-general. For the four Franciscans, Croix vested in them only the spiritual authority for the settlements, but he did not clearly define their roles. The priests would administer to the settlers "as true and legitimate pastors," but the Father Missionaries, as Croix called them, were also "to proceed with the reduction of the Indians in conformance with the sovereign laws and royal cédulas of their Majesties." In other words, the Franciscans were to function as both missionaries to the Quechans and pastors for the settlers.[15]

Spanish missionary practice usually congregated natives around a new mission in order to inculcate, or "reduce," them in the ways of Christianity and Western civilization. However, Croix and Galindo scrapped this formula; they ordered that only those Quechans "who wish voluntarily to join either of the pueblos" were to be under the direction of the priests, and then only in religious matters. For the rest of the tribe, Croix commanded the Franciscans to "teach them with great sweetness and gentleness the certain truths of our religion. Then they shall exhort them to ask for and to receive Holy Baptism of their own accord, after being instructed in the obligations we have as Christians." Obviously, the caballero hoped that in this manner the Franciscans would evangelize and hispanicize the Indians without recourse to the traditional methods used in the missions.[16]

However, for the past six months, Father Garcés and Father Díaz had been using exactly those methods in an attempt to establish a formal mission among the Quechans; clearly, the padres' efforts had been unsuccessful. The plan for two pueblos put forth by Croix and Galindo provided the opportunity to substitute what was essentially a military solution for the failed missionization effort. With the military rather than the Franciscans exercising direct control over the settlements, the Quechans would be spared the forced assimilation that was typical of the missions, an idea that no doubt appealed to the Enlightenment sensibilities of the caballero and the asesor.[17]

Unquestionably, Croix believed that the two "military colonies" could and would function in lieu of the originally conceived presence of a presidio on the Colorado River. He calculated that the settlements would be as militarily effective as a regular presidio, but at a cost to the crown of only 4,704 pesos annually, compared with almost 19,000 to run a presidio. He believed these savings would be achieved without compromising the security of the pueblos. Indeed, twenty soldiers backed up by thirty armed militiamen was a considerable force, numerically equal to the standard presidial garrison. However, the new plan considerably weakened the colony's military value by parceling the men in two places, rather than concentrating them in a single establishment.[18]

The source of the Caballero de Croix's plan has been the subject of much debate among historians. Clearly, regarding the number of soldiers and the use of civilians to bolster them, both Father Garcés and Father Díaz had put forth similar proposals; Garcés had even suggested the establishment of a Spanish civilian pueblo along the Colorado River. However, all of these plans had envisioned traditional missions as the basis for operation, with the padres controlling the military and financial operations. Furthermore, Garcés always maintained that these efforts were eventually to be followed up with the establishment of a formal presidio. The plan to build two pueblos without a presidio and without traditional missions was essentially Croix's own contrivance, with considerable input from Galindo y Navarro.[19]

Once determined to found the settlements, the commandant-general laid the plan before Father Díaz and asked for the Franciscan's comments. Two days later, on February 19, Father Díaz returned with his written opinion. He had no objections to setting up two pueblos of Spaniards at Yuma. He noted that the Quechans were skilled agriculturists, that they practiced individual land ownership, and that any who wished to live in the Spanish villages would be familiar with the parceling out of farm lots. The major problem in the new plan, Díaz felt, lay in removing financial control of the settlements from the Franciscans. Lack of funds for necessities and gifts for the natives had been a constant problem for the missionaries ever since they had arrived at the Colorado River. For the caballero's plan to be successful, the many expenses needed to convert the Quechans could only be met if the priests managed the wealth, or *temporalidades*, of the new establishments, as was practiced in traditional missions. If the caballero did not agree, Díaz asked that he at least give the sum of two hundred pesos per mission to the padres to aid them in their evangelization.[20]

Father Díaz had surprisingly accepted Croix's new arrangement with little debate. Perhaps the Franciscan was overwhelmed by the caballero's plans, or perhaps he felt that he and Father Garcés could manage to utilize traditional mission practices in spite of Croix's order. Regardless, Díaz obviously felt he had to agree with the caballero's plan as the only way of continuing among the Quechans the missionary activity that he and Father Garcés had initiated.[21]

Pleased that Padre Díaz accepted his design without major objections, the caballero sent the Franciscan's response to Asesor Galindo y Navarro for review. In a report of February 29, the asesor reiterated that the finances of the two pueblos should be controlled by their military commander, but he noted that as the king had ordered the Quechans to be converted to the faith, it would be wise to grant the priests the requested supplementary fund of four hundred pesos. Satisfied with Galindo's opinions, three days later Croix ordered that final instructions for the founding of two pueblos of Spaniards along the Colorado River be drawn up. On March 7, he signed the finished decree and commanded its immediate implementation.[22]

In many ways the decree for the settlements reflected both the idealism and ignorance of its authors. Although certain practical elements, such as the recruiting of the settlers, the amount of cattle and tools supplied to them, and the selection and payment of the soldiers, were dealt with in detail, many elements were pure fantasy. Croix and Galindo assumed that there would be vacant land for the villages and fields for planting; their plan called for the lands "presently possessed" by the Quechans to be set aside for the Indians, but the rest would be parceled out to the settlers. Several sections were to be reserved as common land; others would be used to maintain the four Franciscans. "To avoid doubts and quarrels," each village was to set up boundary markers, and "the pasturage, woodlands, and other utilities shall be the common property" of both settlements.[23]

Croix ordered each village to be walled "with a tower at each of the four corners." The soldiers were to stable their horses inside the walls, feeding the animals from a haystack stored nearby. Individual homesteads were to be parceled out by lot and the buildings constructed so "that they be uniform and that the streets be straight in order to avoid disorderly appearance." The houses of the Quechans were to be similarly arranged, "when they have been persuaded by the father missionaries to join the pueblos to which they have been attracted by the good example and gentle treatment of the settlers." Once situated, the villagers were to form a "municipal government . . . made up of an *alcalde* [magistrate] four *regidores* [councilors] and a *síndico* [attorney] or *tesoro* [treasurer]," each elected for one year subject to the confirmation of the commandant-general.[24]

The Caballero de Croix's vision that the arid lands around the Yuma Crossing were abundant in fields, pastures, and woods can be ascribed to sheer ignorance of the terrain. However, his view that fifty families of settlers and soldiers could merge blithely and happily among three thousand independent Quechan Indians was idealistic in the extreme. Croix had seen with his own eyes the failure of presidial garrisons to erect adequate defensive walls, organize effective governance, and reach financial solvency, let alone achieve harmonious assimilation with the surrounding Indians. Yet he expected his two "military colonies" somehow to accomplish these goals along the Colorado River.[25]

Despite the internal contradictions of the decree, by the middle of March 1780 the Caballero de Croix's scheme began to be turned into reality. The commandant-general gave Father Díaz authority to enroll twelve laborers and their families, six for each village, for a period of two years. The government would support these workers with a monthly salary that was "just and fitting." In addition, Croix allotted a total of 2,400 pesos to purchase and transport "vestments, sacred vessels and church utensils" and things "to take care of the most pressing needs of the Indians." From this sum, combined with the four Franciscans' annual salary of four hundred pesos, the commandant-general expected the priests not only to sustain themselves, but also successfully to convert the Quechan nation.[26]

If Father Díaz found himself pressed by this assignment, he was not the only one. Croix selected as military commandant for the two pueblos, Ensign Santiago Yslas, from the presidio of Altar. Nothing in Yslas's career had prepared him for the heavy burden of command that he now faced. Born in 1748 in Monferrato along the Po River in northern Italy, near the border of Piedmont and Lombardy, Yslas was "a soldier of fortune." At age twenty-four he arrived in America and made his way to

Mexico City. On July 25, 1772, he enlisted in the Regiment of the Dragoons of Mexico, and after only five months was promoted to corporal. Four years later he advanced to sergeant. Yslas was then assigned to the fifty-man picket his regiment furnished for service along the northern frontier, then stationed in Chihuahua, the capital of Nueva Vizcaya.[27]

In the caste-oriented Spanish military a European noncommissioned officer, such as Yslas, was highly regarded. As a consequence of this status, when a vacancy occurred in one of the four "flying companies" (*compañías volantes*), independent units supplementing the regular presidial garrisons, on May 20, 1777, Yslas received the rank of *alférez*, or ensign, of the Third Flying Company of Nueva Vizcaya. In this capacity he took part in a single sally against the Apaches, but did not come to grips with the enemy.[28]

In 1778, the Third Flying Company was sent to the Sonoran presidio of San Miguel de Horcasitas to bolster the provincial defenses against the Seris and Apaches. There, Ensign Yslas met and married Doña María Ana Montijo, daughter of militia sergeant Don Felipe Montijo and Loreta Salgado, members of one of the first families of Horcasitas. The Montijos gave their daughter as a dowry a large portion of their sizeable farmland and herds. As a result, Yslas's marriage to Doña María gained him a position as a member of the regional gentry.[29]

Probably this new status enabled him to transfer from the Third Flying Company to the garrison of the presidio of Altar. Appointed second ensign of the company, Yslas commanded the *tropa ligera*, light horsemen, unencumbered by the heavy, leather armor and shield carried by the other presidial soldiers. At Altar, he saw immediate action, riding out seven times in pursuit of Apaches and once against rebellious Pima Indians, on which occasion he killed one of the enemy with his own hands.[30]

With his background as a European regular, Yslas's major duties consisted of training and drilling the frontier soldiers. A 1779 inspection of the presidio noted that "Yslas continues to discipline the troop, and in teaching it to shoot at the mark perfectly, and to aim correctly." His service record noted: "This officer has application for the Royal Service and has dedicated himself to the instruction of the troop of this Presidio." His proficiency in disciplining and training troops probably was a major factor in Yslas's selection as commander of the Colorado River settlements. However, drilling soldiers was a far cry from organizing a self-sufficient colony, and the ensign soon found himself a very busy man.[31]

To this officer fell the task of recruiting, equipping, and transporting twenty families of settlers and twenty families of soldiers to their new homes along the Colorado River. Once there, Yslas was to establish the two settlements on a firm military and financial footing, support Fathers Garcés and Díaz in converting the Quechan, and maintain the peace between the hostile tribes of the region. Separated from the nearest presidio by 150 miles of desert, Ensign Yslas would have to accomplish these tasks in virtual isolation.[32]

The instructions from Commandant-General Croix on erecting the two pueblos detailed three soldiers from Altar and six from the presidio of Buenavista to accompany Ensign Yslas to the Colorado. The majority of soldiers, eight troopers and two corporals, were to come from the Tucson presidio. They would be led by Sergeant Juan de la Vega, who would act as Yslas's second in command. Of the men from Tucson, at least three, Corporal Pascual Rivera, Corporal Juan Miguel Palomino, and soldier Juan Vicente Martínez, had accompanied Lieutenant Colonel Anza on his expeditions to California; therefore, they were somewhat familiar with the Quechans. Contrary to Father Garcés's recommendation, none of the twelve troopers currently serving at the Colorado would be assigned to the permanent garrisons of the two pueblos.[33]

The selection of soldiers had already been decided, but Yslas himself was in charge of enlisting twenty families of colonists for a period of ten years. Though Father Díaz assisted the ensign in this process, the recruiting, nevertheless, took several months. The benefits offered to the settlers had great attraction. In addition to the promise of free land, each family would receive from the government a monthly stipend of ten pesos, along with "a yoke of oxen, two cows, one bull, two mares, and one pointed and one blunted hoe." Gradually, traveling throughout the Pimería Alta, Ensign Yslas filled his quota, many of the families coming from Altar, Tucson, and the former presidio of Tubac.[34]

Slow as the enlistment of settlers was, Yslas faced even more trouble in acquiring the cattle, oxen, and horses necessary for their support. The caballero ordered the Franciscan missions of the region to gather together a herd of 50 cattle and 200 sheep to serve as common stock for the settlements and to help support the four priests at Yuma. The regional missions responded in good time, but Yslas was still unable to gather the total number of animals required for the colonists. By September 1780, after seven months of effort, he had acquired only 192 cattle and horses and 204 sheep for the settlers, and forty-two horses for the soldiers of the garrison—far short of the amount promised in Croix's instructions. More importantly, Yslas failed to locate any oxen, which were essential for plowing and therefore crucial to the self-sufficiency of the new settlements.[35]

While Yslas continued his preparations, Father Díaz had gone to the mission of Tubutama in anticipation of returning to the Colorado River before the main group of colonists. From there he wrote a letter on September 12 to the caballero relaying his concerns about the length of time preparations were taking. The time for harvesting had arrived at the Colorado, and Díaz feared the Indians would "in continued feasts, consume the greater part of their fruits," leaving little for the Spanish settlers. In an attempt to prevent this from occurring, Father Díaz planned to leave for Yuma no later than September 24. A muleteer, two laborers, and half a dozen soldiers would accompany him "in order to lay in at the opportune time the necessary stock of provisions for the whole year." As a further precaution, Díaz asked Captain Pedro Tueros at Altar to forward some funds to Sergeant Juan de la Vega at Tucson to allow the settlers gathered there to purchase grain before journeying on the trail.[36] Díaz was also concerned that Father Garcés had not received any real support since Padre Juan Antonio Barreneche had joined him in January 1780, a period of more than eight months.

Barreneche, in fact, had quickly proved himself to be a fervent and dedicated missionary, confirming his early promise.[37] Born in 1749 in the village of Lacazor in Navarre, Barreneche was one of several children of Juan Miguel and María Catalina de Barreneche. His parents, "honest members of the republic, though not very abundant in good fortune," apprenticed young Juan to a wealthy merchant, Don Martín de Alegría, who took the boy to Cuba to serve as a cashier in the warehouses of the Royal Havana Company.[38] "Ignorant of the frauds of the world," Barreneche soon found himself awash in the earthy atmosphere of cosmopolitan Havana. It did not take long for him to discover "that sea ports exhale libertines, slaves to all that is vicious . . . sectarians in their depravities, customs, uses and methods." In reaction to "the corrupt habits" of the city, at age sixteen Barreneche joined the Third Order of St. Francis, a branch of the Franciscans reserved for laymen. In 1768, having found his vocation, he entered the Franciscan convent of the Province of Santa Elena de la Florida in Havana.[39]

Barreneche proved a fervent and devoted novice. A fellow Franciscan later wrote that "his dwelling was the choir. His fasting was his abstinence. His rest was the vigil in prayer." After ordination, Father Barreneche transferred from the Florida province to the College of Santa Cruz de Querétaro. In 1773, he disembarked at the Mexican port of Tampico and set out to walk the two hundred leagues to his new station, "equipped with only a Breviary, and without any other clothing than the tunic and habit in which he was dressed."[40]

Arriving at the college on September 13, 1773, Father Barreneche continued his rigorous devotions, scourging himself, wearing hair shirts, and continuously mortifying his flesh. "He slept very little or not at all," Father Esteban de Salazar later recalled, "practicing some devotional exercises such as the Stations of the Cross, until the hour when the first Masses were said, at which he would assist, always serving the minister when they lacked Acolytes."[41] Barreneche fasted continuously, to the point that his superiors ordered him to eat properly lest he damage his health. Chocolate, for which he confessed a special delight, and bread were his usual staples. For Father Barreneche, "the virtue of Holy Poverty was his greatest love." However, for more than two years he had told his friend Father José Antonio Bernard of a secret desire to serve as a missionary on the northern frontier. The call for a replacement to be sent to the struggling mission along the Colorado River answered Barreneche's prayers.[42]

Despite the zeal with which the young padre had assisted Father Garcés in proselytizing the Quechans, the situation at Yuma remained dangerous: the natives were expecting much from the Spaniards and to date had received little. Father Garcés confirmed this precarious situation in a dispatch sent to the Caballero de Croix sometime in September 1780. Garcés warned that the Quechans "already irritated by so many delays and evil influences . . . were becoming every day more restless and could not be controlled except by superior force."[43] Garcés identified the instigators of the troubles as Salvador Palma's brother Ygnacio and the son of the deceased Chief Pablo, both of whom had been baptized in Mexico. The padre accused the pair "of stirring up the whole tribe with such fatal influence that the rumor had already spread among the youths that on coming to the Río Colorado, the fathers and Spaniards were to be killed." To make matters worse, Sergeant Arguello and most of his twelve man detachment had returned to Altar, leaving Garcés with only three or four troopers for protection. Furthermore, the remaining soldiers were "without a cigar or anything else which they could barter for a little corn to preserve their lives."[44]

Responding to these appeals, Father Díaz set out at once for the Colorado River with whatever men he could gather. On October 20, Díaz and his party of soldiers and settlers, along with their families, arrived to find mission La Purísima Concepción in desperate straits. Padre Díaz observed that "there was a very scant supply of provisions" among the tribes of the Colorado because the river had failed to flood as usual. The Spaniards, therefore, sought aid from the Kohuana tribe, "which is the one that is richest in supplies." Before these Indians could help, the Quechans, led by Ygnacio Palma, attacked the Kohuanas, "killing some, and capturing others, burned many houses and grain fields, stealing all the corn that they could carry and leaving . . . all of us without means to lay in the necessary store of provisions."[45]

When Fathers Garcés and Díaz castigated the Quechans for this attack, the Indians became angry "and were on less friendly terms even with the Spaniards." Díaz wrote Croix on November 8, blaming these events on the lack of soldiers in the mission's escort. "In consequence," the padre noted, "the Indians lose their fear and respect and do what they like without our being able to prevent their disorders." He asked the commandant-general immediately to send supplies for the troopers and their families who had accompanied him. Díaz also felt that with the shortage of food, it might be prudent for Ensign Yslas to delay bringing the bulk of the colonists until the spring, when new crops would be harvested.[46]

The Quechan attack upon the Kohuana had resulted not only from a lack food, but, in Father Díaz's opinion, as a direct result of "the interest they have in capturing prisoners" to be sold as slaves. The tribes of the Colorado and Gila Rivers continuously sold captives to the Spaniards in the Pimería Alta and at the Papago villages. Díaz felt that unless Commandant-General Croix took steps to stop the trade, the Quechans and their neighbors would continue to attack each other for slaves. Until then, the pueblos at Yuma would "not be freed here from these unjust outbursts, so pernicious and so contrary to law."[47]

Father Díaz concluded his letter by warning Croix against the growing power of Ygnacio Palma among the Quechans. The padre claimed that Ygnacio "has a large following among the youth of this tribe," and that he had not only attempted to kill his brother Salvador Palma, but that he "has incited his followers to take the life of the fathers and soldiers." "It would be wise," the Franciscan recommended, " . . . to remove from the tribe so wicked a counsellor." But he left the final decision on how to proceed up to the commandant-general.[48]

This letter offered an indication of the substantial changes that the internal politics of the Quechans had undergone. Ygnacio Palma obviously had begun to emerge as a powerful force, challenging his brother Salvador for the position of kwoxot. Ygnacio's icama, or dream power, was decidedly anti-Spanish and perhaps anti-Christian, rejecting the alliance with the white men in favor of traditional Quechan policies. Ygnacio's leadership in the attack against the Kohuanas was an obvious repudiation of the Spanish priests' efforts to end the wars of the region. More importantly, the attack was seen as a determination on the part of Ygnacio and other tribesmen to maintain the leadership of the Quechan League.[49]

However, among the Quechans substantial support still existed for continued relationships with the Spanish. Father Juan Barreneche reflected this fact in his letter of November 26 to Father Sebastián de Flores, the new guardian of the Santa Cruz College in Querétaro. Unlike Padre Díaz, Barreneche was much more hopeful about the situation at Yuma. He began by requesting the college to pray for the soul of his mother, María Catalina, as he had just learned of her death. Quickly putting aside his personal grief, Barreneche informed his fellow Franciscans, "I also want to tell something . . . of . . . the conversion of the infidels." "First of all," he reported, "of the small children voluntarily brought by their Gentile parents, there are found baptized 200, of which some have died." Barreneche felt that if the Franciscans had been given more support, all the Quechan children could have received the sacrament by now. Together with some older people and some "marriageable youths," overall about 340 Quechans had been baptized, representing a respectable portion of the entire tribe, perhaps 10 percent. Considering the handicaps under which the Yuma missionaries labored, this was a considerable achievement.[50]

The padre noted that many adult Quechans came to be catechized, but somewhat irregularly. He attributed this sporadic attendance to the fact that the tribe was "very spread out throughout all the environs of this Río Colorado for a distance of about eight or nine leagues, one house here, another one there, and very few together." Only those Indians living near the mission had been instructed in the faith. Barreneche thought that if the Quechans could be concentrated into two or four pueblos, each with its own mission, the entire tribe could soon be converted. But as things now stood, "even if they assign eight ministers only for this nation, the way they are so spread out it would be very difficult." The padre believed that "with some labor it could be done."[51]

Barreneche concluded by telling his brothers at the Santa Cruz College that the Quechans were not the only group ripe for conversion. The Kohuanas, Halykwamais, Cocopas, Halchidomas, Mohaves, and Maricopas were "all wishing ministers so they can baptize their children"; however, because of Spain's war with Britain, Barreneche held out little hope for increased aid from the crown at this time. The padre prayed that, nevertheless, when hostilities ended, support would be forthcoming "so that so many souls may not be lost, but redeemed through Jesus' blood."[52]

The optimistic nature of Father Barreneche's letter stood in stark contrast to the dire warnings of Father Díaz to the caballero. The difference probably reflected that among the Quechans neither the icama of Salvador Palma, who favored allying with the Spaniards, nor that of Ygnacio, who rejected the Europeans, had proven decisive. However, soon after Díaz and his advance group of colonists arrived, a marked change occurred. Father Díaz had brought half a dozen soldiers from Tucson, a carpenter, and a blacksmith, all with their families, probably accompanied by a substantial escort. Added to the small group of soldiers that had remained at Yuma, Spanish forces along the Colorado increased dramatically. When the Franciscans told the Quechans that even more soldiers and settlers were on their way, the pro-Spanish policies advocated by Salvador Palma once again came to the fore.[53]

Seeing the way the wind was blowing, Ygnacio Palma quickly reversed his actions and began to ingratiate himself with the white men; indeed, his new assistance became so marked that the Spaniards officially appointed him as one of the magistrates for the tribe. Father Garcés commented that "although the Indian Palma has been troublesome he has changed completely ever since we appointed him *justicia* [the staff of office, however, was withheld from him until he should be married within the church] . . . and he is a great assistance to the catechizing, bringing many to mass and to pray."[54]

Whatever the true disposition of Ygnacio Palma and the Quechan tribe toward the Spanish may have been, the arrival of the main body of colonists brought the issue to a head a few weeks later. On December 27, 1780, Ensign Santiago Yslas, with more than one hundred settlers, a large escort of soldiers, and hundreds of cattle, horses, and pack mules, reached the Colorado River. He informed the Indians that they were there to build two military colonies and to secure the Yuma Crossing for Spain. If the Quechans had any doubt about Spanish intentions before this, one thing was now crystal clear—the white men had come to stay.[55]

7

The Respectable Union

The Spanish Settlement, December 1780
to June 1781

ENSIGN YSLAS realized at once that the hill atop which lay the sixteen-month-old mission of La Purísima Concepción was a perfect site for settlement. Rising more than fifty feet from the surrounding valley, it commanded a view in all directions. The broad summit offered ample space for building, while the steep, almost precipitous, slopes provided a natural defense. To the south, the muddy Colorado had cut a path between this hill and an identical one on the Sonoran side, forming a natural pass. Upstream, to the east, lay the junction of the Gila and Colorado. Thick groves of cottonwoods and willows lined both streams far into the distance. Fertile bottomlands, amply irrigated by the rivers' overflow, were near at hand, as were several Quechan villages *(rancherías)*. Most importantly, the hill commanded the ford across the Colorado on which lay the new road to California.[1]

Atop the summit, Yslas found the crude adobe walls of the mission's small church and the wood and thatch huts, or *jacales*, built by Father Díaz and the advance group of colonists since their arrival the previous month. Yslas and his party soon began to set up similar shelters, to serve until they could construct more permanent houses. Already, the ramshackle new settlement had adopted the name of Garcés mission, La Purísima Concepción del Río Colorado.[2]

When the ensign and his command first arrived on December 27, 1780, the Quechans greeted them "with much applause, pleasure and rejoicing." He had made a speech before the assembled Indians and informed them that "the will of the King, my master" had ordered the establishment of two pueblos of Spaniards along the Colorado River. "After I had given them some advice," Yslas later commented, "they were well satisfied, replying that they would not be found wanting in any respect. . . . I observed in them much good will so that all the Indians are very quiet and peaceful and without any sign of disorder."[3]

However, despite this auspicious beginning, problems quickly arose. Although there was an abundance of beans and squash for the newcomers to eat, there was a marked shortage of corn. Ensign Yslas discovered that the lack of oxen had prevented the advance group of Spaniards from planting any crops or gathering any wood for the construction of houses. He had no one to blame but himself, for providing the draft animals had been his responsibility in the first place. Regardless, he immediately began to organize the colonists in the construction of an irrigation canal to water the fields around the pueblo of La Concepción.[4]

Yslas discovered that the master carpenter and master blacksmith, both of whom had arrived in November, had failed to deliver on the amount of work for which they had contracted. As punishment, the ensign made the blacksmith sign a statement declaring "that he would make all the ironwork belonging to the construction of the church, house of the reverend father ministers, commandant, and other public buildings" without charge to the government. In the case of the carpenter, Yslas decreed that the man would not receive any payment for the time he had wasted.[5]

The ensign then turned to choosing residents for the town of La Concepción, where he and his wife Doña María Ana Montijo would reside. To be his second in command, he chose thirty-eight-year-old Cpl. Pascual Rivera, of Tucson, and assigned four other leather-jacket soldiers, or soldados de cuera, also of Tucson, to the town: José Ygnacio Zamora, age twenty-eight; José Ygnacio Martínez, age thirty-three; and Bernardo (Fernando) Morales and Juan Joachin Gallardo, ages unknown. Two light troopers, or tropa ligera, from Yslas's old command at Altar, Faustino Zelaya and twenty-two-year-old Pedro Solares, along with two soldiers from the presidio of Buenavista, Pedro Bohorques and Manuel Duarte, comprised the remainder of the garrison. To support the military, approximately fifteen civilian heads of household and their families would also settle in La Concepción. Father Garcés and Father Barreneche would serve as the pastors of the community. In total, about eighty-six men, women, and children populated the new town.[6]

As the citizens, or vecinos, of La Concepción began to organize themselves, Ensign Yslas turned to the establishment of a second "military colony." After consultation with Fathers Garcés and Díaz, Yslas examined a site about ten miles northeast of the Yuma Crossing, near present-day Laguna Dam. In 1776, Father Garcés had identified this location, which he named the Puerto de San Pablo, as being "very advantageous, between the sierra and the shore, among some high hills that are beyond the puerto, in whose immediate vicinity there is a channel through which runs the water when the river is high. . . . This situation affords plenty of grass and I consider it as very much to the purpose of founding a mission."[7]

Commandant Yslas agreed with Garcés's assessment. He decided to place the second Spanish pueblo there, "on the same side of the river as this first town of La Concepción at a distance of five leagues up stream towards the east." On January 7, 1781, in a formal ceremony, the colonists marked out the new settlement of San Pedro y San Pablo de Bicuñer. "I gave over possession," Yslas described the scene, "of the aforesaid town and the lands belonging to it to the Reverend Fray Juan Díaz and settlers in the name of the King my master, and some Yuma Indians and justicias looked on and saluted us with shouts, each one by himself crying hurrah for the King, our Lord." Whether this affair was stage-managed or genuine, the Quechans by their actions once again acknowledged the Spanish presence in their land.[8]

In command of the village of Bicuñer, the ensign placed 1st Sgt. Juan de la Vega, of Tucson. Juan Miguel Palomino, a thirty-seven-year-old corporal from Tucson, seconded Vega. Three leather-jacket troopers from Tucson served under their former noncommissioned officers: thirty-one-year-old José Cayetano Mesa, and Francisco Xavier Díaz and Juan Vicente

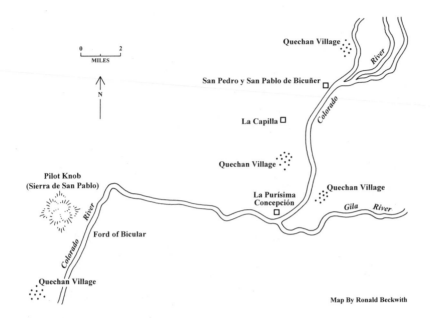

MAP 2. The Yuma Crossing, ca. 1781.

Martínez, both age thirty-two. Four soldiers from the presidio of Buena-vista, thirty-year-old Miguel Antonio Romero, Xavier Luque, Matías de la Vega, and Esteban Romero, ages unknown, along with José Reyes Pacheco, age thirty eight, a soldado de cuera from Altar, rounded out the troop. In addition, more than a dozen civilian families took up residence at Bicuñer, taking the total population to about seventy-seven—slightly less than that of La Concepción.[9]

To serve the spiritual needs of the residents of Bicuñer, thirty-seven-year-old Father José Matías Moreno joined Father Díaz. Father Moreno was born in 1744 in northern Spain, the son of Mathias Moreno and Catalina Gil. He entered the Franciscan order on June 21, 1761, in his native city of Logroño, at the age of sixteen. After ordination, he attended university studies for several years and became renowned for having "a great wealth of philosophical and theological knowledge." In 1769, Moreno enlisted to serve as a missionary in the College of Santa Cruz de Querétaro in Mexico.[10]

Before leaving Spain, Father Moreno expressed to his sister his inner-most feelings on his new assignment. Moreno was disturbed that his "zeal for the faith, the conversion of souls and the longing for martyrdom" led him to leave his parents, family, and homeland. He worried that perhaps his motivation came from a false sense of pride, that he loved himself more than his family, and he confessed to his sister that he had been "battling with these desires." Still, "all the sophistries of proper love" had not swayed Moreno's trust in his convictions. He told his sister that he anxiously looked forward to serving as a missionary and for the "occasions to plant the faith of Christ and to suffer martyrdom."[11]

His opportunities to convert souls came soon enough. In 1773, the college's superiors sent Moreno to the missions in the Pimería Alta. For more than a year, he labored among the Pimas and Papagos gathered at Mission San José de Tumacácori, located near the presidio of Tubac. About forty miles to the north lay Father Garcés's mission of San Xavier, and consequently Padre Moreno became familiar with Garcés's plans for evangelizing the natives of the Gila and Colorado Rivers. These efforts would, ultimately, lead Father Moreno to his destiny.[12]

In 1775, he was reassigned more than one hundred miles to the south, to the mission at Caborca in the Altar River valley. For the next five years, along with his compañero Father Pedro Font, Moreno dutifully continued his labors among the heathen. When Font accompanied the second Anza expedition to California in 1775/1776, Moreno was again impacted by Garcés's plans for expanding the mission frontier into the unknown. But after Font's return, the designs of Garcés seemed to stall, and the rigors of daily life at Caborca soon obscured any vision of glory for Father Moreno. Instead, he and Padre Font concentrated their efforts on other projects, including overseeing the construction of a substantial brick church at their *visita* of San Diego del Pitiquito, several miles to the east of Caborca.[13] By the time the call came, in late 1780, for Father Moreno to aid in the conversion of the Quechans and to minister to the new settlements of the Colorado River, he had become one of the most experienced Franciscans on the frontier, having accumulated almost twenty years in the order, twelve of which had been as a missionary for the Querétaro college.[14]

When Father Moreno and the other colonists arrived at the Yuma Crossing, Father Garcés had been among the Quechans for more than a year and a half. Despite the presence of the soldiers and settlers, Garcés remained disappointed with what he viewed as a lack of support for the conversion of the Indians. The Caballero de Croix's instructions for governing the two pueblos had essentially forbidden the Franciscans from concentrating the natives into traditional mission communities; however, if the padres were successfully to evangelize the Quechans without gathering them together, more priests and more resources would have to be committed by the Spanish government.

Garcés gently chided Croix on the situation in a letter dated December 30, 1780. The priest pointed out that now that the two villages of Spaniards had arrived, the time had come for the caballero to give more attention to converting the Quechans. "I hope that your lordship, out of the goodness of your heart . . . will take additional steps for the complete reduction of the tribe, for with the establishment of the two missions more than half the tribe cannot receive Christian instruction without removing from their lands, a thing difficult to bring about, because they are attached to the soil and derive profit from it." If Croix did not want the Quechans to go into missions, then Garcés felt that more missions should be established among the Quechans.[15]

To that end, Garcés and Father Barreneche drafted a letter to their superiors at the Querétaro college on January 16, 1781. The priests had received word that a potential donation of four thousand pesos had been offered to the college for the founding of another mission among the Quechans. The only condition was that it be named San Lorenzo. This offer must have seemed a godsend to the padres, and they set out to assure their fellow Franciscans that the donation would achieve great success. If funded, Garcés and Barreneche wrote, Mission San Lorenzo would "be located within four or five leagues of this [mission of La] Purísima, among the same Yuma Nation, where there are plenty of Indians." The amount offered would not pay for another colony of Spanish settlers, but "for Ministers and their escort, it is sufficient"; yet if the Querétaro college could convince the caballero to approve the new mission, another Spanish village might eventually be established.[16]

The two priests assured their superiors that the founding of the San Lorenzo mission would not intrude on the development of the two pueblos already at Yuma. Garcés and Barreneche had consulted with Father Díaz on the matter, and he believed that if the funds for any new mission were also to pay for a military escort, the Caballero de Croix would not oppose the establishment. The priests noted that Díaz's opinion was shared "by the Commander of these establishments Dn. Santiago Yslas."[17]

Fathers Garcés and Barreneche continued to stress the pressing need for another mission to the Quechans. "Even though there have [been] placed in this nation two missions," the Franciscans believed that they had only been able to reach about one-third of the population. For the remainder, they lamented that "we are without power to catechize [the adults] nor baptize the infants, since the Mission of San Pablo [at Bicuñer] has been placed at a point above the last of this nation, about four leagues from this [mission], for not being able to find another place suitable for the Spanish citizens."[18]

The priests' report on the conversion of those Quechans they had been able to reach was less than glowing. The Indians were still not satisfied with the amount of material benefits they had received from the white men. "The reduction has had its highs and lows, but the day will come, thanks be to God, that it will come to prosperity, although not like it was thought, because Palma and the gifts from Mexico have done more harm than advantage." Still, Garcés and Barreneche remained hopeful that with more effort on their part and with greater support from the government, they would eventually be successful.[19]

Despite the Franciscans' hopes, the isolation of the command concerned Santiago Yslas. Since the main party's arrival, tensions between the Spanish settlers and the Quechans had emerged, though slowly. The origin of the problems revolved around land. Much of the area appropriated by the Spaniards for their two villages had been in the actual possession, or had at least been claimed by, groups of Quechans. In addition, the settlers allowed their animals to pasture on unoccupied parcels, heedless of the fact that these fields belonged to the Quechans. "The pasturage for maintaining herds of mares and sheep is very scarce," Yslas informed Croix, "and it will be necessary to retire toward Monterey for breeding"; however, in the meantime the scarcity of pasture resulted in the settlers' cattle eating up some of the fields of the Quechans. The Franciscan chronicler Father Juan Domingo Arricivita later admitted, "The result was that much damage was done by this multitude of animals in the maize-fields and sown lands of the Indians."[20]

The lack of oxen among the Spaniards exacerbated the problems. Not being able or willing to clear the underbrush from much of their land, the settlers expropriated cleared fields from the Quechans. "A grievous error it was," Father Arricivata noted, "for the Spaniards to think that the best lands should be for them." The colonists "began to desire to make use of the patches or clearings that were in the mountain groves, and in which the Indians had sown." The Quechans objected to these events, but "showed a moderation very unusual for savages, which was to complain to the ensign-commandant, bringing to his knowledge not only these damages, but also those that the cows and horses were doing."[21]

In letters to the caballero dated January, 1781, Ensign Yslas stressed the positive aspects of the founding of the two Colorado River settlements, hinting only obtusely at the growing friction over ownership of land. In describing the construction of the irrigation ditch for the village of La Concepción, Yslas wrote, "If the settlers had given their attention to obtaining water from the river, they would always have remained in arrears, and could not have made gardens for vegetables and fruit trees, and there would undoubtedly have been some discord with the Yuma Indians for the lands which the irrigating canal would water do not belong to them." By mentioning the tensions in this manner, it is unclear if Yslas took any definitive action to deal with the situation. However, in a moment of candor, the ensign flatly informed Croix that he felt he needed "ten pairs of irons and two pieces of artillery, for they would not fail to be of use some day in case there should be an uprising among these Indians."[22]

As tensions mounted, confrontations between Spaniards and the natives did occur. In one instance, a Quechan struck back by attacking an animal loose in his field. In response, the ensign-commandant "ordered one of them [the Quechans] beaten for having wounded a horse belonging to a corporal." Yslas's failure to understand the situation is apparent in his report to Croix about the flogging incident, wherein he quixotically commented, "In dealing with the Indians I have discovered up to the present that they are of all sorts, some good and others bad." He continued that "the punishment was administered by the hand of Captain [Salvador] Palma, who obeys me in whatever cases and matters I give him instructions, and with much loyalty and promptness he does everything."[23]

However, even those Indians the Spaniards deemed good were not always so accommodating. The underlying cause for the disaffection was the Quechans' desire for material benefits. Salvador Palma, for example, complained to the ensign that he had not received all the gifts he had been promised. "Captain Palma wished to go over and see your Lordship [Croix] complaining that he had not been given the clothes which his Excellency the late viceroy [Bucareli] had promised him." Somewhat tactlessly, Yslas informed Palma "that the time had already passed" for the Quechan leader to receive the gift of clothes, "and that he should take for an example the industry of the Spaniards, for by this means they would be clothed and in no other way." The ensign, despite the Spaniards' inability to sustain themselves, told Palma to emulate the industriousness of the white men, and "that to teach him this and various other things we had come to his lands." Putting up a good front, Yslas declared that "Palma remained satisfied and since then he has not spoken again."[24]

The clamoring for gifts among the Indians was not limited to Salvador Palma. A Kohuana, "The Captain" of the tribe, came before Santiago Yslas to complain of the attacks his people had suffered at the hands of the Quechans. Yslas "consoled" the Kohuana chieftain, no doubt with gifts and promises of more gifts, and "left him well content." When news of this reception circulated, other nations began to send delegations to the new Spanish settlements. "Every day," Yslas reported, "Indians from various tribes come to visit me with their justicias and to all of them I give very good counsel and leave them much consoled."[25]

When Commandant-General Croix, at his headquarters in Arizpe, received the first reports of Yslas, Father Garcés, and Father Díaz, he got a rather confused picture of happenings at Yuma. Undoubtedly, the fact that most of his information was two to three months out of date by the time it arrived enhanced the confusion. For example, Father Díaz had written in November that Ygnacio Palma was causing trouble, but Father Garcés's December letter indicated that the problem had been solved; then Santiago Yslas's letters of January made no mention of that issue, but instead had requested cannon and irons in case there was an uprising. Nevertheless, the commandant-general remained confident that his two "military colonies" would flourish. However, realizing that he was operating in the dark, the caballero contented himself with issuing a series of orders filled with cautionary instructions and what he felt to be practical advice.[26]

Croix responded first to Father Díaz's concerns about the lack of provisions along the Colorado River. He told Father Díaz he had ordered the paymaster of Altar presidio, Lieutenant Andrés Arías Caballero, "to proceed to your settlements for the purpose of transporting the yokes of oxen and the cattle for the aid of the said colonists." The commandant-general also issued instructions for the next supply train to include "some provisions and articles of equipment to remedy . . . the lack of clothing experienced by the soldiers and their families."[27]

In regard to the sale of Indian slaves that Díaz felt exacerbated the wars between the Quechan and Maricopa–Gila Pima Leagues, Croix declared that he had not known of "this iniquitous trade." He issued orders for the practice to be stopped immediately "at the presidio of Altar and in the towns of la Pimería." Turning finally to the anti-Spanish actions of Ygnacio Palma, Croix issued a secret order to Ensign Yslas to the effect that "if it be necessary, to remove the aforesaid Indian from his country . . . in such a way that disorders shall not result." The caballero warned that the removal be handled in such a fashion that "we may not be exposed to the danger of the culprit taking flight and stirring up his compatriots." In a separate letter of January 12, Croix informed Father Díaz of the actions he had taken concerning Ygnacio Palma.[28]

Having satisfied the concerns of Father Díaz, Croix next responded to the issues raised by Father Garcés. In a letter dated January 28, Croix praised "the constant zeal of your Reverence for the spreading of the gospel and the extension of the King's domain." However, in response to the padre's request for greater support to his evangelizing efforts at Yuma, the caballero pleaded that although he might wish to send more aid, "often it may be necessary to leave something to time because of my attention being occupied with many prior claims of the royal service. Nevertheless, your Reverence . . . can report to me the assistance you deem necessary so that if it is possible, I can grant it."[29]

The commandant-general now focused his attention on the reports from Ensign Yslas. For the most part, the caballero approved of the ensign's actions. However, in a letter of February 22 Croix took Yslas to task for requesting additional arms. Pointing out that the Quechans had voluntarily invited the Spaniards to settle among them, the caballero wrote sternly:

> I do not understand why there is a need of the irons or the cannon that you ask for . . . rather much gentleness, kind treatment, and discretion. Severity would be only . . . suitable for the purpose of proving to them that they have been deceived in requesting our friendship. . . . These just considerations I want you to hold in mind, and let them serve as a rule for your conduct toward these Indians, certain that observing them you might avoid the necessity of arms and chains, to use which is violence and might cause my displeasure.[30]

Sometime in late February or early March 1781, Lt. Arías Caballero, the Altar paymaster, having received the commandant-general's orders, conveyed a herd of oxen and an abundance of goods and supplies for the maintenance of the settlers. He also carried Croix's dispatches to Díaz, Garcés, and Yslas. Croix, feeling that he had done all that he could for the moment for the two Spanish villages along the Colorado River, was now free to return to his major concern of dealing with the Apaches.[31]

However, by the time the lieutenant arrived at Yuma with the commandant-general's orders and instructions, the situation had stabilized somewhat. Several families of Quechans, including Salvador Palma's, had taken up residence at the village of La Concepción, mingling closely with the settlers. Even Palma's brother Ygnacio, who earlier had manifested markedly anti-Spanish sentiments, seemed to have settled into his duties as a justicia for the tribe. He had performed his responsibilities so well that the Spaniards had come to view him as a great asset. In March, Santiago Yslas updated the Caballero de Croix on the situation, writing that Ygnacio Palma "has done all that has been commanded of him, whether it be to admonish the faults of the . . . Indians or to punish them, and moreover, I have noted his attachment to the Spaniards."[32]

When one of the primary Quechan tribal leaders—a man the Spaniards called Pablo—died, Ensign Yslas appointed Ygnacio Palma to replace the deceased chief. "Perceiving that he [Ygnacio] was so efficient, and that all the Indians had considerable respect for him as well as for another, a companion of his, I made the resolution and carried it into effect of giving him the office of governor in place of the deceased Pablo, and the second was appointed *fiscal.*" Ygnacio thus became the leader of those Quechans settled in or around the village of Bicuñer. His close friend and supporter, Pablo, son of the deceased chief of the same name, would serve as his lieutenant.[33]

As evidenced by these appointments, the Spaniards began to exercise direct control over the internal social and political leadership of the Quechan tribe. Whether the people still regarded Salvador Palma as kwoxot is difficult to tell; it might have been that his brother Ygnacio had emerged to challenge him for that position. Either by design or default, Ensign Yslas's elevation of Ygnacio to a position of authority allied both Quechan brothers and their factions with the Spaniards. Salvador and Ygnacio both followed the orders of Yslas to the point of chastising their own people. The icama of both Quechan leaders clearly had turned in favor of the white men. How long the newcomers could control this situation remained to be seen.[34]

During spring 1781, the two pueblos along the Colorado River put down roots. At the village of La Concepción, the settlers and natives constructed a dozen or so structures atop the hill for which the town had been named. The buildings consisted of "mud, between upright poles or forks to support the roof," placed over stone foundations, each one being "fifteen or twenty feet, nearly square." The settlers' houses were "irregularly placed covering an area of about an acre," arranged in a rough rectangle forming a small plaza. The houses flanked the stone and adobe church, which, with the attached rectory, constituted the largest building in the village. The site was "an excellent position for defense . . . commanding a fine view of the surrounding country." As the construction proceeded at La Concepción, similar structures were underway upriver at the village of San Pedro y San Pablo de Bicuñer.[35]

While the Spanish settlers and the Quechans had reached a temporary modus vivendi, the four Franciscans' attempt to evangelize the tribe was still being sorely tested. Having been forbidden to congregate the Quechans for religious instruction, Father Garcés and his companions tried other unorthodox methods of conversion. The priests offered baptism and the teaching of catechism to any Quechan, not just those who had voluntarily settled at the Spanish villages. Yet the results had been ambiguous, and although Father Garcés and Father Barreneche, at the village of La Concepción, were in favor of continuing this method, Father Díaz was not so sure. As a result, the padres wrote to their superiors explaining the situation and asking for guidance.[36]

In a March 23 letter to the guardian and directory of the Querétaro college, Garcés noted that circumstances had changed much since the project had started. "When the Caballero [de Croix] ordered me to come to this tribe, he ordered me to catechize and baptize them generally having formed a high conception of the inclination of the tribe towards Christianity and of the chimerical authority of Palma." Furthermore, Garcés said he had understood "the Caballero was to come in person and I supposed . . . that at least eighty men were to be assigned to this River." Instead, Croix had canceled his planned review of the Colorado River and sent out a far weaker military force than Garcés had expected.[37]

Padre Garcés also believed that the Quechans were not as willing to accept Christianity as he previously believed. He observed they had qualities that both suited and inhibited their conversion. For example, because they were "unaccustomed to hunting, drunkenness, roving over the mountains, drinking mescal, or eating foods outside of what they raise on their river bottoms, and because no idolatry is practiced among them, [they] are well adapted to become Christians." On the other hand, the Franciscan acknowledged "there are hindrances because of their insubordination, their small need for food, which is usually the principal inducement with Indians, and the fact that this tribe is scattered over both banks of the river."[38]

Garcés and the other missionaries criticized several aspects of Quechan culture and experienced difficulty in convincing the natives to act in a "civilized" fashion. The tribe's sexual habits were one of the major obstacles. Young Quechan adults took multiple sexual partners, and many men practiced polygamy. In a letter to a friend, Father Barreneche admitted, "As regards the adults from 15 or 20 to sixty they are not able to be baptized because they do not care to be catechumens." When Quechan adults did seek to become Christians, their sexual habits affronted the priests' sensibilities. "The experience we have . . . is that if they remain single after Baptism they do not refrain from living like the gentiles, and if they are married by us, there is little hope they will be content with one woman." Barreneche did find some Quechans who lived monogamously, mostly elderly people. For the majority, he concluded that "if God does not move them voluntarily and enlighten their understanding," they could not be baptized at the present time. Father Garcés further observed, "These people are the wildest on the frontier and too stupid to be attracted by spiritual things, and so, few can be baptized of those that reach twenty years and are under sixty, because of the concubines that they habitually take and leave."[39]

Unable to control the behavior—the "barbarity"—of the adult Quechans, the Franciscans turned their attention to the children of the tribe as their best hope for conversion. Father Garcés baptized all the infants and young children brought in by their parents, even if they did not live near La Concepción. Whether or not the college would approve of this method, Padres Barreneche and Garcés felt something had to be done. Many Quechan children died before the priests could baptize them, troubling Barreneche greatly: "The sad thing is that, within our sight, many innocent souls . . . die . . . without the grace of Baptism."[40]

However, the padre continued to be optimistic and claimed that "over here the conversion . . . is going well; the gentile parents bring their infants for baptism, and they like to come to Mass and to pray." Father

Garcés, however, took a more pessimistic view toward those Quechans who came forward voluntarily. He commented that "they have regularly presented [for baptism] their infants and many older children." But the padre feared they did so more out of an interest in tobacco, because he had seen Indians travel more than two leagues to obtain cigarettes. He concluded that the Spaniards' gifts, more than their faith, attracted the Quechans. Garcés lamented:

> When I reached this tribe, I found just this one thing, the expectation of gain so impressed upon them by the conversations of Palma (who I know received any amount of promises in Mexico) that I formed the idea that their disposition was very bad and influenced by the Devil; but knowing that God is more powerful and that the gifts which they were expecting would be forgotten in time and they would be contented with gifts of little value, I . . . resolved to set in motion the affairs of the mission and lay the foundations of the establishments.[41]

However, Garcés still doubted his ability to attract the Quechans to Christianity. He had some success among the old people, and hoped that "their baptism will secure the total reduction of the tribe, which regularly follows the examples of their elders." He had also baptized many Quechans who lived in or near the Spanish village of La Concepción, "although they are absent five or six months," tending their crops. The padre felt this method was proper because the missionaries could then instruct these people at the Sunday masses inside the village or go out and preach to them in the fields. "Both methods," Garcés believed, "should be practiced."[42]

Father Barreneche concurred with Garcés's method. He reported that the missionaries had baptized some elderly Quechans, who were capable of understanding "the principal mysteries of our Holy Faith," and other adults from the tribe, who were "sick and in danger of death." Although he felt "some misgivings about their disposition to receive the grace of Baptism . . . charity obliges us to favor them . . . piously hoping in the goodness of our Great God and in the petitions of the many holy souls that beg ceaselessly for the conversion of the Infidels."[43]

The real problem in the attempted conversion of the Quechans revolved around those people living outside the Spanish settlements, in places the Franciscans could not reach on a regular basis. The tribe was spread out over a large area, "a district of eight leagues by ten," and the four Franciscans simply could not cover all the ground. Father Barreneche saw only two possible solutions: either more priests must be sent, or he and his *compañeros* must be allowed to congregate the Quechans in proper "reductions." As to the first, Padre Juan asked his brothers at the college to "beg God to send zealous workers to the Vineyard: *quia messis quidem multa, operarii autem pauci* [the harvest truly is plenteous, but the laborers are few]." Barreneche understood that the workers had not been sent due to a lack of funds; he believed that the Caballero de Croix would pay for additional missionaries, but "it appears they are prevented only by the Wars that are in Spain."[44] As to the alternative of congregating the Quechans, Father Barreneche felt that this would inevitably occur over time: when the baptized children grew older, they could be "brought together in Missions . . . having their pueblos joined to [those of] the Spaniards," along with those older Indians who had become Christians and been married by the priests. Barreneche foresaw that this process "would be very easy, because these people are very timid." Even if some of the Quechans objected to the reductions, the padre was confident that "the Christians will assemble . . . bold forces of soldiers and citizens," and force the issue.[45]

Whereas Father Barreneche remained confident that the Quechans would ultimately be converted to Christianity, Father Garcés was not so sanguine. Continuing with his unorthodox methods, Garcés decided to follow the example of the priests at the California missions of Monterey and San Diego, who had baptized numerous Indians who did not reside at those missions. "This conversion would be very barren," he concluded, "if we labored in the rigorous method . . . always practiced by the Church." Furthermore, by baptizing as many Quechan children as possible, Padre Garcés hoped to win more friends for the Spaniards, noting "that we have had many fears and cares with this nation, which is moved by the Devil, and motivated in part by having seen so little force until the families arrived."[46]

The Franciscans' inability to provide regular Christian indoctrination to baptized Quechans was another of Father Garcés's concerns. "I refrained at first in baptizing those outside the pueblo . . . born by the fear of error and impelled by the desire to have . . . total perfection." Even after he had started performing general baptisms, trouble plagued Garcés. An epidemic broke out among the tribe "in which there died some baptized infants, which they attributed to my coming . . . and they totally ceased to bring their infants." To add insult to injury, some Quechans complained about the sparse amount of gifts they received when they visited the missions. If the priests tried to talk to these Indians about baptism, Garcés reported, "they mock you."[47]

The presence of several "ringleaders that disturbed the tribe against us" did not deter Garcés from pressing ahead with his plans. He baptized all the children he could, "which were the boys and girls of seven to ten and twelve years." Father Barreneche agreed with this tactic, and even wanted to include "all the very old people, both inside the pueblo and those outside for a distance of two leagues." On the other hand, Father Díaz at Bicuñer initially hesitated to baptize any of the Indians before they had been congregated and instructed. Díaz, however, eventually moderated his views and agreed that they should at least "baptize indiscriminately all the children of the tribe which are not passed two years."[48]

Once agreed on a general strategy, the four Franciscans immediately took steps to implement it. Many of the Christianized Quechans lived between the Spanish villages, a distance of nearly ten miles. However, "of the rest of the nation, which is the larger part, there have been baptized only some sick and in danger of death." In an attempt to proselytize more of the tribe, Garcés set up a chapel in a small *jacal* (hut) "about a league and a half from the mission [of La Concepción]." At this location he thought the Franciscans could more readily preach to the Quechans, "because they sow [crops] there," and it was also a convenient place "for saying Mass on Feast days."[49]

In his March 23 letter to the guardian and directory of the Querétaro college, Father Garcés once again stressed the need for more support for the Yuma enterprise. Four missionaries simply were not enough to catechize the whole tribe effectively, even if the priests split up to cover more ground. In fact, Garcés stated that if funds for the new mission of San Lorenzo were ever sent, they would have to be spent on the Quechans alone rather than other tribes along the Colorado. As for the propriety of the method of general baptism, Garcés asked his superiors to give him their opinions on the matter. He had already written for guidance to Father Francisco Antonio de Barbastro, president of the missions of Pimería Alta, but had yet to receive a reply. Whatever the final decision, he assured the guardian and the directory of the Querétaro college that he and his companions would submit to their directives.[50]

The difficulties that the four Franciscans faced in converting the

Quechans was not reflected in the reports Santiago Yslas sent to the Caballero de Croix. The ensign painted a generally optimistic picture, although the situation was not nearly so mundane as his dispatches indicated. He described the progress in the construction of the irrigation canal: "I announce to your Lordship that already the water is flowing in the canal drawn from the arm of the water from the river and the work extends for more than a league. I sincerely hope that with diligence it may be completed for this soil on account of its looseness requires some ingenuity to make it profitable."[51]

Yslas also noted that he continued working for peace among the tribes of the Colorado River. He boasted that not only had he overseen "the reconciliation of the Cajuenes (Kohuanas) with the Yumas . . . I also brought about peace between the Cachadunes (Halchidomas) and Yumas for the latter were at war with all." The Halchidomas even asked Yslas to see if missions could be sent to their territory. "They assure me that their soil is better than this of the Yumas and the Indians are also known to be more civilized; they sow considerable cotton and they weave many blankets." Although Yslas favored the idea, he believed there was a lack of missionaries for such an endeavor. Therefore, he deferred final judgment on the request to Croix.[52]

Despite these optimistic reports on external events, Yslas still faced several internal problems. Stung by the caballero's admonishment of his request for cannon and irons for the two villages, the ensign again tried to impress upon Croix the vulnerability of his command. "I did not ask for cannon and irons with the intention of treating the Yuma Indians severely, but I was seeking to be prepared in case some day there might be some trouble among these people or among the other tribes as we are very far away from obtaining soldiers quickly to aid us." He claimed that his management of the Quechans "is such that when I give an order to one of them and he commits some offense deserving of punishment, I make use of his own *justicias* for his punishment in order that no feeling may be aroused against me."[53]

However, these reports did not inform the Caballero de Croix that the Quechans had become extremely aroused against Santiago Yslas. During the early months of 1781, Ygnacio Palma and his friend Pablo, the *fiscal* at Bicuñer, came into conflict with José Cayetano Mesa, one of the soldiers of the garrison. For a reason now unknown, Ygnacio Palma and Pablo threatened or attempted to kill Mesa. When word of the altercation got out, Commandant Yslas summarily arrested both of the Quechans and placed them in the stocks.[54]

Whatever the true nature of the dispute, Yslas's actions outraged many Quechans and they remonstrated with the ensign to free the prisoners. Yslas eventually released Ygnacio Palma and Pablo, but the damage had already been done. As he was one of the major powers in the tribe, Palma's status approached, or possibly was, that of kwoxot. To treat one of the most respected members of the community in such a humiliating and arbitrary fashion affronted the entire people. The Franciscan chronicler Arricivata later amply summed up the results of Yslas's actions: "This was one of the most regrettable incidents . . . for this officer ought to have reflected that a savage could not understand nor observe military discipline and that being of a rebellious and haughty nature even when he took him [Ygnacio] out of confinement, he would depart with more irritation than correction; nor could it affect his turbulent followers otherwise than to arouse them all."

The effect of Ygnacio Palma's incarceration proved decisive. Whatever goodwill he and his followers may have had toward the Spaniards immediately evaporated.[55] Once again Ygnacio's dream power, his icama, called for an end to dealings with the newcomers and he now set about to persuade his people to follow his lead. For many Quechans, persuasion was unnecessary; the Spaniards had proven a constant source of disappointment and annoyance. Salvador Palma had promised his people that when the white men came, they would bring an abundance of clothing, bales of fabric, blankets, horses, and other presents. However, the material benefits received so far had been limited and in no way fulfilled their heightened expectations. Instead, the Spaniards had actually been detrimental to tribal resources, straining their already fragile food reserves. The continuous damage to crops by the settlers' and soldiers' untended animals exacerbated the drain on the limited stores. With these causes for discontent, Ygnacio Palma found a receptive audience for his anti-Spanish feelings.[56]

By mid-spring 1781, fewer and fewer Quechans tolerated the Spaniards. Although Yslas heralded to Croix the near completion of an irrigation canal, the settlers were still unable to supply themselves adequately with food. When they tried to purchase grain from the Quechans, many in the tribe expressed their discontent by demanding exorbitant prices, or even by refusing to sell at all. As a result, probably during the spring,

Yslas had to send a small detachment of soldiers and settlers, led by Cpl. Pascual Rivera, to the California Mission of San Gabriel to obtain food in exchange for money and clothing.[57]

The departure of Corporal Rivera provided an unforeseen ally to Ygnacio Palma and his followers. Soon after Rivera's party left, a rumor began circulating among the Quechans that the real purpose of the expedition was to gather reinforcements to arrest Ygnacio and enslave the whole tribe. Surprisingly, several of the Indian interpreters employed by the Spaniards originated the rumor. Most prominent was Francisco Xavier, a Halykwamai Indian. Sold as a *nifora*, or war slave, at an early age at the presidio of Altar, he was raised in the house of the former commander, Capt. Bernardo de Urrea. Having been retained as an interpreter for the Colorado River settlements, Francisco Xavier now used his position to foster hatred and suspicion against the Spaniards.[58]

Ygnacio Palma welcomed Francisco Xavier's advice, and together they gathered more and more support for their anti-Spanish position. Whether Ygnacio actually believed the stories that the interpreter told him is impossible to tell, especially in light of his having been recently mistreated by Commandant Yslas. However this went, Ygnacio used the opportunity to appeal to his people to reestablish their independence. To many, his rhetoric was compelling: Since their arrival, the Spaniards had disrupted the tribe's traditional cultural patterns, hindered its wars, and disrupted its leadership of the Quechan League; the efforts to convert the people to Christianity were, in fact, an attempt to force them into slavery; by allowing the white men to settle among them, the Quechans had actually assisted in their own subjugation.[59]

Added to these "nationalistic" appeals, Ygnacio undoubtedly recalled many examples of personal slights and grievances suffered by tribal members at the hands of the Spaniards. For example, it was later reported that Yslas erected a stake upon which many Quechans had been flogged when he felt they were "deserving of punishment." Although the beatings had been carried out by Quechan leaders, the ones who suffered the punishment obviously held Yslas responsible.[60]

The majority of settlers and soldiers sent out to Yuma also apparently treated the Quechans poorly, showing little understanding or tolerance for the Indians, whom they regarded as "savages." However, these same settlers have been described by the historian Jack D. Forbes as "improvident, apparently lazy, mostly or wholly illiterate and self-centered . . .

racially mixed or Indian people of a very low economic class." Ultimately, many of the Quechans who had earlier welcomed the Spaniards now despised them.[61]

The behavior of Salvador Palma provided the clearest evidence of this turn of events. For years, Palma had been the guiding force behind the Quechans' call for the Spaniards to settle along the Colorado River. His friendship with Father Garcés and Commander Anza and his acceptance of Christianity had cemented his peoples' alliance with the white men. When the Spaniards had finally arrived in force at Yuma, Palma was the one who led the way in welcoming the newcomers by settling with his family in the village of La Concepción. However, the humiliation of his brother Ygnacio, combined with the continuing problems between natives and colonists, led many Quechans to reject Salvador Palma's leadership and his pro-Spanish sympathies. He apparently lost his position as kwoxot among the tribe, possibly being replaced by his brother. The loss of prestige, coupled with the rising tensions, finally proved too much even for Salvador Palma. During the spring of 1781 he moved his family out of La Concepción and separated himself from the settlers.[62]

Perhaps in a bid to reestablish his position within the tribe, Salvador Palma actively participated in plans to oust the Spaniards from Quechan territory. Together with his son, José Antonio, he met with his brother Ygnacio and the disaffected interpreter Francisco Xavier. The rumors that the Spaniards had sent for reinforcements from California and Sonora to arrest Ygnacio and his followers and attack the tribe continued to circulate, and were apparently believed by many of the tribal leaders. Even after Corporal Rivera and his party returned from San Gabriel with only provisions, reports that a large number of Spanish soldiers were on their way to Yuma persisted. In this charged atmosphere, the slightest spark threatened to explode into violence.[63]

8

The Fury of the Yumas

The Settlements Destroyed, July 1781

IN THE FIRST WEEK of June 1781, a group of forty Spanish soldiers and their families arrived at the Yuma Crossing under the command of Capt. Fernando Rivera y Moncada. Driving a herd of almost a thousand cattle, horses, and mules, Rivera's party was on its way to California to colonize the new presidio and mission of Santa Bárbara. The expedition was escorted by a detachment from several Sonoran presidios. Once they reached the Colorado, the men from Sonora were to be relieved by troopers from California. This second detachment appeared a few days after Rivera's arrival, and suddenly close to a hundred Spanish soldiers gathered at Yuma. To the Quechan leaders, their deepest fears were seemingly realized: the rumors had been true; the Spaniards had come to destroy them. The Quechans were now convinced that they would have to fight the white men; the only questions left were where and when.[1]

By June 9, 1781, Rivera and his California-bound colonists had begun to settle in for their anticipated brief stay at Yuma. The 961 cows, horses, and mules that the expedition had driven across the Camino del Diablo arrived at the Colorado River in poor condition. Almost immediately, the famished and parched animals devastated the mesquite trees and planted fields of the Quechans. In addition, the people in Rivera's party were themselves short of food, and not only did the new arrivals begin to strain the reserves of the Quechans, but the Spaniards also even sent out requisitioning parties to obtain food from the Kohuana and Halchidoma tribes.[2]

To the Quechans, the situation was infuriating. For months they had complained to Santiago Yslas about the damage to their fields done by the animals of the two villages. "The commandant knew well what reason the Indians had to complain," the Franciscan historian Arricivata later wrote, "but it was impossible for him to prevent the injuries which provoked them." With the arrival of Captain Rivera's animal herd, the loss to the tribe's food stores increased enormously.[3]

However, the Quechans found themselves in a dire predicament. Rivera's men were well armed and mounted, presenting a considerable military force against which the tribe could not hope to prevail unaided. Only if they received substantial support from their allies in the Quechan League, or if the number of soldiers decreased, would the Indians have a reasonable hope for success. Until such a situation occurred, they would have to continue to suffer the presence of the white men as best they could.

The animosity of the Quechans toward the Spaniards was very thinly veiled, and several of the officers accompanying Captain Rivera noticed it. Ensign Cayetano Limón of the Sonoran presidio of Buenavista commented that Salvador Palma had moved out of the village of La Concepción, and although the Quechan leader and "other Indians associated with him" continued to deal with the Spaniards, relations were less than friendly. "Their manner of treating these settlers was not consistent," Limón later recalled, "and seemed to me to pass over to insolence."[4]

Sergeant José Dario Arguello, from the presidio of Tucson, also observed the growing enmity of the Indians. Arguello had commanded the first detachment of soldiers sent out to guard the Yuma mission back in 1779, and he understood how fragile the food supply of the Indians actually was. When Captain Rivera ordered him to requisition supplies from the Quechans, Arguello later reported that at every ranchería "the Indians screamed out to me that the cows and horses destroyed their mesquite, tornillo, and corn fields, and that they did not understand why [the animals] were not fenced in."[5]

Apprised of this situation, Captain Rivera put his men on guard against the Indians. He also kept close watch over his animals, especially after reports that the Halchidomas planned to raid the horse herd. However, Rivera and his officers were astonished that Commandant Yslas did not seem concerned. Ensign Cayetano Limón remarked, "I noticed an indifference or blind confidence among the soldiers and Spanish residents who occupied that region, and this was remarked also by . . . Captain [Rivera] himself, who mentioned it to the said Yslas, for they did not post a single sentinel at night although they were so well informed of the bad faith of the natives."[6]

After ten days at Yuma, Rivera decided that the California-bound colonists had recuperated enough to continue their journey. As a result, on June 19 the majority of the expedition headed west bound for Mission San Gabriel. However, Captain Rivera decided that he would remain at Yuma with about 257 horses and mules too weak to travel. To assist him with these animals, he kept nineteen soldiers and a few servants under his command. Once the California colonists were safely on their way, Rivera and his troopers remained on the southern, or Sonoran, bank of the Colorado River, directly across from the village of La Concepción. Setting up a series of brush jacales for the men, Rivera allowed the animals to graze freely. The only problem the captain encountered was when one of his men, recruit Francisco Xavier Castro, deserted.[7]

For Salvador Palma and the other Quechan leaders, Rivera's movements presented a golden opportunity. The Spaniards were now divided into three, separate groups: two were in the towns of Concepción and Bicuñer, located about ten miles apart; Rivera's men were across the Colorado. With careful planning, it would be possible to strike separately at each group, isolate them, and overwhelm them. Throughout late June and early July, the Quechan leaders prepared. They began to gather weapons and secretly sent for aid to the other tribes of the region. Eventually, a substantial number of Mohaves responded to the appeals of their kinsmen and allies, and even a few Halykwamais and Halchidomas, old enemies, appeared. As the summer lengthened, the Quechans were at last ready to liberate themselves from Spanish oppression.[8]

The morning of Tuesday, July 17, 1781, promised another hot, summer day at Bicuñer. The routine toils of working the fields, digging the irrigation ditch, and guarding the horses and mules awaited most of the adult men, and the women set about the no less demanding domestic labors. Father Díaz and Father Moreno had already been up for several hours. The family of an elderly, sick woman had summoned them to her bedside in the early morning, while it was still dark. Judging that she was near death, the two padres administered the last rites, anointed the woman with holy oil, and gave her communion.[9]

As the sun broke over the mountains, Díaz and Moreno walked across the town plaza, heading back to their church. Morning mass would have to be said and they needed to prepare. The priests saw several people gathering outside the church as other settlers walked out toward the fields. Sgt. Juan de la Vega had routinely dispatched a single soldier to guard the horse herd, but not suspecting trouble he had not placed sentries.[10]

In a moment, the quiet of the dawn was rent by the screams of war. Scores, perhaps hundreds, of Quechan and Mohave warriors leaped from concealment, rushing the plaza from all sides. Painted for battle and brandishing lances, bows, and war clubs, the Indians killed every Spaniard they could catch. Breaking into the houses of the citizens, the Quechans dragged many Spaniards outside, killing some, sparing others. Any control that the war leaders had over the warriors broke down immediately.

Standing in the plaza watching the attack in horror, Father Díaz and Father Moreno were among the first casualties. Wielding a captured gun, a Quechan shot Díaz through the body. As he crumpled to his knees, the priest was then set upon by other warriors, who crushed his skull with their war clubs. Father Moreno was also clubbed to the ground, and perhaps while he was still alive they hacked off his head with an axe. The "palm of martyrdom" that he had so long wished for had come at last.[11]

With Bicuñer's plaza secure, some Quechans set about ransacking the houses, while smaller groups of warriors headed out to hunt down the Spaniards working in the fields. In the panic and confusion of the initial onslaught, Miguel Antonio Romero, a soldier from the presidio of Buenavista, ran to the banks of the Colorado River. Diving into the water, he swam to the far shore, concealing himself among the brush. He watched and waited, unsure what to do. At the time he could not have known that his wife, María Juana Cota, and their two children lay dead within the town.[12]

One of Romero's civilian neighbors, the town carpenter, Juan José Miranda, also managed to escape to the river. After seeing the destruction of Bicuñer, Miranda made a desperate choice: moving stealthily among the cottonwood and willows that lined the river bank, he began to make his way downstream to La Concepción and, he no doubt hoped, rescue.[13]

Miranda's hopes were vain, for La Concepción had experienced a similar ordeal. Before 8:00 A.M., Commandant Yslas left his house and headed toward the town's adobe church; he was scheduled to serve as Father Garcés's altar attendant for the second mass of the day. Before sunrise, Yslas's wife, María Ana Montijo, had attended the earlier mass conducted by Father Barreneche. Looking out over the rim of the hill on which La Concepción lay, the commandant noticed some groups of armed Quechans milling about below the town. Checking out the situation, Yslas found that Cpl. Pascual Rivera was the only other soldier in town that morning, the rest having gone to work in the fields. Yslas ordered Rivera to arm himself and stand guard outside the church. Satisfied with this precaution, Yslas entered the church and helped Father Garcés prepare for mass. In the priests' house next to the church, Father Barreneche engaged in private meditation.[14]

Meanwhile, outside town, Quechan warriors silently scaled the hill and infiltrated La Concepción. Outside the door of the church, Corporal Rivera watched as several townsmen and women entered to attend mass. He noticed some Quechans enter the plaza, but raised no alarm. As the service began inside the church, three or four Indians cautiously came toward Rivera, holding out to him a gift of firewood. Surprised by their manner, the corporal approached them. In an instant, the Quechans dropped the bundle of wood and began to batter Rivera with their clubs, simultaneously raising a great war whoop. At this signal, other Indians outside the plaza launched a general attack.[15]

Inside the church, Yslas had just moved the scriptures from the epistle to the gospel side of the altar when he heard the war cries of the Indians. Dashing outside, he saw Rivera struggling with the Quechans. Running through the plaza to his house, Yslas grabbed his weapons and armed himself. Warned by her husband, Doña María shouted the alarm to several of her neighbors.[16] Gathering up a few women and children, she fled hurriedly to the church. Once inside, she found an incredible scene: several townspeople were accosting Father Garcés, arguing with him over who was to blame for the revolt. Although Doña María later recalled that the padre's face was "ashen grey," the priest managed a brave reply. "Let's forget now whose fault it is," he told the panicking Spaniards, "and simply consider it God's punishment for our sins."[17]

Father Barreneche had also heard the assault begin. Rushing from his apartments, he ran into the plaza and saw the Indians clubbing Rivera. Wading into them, Barreneche managed to squeeze the hand of the doomed corporal and give him a general absolution. Turning on the priest, the Quechans struck him several times with their war clubs. Driven back, Barreneche somehow managed to regain the safety of the church.[18]

Having gathered his weapons, Ensign Yslas emerged from his house and headed into the plaza; however, before he could do anything the Quechans surrounded him. From the doorway of the church, Doña María watched in horror as her husband was clubbed to death. After stripping him of his clothes and weapons, the warriors eventually dragged his body to the side of the hill and cast it down into the river.[19]

Although the Quechans killed several in their initial assault, many Spaniards succeeded in barricading themselves in their houses; others joined the group inside the church. Leaving these people alone for the moment, groups of warriors scattered down the hill and into the fields around La Concepción, seeking those Spaniards tending the crops. Pedro Solares, a soldier of the Altar presidio, was guarding the twenty-one horses and mules of the town's garrison when he was attacked. Running for his life, Solares made it to the river, where he hid in the brush. He knew Rivera and his men were on the other side, and perhaps Solares hoped to bring word to the captain of the Quechan attack.[20]

For his part, Rivera needed no warning. From the small bluff where his jacal sat, the captain clearly saw and heard the assault on La Concepción. He immediately assembled all the men left in camp and sent word for those guarding the *caballada* (horse herd) to return at once. Although he possibly considered crossing the river and aiding the townspeople, Rivera rejected the idea. Fording the Colorado would have been suicidal, especially in view of his small numbers. Most likely, the Quechans had already sent warriors across the river to skirmish with Rivera's men, and the captain must have realized that his position was desperate.[21]

Once his command assembled, Rivera took stock of his situation. Along with Sergeant Juan José Robles, there were fourteen veteran soldiers and three recruits. Rivera set out a small mounted advance guard, while the bulk of the troopers set to work digging a field entrenchment.

Two women, María Manuela Ochoa, wife of deserter Ysidro Germán, and María Rita, wife of Xavier Romero, a soldier from the presidio of Pitic, joined in the desperate work. While Rivera supervised his command's defensive preparations, inexplicably he apparently made no attempt to retreat his force or to send to Sonora for help.[22]

While Rivera prepared his defenses, upstream at Bicuñer the Quechan attack had ended. By midday, the Indians had killed or enslaved all the residents of the town. After securing their prisoners, the Quechans looted the houses of all valuables and supplies; the bodies of the dead were stripped naked and the clothing shared out among the victors. From the church, the Indians took out the chasubles, albs, and other vestments that Father Díaz and Father Moreno had used for mass, wearing them as ponchos and shirts. The chalices and other vessels were also saved, but the priests' missals and bibles were of no use to the Quechans. The warriors forced José Urrea, a Kohuana Indian interpreter for the Spaniards, and José Ygnacio Bengochea, a Halchidoma Indian who had been Father Moreno's servant, to gather up the books, the candlesticks, and other paraphernalia from the church and take it to the river. While the other citizens looked on helplessly, the Quechans made Urrea and Bengochea hurl the sacred books and trappings into the river.[23]

José Reyes Pacheco, a soldier from Altar, was one of the few Spanish men not killed outright by the Quechans. He begged the Indians to be allowed to bury his wife, Leonarda Brava, and their daughter. Other captives, too, spoke up, pleading to tend their dead. The Quechans refused, and the bodies of the slain were left to putrefy where they fell. The Indians then systematically set fire to the whole village. Many of the warriors returned to their homes with the captives and booty, but others headed south to join in the attack on La Concepción.[24]

The destruction of San Pedro y San Pablo de Bicuñer had been extremely bloody. Of the approximately seventy-seven men, women, and children in the town that morning, forty-five lay dead. Modern historians later claimed that only male Spaniards were killed, the Quechans uniformly sparing the women and children; in fact, there was no such consistency. Manuel Barragan, a former resident of Tubac, and his wife Francisca Olguin both died, as did Doña Francisca's kinsman José Olguin; however, the latter's wife, María Ygnacia Hurtado and their three children survived. Eight-year-old Juan José Garrigosa was spared, but saw his father, mother, and sister slain. Settler José Antonio Romero and his entire family—mother, wife, and daughter—were all killed, whereas José Joaquín de León, his wife Juana Coronado, and all three of their children lived. In the heat of the attack, survival depended on luck and the mercy of individual Quechans.[25]

While Bicuñer burned, the Quechan attack against La Concepción subsided. Although many residents had been killed, others remained barricaded in their houses and in the church. Around noon, hostilities ceased for several hours. Father Barreneche left the church alone and went into the plaza. Finding some victims of the assault still alive, Barreneche heard their confessions before they died. During this lull, apparently those Spaniards holed up in the church or barricaded in their homes made no attempt to escape or join together in a unified defense, possibly because numbers of Quechan warriors remained around the plaza.[26]

But while the Spaniards remained inactive, throughout the afternoon the Quechans reorganized their forces. By sunset, large numbers of warriors again assembled outside La Concepción, no doubt reinforced by victorious tribesmen from Bicuñer. Early in the evening, they renewed the attack on the town in great force. The night favored the assailants, enabling them to approach close to the houses before being seen. The assault quickly carried all before it. The Indians set fire to the houses, forcing many of the inhabitants into the open, where they were killed. Several other Spaniards perished in the flames. At the house of the commandant, the rebels looted or smashed all the goods and furnishings they could find and destroyed a large supply of grain that Yslas had hoarded for emergencies. Although they heavily attacked the church, filling the doors and walls with arrows, the Quechans once again did not assault the Spaniards inside.[27]

In the midst of the attack, Ensign Yslas's wife, María Ana Montijo, and the other refugees watched incredulously as Father Garcés and Father Barreneche stealthily crept out of the church and into the plaza. Under the cover of darkness, the two Franciscans moved through the town, ministering to the dead and dying. At midnight, with La Concepción thoroughly looted and in flames, the Quechans retired. Sometime later, Garcés and Barreneche returned to their church. For the rest of the night, one by one, they heard the confessions of the remnants of their flock.[28]

Wednesday, July 18, saw the sun rise over the smoldering ruins of La Purísima Concepción. Inside the church with Padres Garcés and Barreneche were about a dozen Spaniards, mostly women and children.

Among the small group was settler Matías de Castro and his wife and son. Castro was fortunate in that his whole family had survived. Many of the other refugees had seen their loved ones killed; others agonized in uncertainty over the fate of their families. Instinctively, the small group of Spaniards turned toward the priests for guidance.[29]

At this juncture, Father Barreneche demonstrated true courage and leadership. Buoyed by the fact that the Indians had not destroyed the little group, the priest gathered the people in the church together. "The devil is on the side of the enemy, but God is on ours," he assured them. "Let us sing a hymn to Mary, most holy, that she favor us with her help, and let us praise God for sending us these trials." The padre then began to sing the hymn *Arise, Arise,* "with great fervor of spirit." Soon all were singing. After the hymn, the priests held what would prove to be their last mass in the church of La Concepción. María Ana Montijo later recalled that as mass was being said "we awaited death at any moment."[30]

After mass, Father Barreneche, Father Garcés, and one or two other men climbed up on the roof of the church and of the priests' adjoining house. They took down the thatch in anticipation that the Quechans would launch another fire attack. Still, the expected assault failed to materialize, and the Indians were nowhere to be seen. Barreneche then pulled out the arrows and spears from the walls and doors of the church, and he did the same to the burned buildings around the plaza. About noon, he climbed to the roof of the church to see if he could locate the Quechans. It soon became clear to the priest and the other Spaniards in La Concepción why they had been spared. Across the Colorado River, several hundred Indian warriors were massing to attack Captain Rivera's isolated command of eighteen troopers and two women.[31]

Rivera had made no movements since he had first seen La Concepción attacked on the previous morning. Throughout that day, his men had completed their field defenses. Although the Spaniards were not attacked in force, the Quechans gradually began to isolate Rivera's men. During the night, Rivera again made no effort to escape, and it is likely that by this time his position was becoming untenable. By Wednesday morning, the Quechans crossed the Colorado in large numbers and soon the captain and his men were completely surrounded. Why Rivera chose not to break out when he could will never be known.[32]

Around noon, the Quechans began to mass for an assault. Entrenched atop the small knoll, Rivera ordered some of his troopers to mount their horses and form up in front of the breastwork; others he stationed inside to shoot down upon the Indians. When the Quechans charged, the horsemen fired a concerted volley from their guns, killing many and momentarily breaking the impetus of the assault. The Indians quickly returned to the attack and, getting in among the mounted troopers, began to strike with their war clubs at the legs and bodies of the horses, crippling the animals and causing the riders to be thrown. As the soldiers fell, the warriors immediately pounced upon them, killing some. In desperation, Rivera had his men dismount and unite inside the breastwork. Although few in number, the soldiers sold their lives dearly, killing many of their attackers. Finally, after a protracted combat, the Quechans overwhelmed the breastwork and annihilated Rivera and his men. Among the mound of dead inside the entrenchment, the Quechans were surprised to find two women. María Rita had been killed with the rest, but María Manuela Ochoa was pulled out of the heap, dazed but alive. An unnamed servant of Rivera, possibly a California Indian, had also survived. Both were taken captive.[33]

The victorious Quechans stripped the dead soldiers of their leather jackets and clothing and gathered up the Spaniards' firearms, lances, swords, and shields. Salvador Palma garnered for himself Captain Rivera's uniform and *adarga* (shield). Palma then ordered his men to search the jacales of Rivera and his men. Inside Rivera's hut, they found documents and books, along with the payroll that the captain had been taking to the California presidios. Palma allowed the papers to be destroyed, but had the chest of coins sent to his own house for safekeeping; undoubtedly, he realized that the money might prove useful in future dealings with the Spaniards.[34] Around three o'clock in the afternoon, Palma ordered the warriors to recross the Colorado River and head back toward La Concepción. Obviously aware that several Spaniards were still alive in the town, he told his tribesmen to round them up and bring them to his ranchería. He specifically commanded that Father Garcés and Father Barreneche not be harmed.[35]

From the roof of La Concepción's church, the padres had watched helplessly as the Quechans destroyed Captain Rivera's command. When the Indians began to recross the river and head back toward the town, Father Barreneche shouted to his comrades to flee, "for in some way or other, we are exposed to die at the hand of the enemy." Barreneche then turned to Garcés and asked if they should try to reach Bicuñer. In what was later held to be a supernatural insight, Garcés told Barreneche that he was certain that Bicuñer had been totally destroyed and all its residents killed or taken.[36]

The two priests decided to head toward the small chapel that Garcés had termed a visita, located four miles to the north, about midway between Concepción and Bicuñer. Despite Barreneche's counsel that they flee as best they could, the small group of Spaniards instinctively stayed close to the two Franciscans. Father Barreneche quickly retrieved his breviary and a crucifix from the priests' house and the refugees set out, as María Ana Montijo recalled, "leaving behind forever the new mission of La Purísima Concepción."[37]

Descending the hill on which the town stood, the Spaniards followed the course of the Colorado past the juncture of the Gila, warily creeping through the trees and brush. After walking for some time, they came to "a long but narrow lagoon." As they paused to search for a place to cross, from the other side they heard the shouts of a wounded Spaniard. Pedro Bohorques, a soldier of La Concepción, had been attacked at the lagoon and left for dead. Seeing the small group of people led by the padres coming toward him, Bohorques gathered the last of his strength and shouted to them, begging for confession. Among those gathered across the lagoon from him were his wife María Gertrudis Cantú and their daughter.[38]

Instantly, Father Barreneche jumped into the water and headed toward the dying man. But the lagoon was deeper than it appeared and Barreneche soon found himself sinking. Unable to swim, the Franciscan thrashed about, dropping his breviary and crucifix into the muddy water. Grasping a nearby log, Barreneche caught his breath and then pulled himself along by the roots of the trees and brush along the bank, managing to reach the other side. Dragging himself out of the lagoon, Barreneche quickly found where Bohorques lay, in time to hear the soldier's confession before he died.[39]

At this point Father Garcés faced a difficult choice. There seemed to be little chance of Barreneche getting back across the lagoon, and even less of getting the women and children over to Barreneche's side. After some moments, he decided to leave the rest of the Spaniards and try to cross the lagoon alone. Garcés might have felt that he and Barreneche endangered the safety of the others, in the perhaps mistaken belief that the priests were especially tempting targets for roving groups of Quechans. Whatever the reason, he gave the Spaniards strict orders that, as it turned out, saved their lives. "Stay together," he warned them, "do not resist capture, and the Yumas will not harm you." Seeing that some of the refugees were half naked, Garcés took off his mantle and habit and covered those most in need. Clad only in his tunic, the padre jumped into the lagoon and swam to the other side. "This was the last we saw of the two fathers," María Ana Montijo later remembered, "as we sat huddled together awaiting death at any moment."[40]

Continuing northward, the two Franciscans again made for their visita. Once there, the fathers came upon the husband of a Quechan woman who had become a Christian and "always shown affection for the missionaries." Treating the priests kindly, the man brought them to his ranchería, where his wife waited. The woman invited the priests to enter and gave them sanctuary. No doubt exhausted, Garcés and Barreneche spent the rest of the night with the Quechan couple.[41]

Back at La Concepción, Salvador Palma and his warriors entered the deserted town. No matter what amount of authority he might have lost since the coming of the Spanish colony, many Quechans still heeded his orders. Seeing no one left in the town, Palma had the vestments, missals, and religious images taken from the church, along with some books and other items from the priests' house. When everything of value had been located, Palma had his men set fire to the church. He then sent those warriors who lived in nearby rancherías to seek Father Garcés and Father Barreneche, again commanding that they not be harmed, "for they had a good heart." Satisfied, Palma returned to his own village across the river, ordering the church valuables brought to his house.[42]

Several miles upstream, María Ana Montijo and the other refugees from La Concepción still waited by the lagoon. In the group were seven women and an unknown number of children. Matías de Castro and his family were still together, but he was no longer the only man among the group; at some point during the day, Juan José Miranda, the carpenter who had fled from Bicuñer early Tuesday morning, had joined the fleeing residents of La Concepción.[43]

Before nightfall, three Quechans found the terrified Spaniards beside the lagoon. The Indians assured the women and children that they would not be harmed and divided them up, each warrior taking those he wanted captive. Turning to Castro and Miranda, the Quechans told the two men that it was still too dangerous for them to come out, "for there were many people, and they would kill them." The Quechans advised the two men to remain in hiding for a few days and then seek out Salvador Palma. With this warning, the Indians left with their prisoners, leaving Castro and Miranda alone, as the night closed about them.[44]

On the morning of Thursday, July 19, Father Garcés and Father Barreneche were still sheltered in the home of the Christian Quechan woman and her husband. Several other Spanish captives had arrived at the same village, including María Gertrudis Cantú, one of the group from La Concepción that had been left by the lagoon the previous day. It had been her husband, Pedro Bohorques, that Father Barreneche had confessed at the lagoon, and if she did not know already, the padre no doubt told her of her husband's death.[45]

The new day found Salvador Palma in his home village. Seeing that Father Garcés and Father Barreneche still had not been located, Palma again sent out search parties. If the priests still lived, they were to be brought back to Palma immediately, and he reminded the search parties that "what the fathers said was good, and they did no harm to anyone." Leaving the village in small groups, the Quechans fanned out north and south along the river banks. Among the searchers was the interpreter Francisco Xavier, the Halykwamai Indian who had been instrumental in persuading the Quechans to destroy the Spanish settlements.[46]

About ten o'clock several of Palma's searchers, including Francisco Xavier, reached the Quechan village near the visita. María Gertrudis Cantú watched as events unfolded. Garcés and Barreneche were still inside the house of the their Christian protector when the warriors discovered them. The two Franciscans were drinking hot chocolate that their host had prepared for them. Immediately upon seeing the two priests, Francisco Xavier shouted out, "If these survive all is lost, for these are the worst." Continuing to shout, he persuaded his companions to disobey Palma and kill the priests. One of the warriors entered the house and told the Franciscans, "Stop drinking that and come outside. We're going to kill you." Father Barreneche said nothing, but Father Garcés, calmly sipping his drink, replied, "we'd like to finish our chocolate first." Enraged, the warrior screamed, "Just leave it!" The two priests obediently stood up and followed him outside. Once they were in the open, María Gertrudis Cantú watched in horror as the warriors immediately began clubbing them. She was so close to the Franciscans as to "hear their piteous moans as they lay dying." Some Quechans later maintained that at the first swipe of the war clubs, "Father Garcés disappeared from their sight and they were left clubbing the air." Whatever else they might have thought of him, the Quechans had always regarded Garcés as a powerful spiritual force.[47] The two priests having been killed, Francisco Xavier and the other members of the search party returned the way they had come. The husband of the Christian Quechan woman who had sheltered the Franciscans had been unable to stop the killing; he now carried the bleeding corpses a short distance to a small sandy rise, where he dug a shallow pit and buried Garcés and Barreneche side by side. His wife then had him make two small wooden crosses and place them atop the grave to mark the site.[48]

As the days passed, the fury of the Quechans subsided. Salvador Palma had as many Spaniards as he could brought into his own village, but many were held in other rancherías scattered along both banks of the Colorado. Palma ordered his followers to round up the horses, mules, cattle, and sheep from La Concepción and Bicuñer as well as the 257 animals from Captain Rivera's *caballada* scattered in the fighting. Prudently, he also gathered fifteen muskets and half a case of pistols, placing them in his house. He knew the Spaniards would return to seek vengeance.[49]

For three days, Matías de Castro, of La Concepción, and Juan José Miranda, of Bicuñer, hid near the lagoon, waiting for things to calm down. At one point, Castro had set out alone to try to find Salvador Palma, but he had been unable to locate the Quechan leader. Dispirited, he returned to where Miranda was waiting and the two men continued their vigil. Shortly afterward, a couple of Quechans stumbled upon their hiding place. The two Spaniards requested to be taken to Palma, and the Indians obliged.[50]

When they arrived at Palma's village, Castro and Miranda found Palma amid many of his people. In a public repudiation of the Christian faith, the Quechan leader was throwing the religious images from the church of La Purísima Concepción into the river. He then placed the gospels and missals in a wooden box, locked it, and hurled it, too, into the water. Then Palma had Castro and Miranda brought to his house. Upon entering the hut, the two Spaniards observed the large amount of loot accumulated by the erstwhile kwoxot. Seeing a small box containing the chrism oil and cruets used for saying mass, Miranda managed to retrieve and keep the box and its vessels. The other items, Palma later bartered away or divided up among his followers, and Castro said he had seen the Indian give out more than nine hundred dollars' worth of coins from the payroll seized from Captain Rivera.[51]

A few days afterwards, a group of seven Quechans found twenty-two-year-old trooper Pedro Solares, who had been guarding the horses of La Concepción when the attack began, hiding along the banks of the river. He had survived in the open for almost a week. Similarly, the Quechans at this time captured soldier Miguel Antonio Romero, of Bicuñer. The Spaniard had swum across the Colorado at the start of the attack, and he had tried unsuccessfully to catch a horse and escape. Eventually, both soldiers were turned over to Palma.[52]

With the capture of Romero and Solares, the Quechans accounted for all of the Spaniards. In all, 105 Spanish men, women, and children had been killed: 37 soldiers, 23 male settlers, 20 women, 21 boys and girls, and the 4 Franciscan priests. The Quechans had also seized 76 captives: 3 soldiers, 2 male settlers, 4 male Indian interpreters or servants, 30 adult women, and 37 children. The Indians put them to work fetching and weeding, but otherwise they were not mistreated.[53]

The Quechans had also suffered a number of dead and wounded, almost all of them from the assault on Rivera's men. To many in the tribe, these losses probably seemed a small price to pay. They had regained their land and their liberties and destroyed the power of the foreign soldiers and holy men. They had substantially enriched the nation with slaves, horses, cattle and firearms, and they had shown to their neighbors the weakness of the white men and the power of the Quechan. With their victory, "the Respectable Union" that the Caballero de Croix had so hopefully initiated, eight months before, had come to an end.[54]

Ransom and Retribution

Spanish Rescue Operations, August to December 1781

As he sat writing at his desk in his headquarters at Arizpe, Teodoro de Croix was quite pleased with himself. During the months of April, May, and June, 1781, he had been laboring over a lengthy report to be sent to José de Gálvez, chief minister of the Council of the Indies. In this document, Croix unabashedly detailed the successful measures and policies that he had instituted in the past several years throughout the Interior Provinces.[1]

Among his many accomplishments, Croix was particularly pleased with the results of his two "military colonies" along the Colorado River. Not only had he secured the new road between Sonora and California, but he had done so at much less cost to the crown than anyone had expected. "I have brought about the erection of two pueblos of Spaniards among the Yumas," he boasted, "so that these fortunate Indians may embrace, voluntarily and happily, religion and vassalage."[2]

Certain that the settlements would be successful, he predicted that they would soon be "covered with grain fields, fruits, and herds, settled by faithful vassals of the king." As for the Quechans, the caballero was equally confident. "I do not doubt they will be happy, because the respectable union of the two pueblos of Spaniards offers the advantage of attracting docilely the heathen Indians to reduction and vassalage." But Yuma was far away from Arizpe, and the caballero's smug assessment was about to be shattered.[3]

Father Juan Bautista de Velderrain had been a missionary at San Xavier del Bac for four years and had seen many things along the frontier. He knew that news traveled fast among the many Indian nations and was usually reliable. However, Father Velderrain simply could not believe the Gila Pima messenger who arrived at the mission on August 5, 1781. The Indian told the priest that the Quechans had totally destroyed the missions on the Colorado River, killing all the people in them. A single soldier had managed to flee and was even now at the Papago village of Quitovac.[4]

Velderrain had been Padre Garcés's compañero at San Xavier when the latter had left for the Yuma missions, and Velderrain thought that the Quechans would never harm him. Besides, Quitovac lay close to the presidio of Altar, and no word of an attack had come from there. Finally, Father Velderrain knew that Captain Rivera y Moncada had been on the Sonoran side of the Colorado River, and "not a single soldier went forth at the bidding of the said captain to seek help." All this seemed to contradict the story of the Gila Pima, but Velderrain decided to investigate the matter further.[5]

The priest sent word to Capt. Juan Manuel de Bonilla, temporary commander of the nearby presidio of Tucson. The captain quickly rode the nine miles out to San Xavier and, with Father Velderrain as translator, listened to the Pima messenger's tale of destruction at the Colorado River settlements. The Papagos of Quitovac had sent word that, about July 23, the Quechans "fell by night upon the houses of a town of said river where they killed all, and that when the other town . . . was hurrying to help them, the rebels went out to meet them . . . [and] killed all of them." The Pima continued that "a fugitive soldier had hurried to . . . Quitovac" and that the Papagos of that ranchería had then gone to Yuma and seen the destroyed towns for themselves. When Bonilla questioned the Pima messenger about the circumstances of the attack, the Indian answered that he only knew what the Papagos from Quitovac had said.[6]

After the messenger headed home, Father Velderrain and Captain Bonilla spoke with the headman of the Papago village at San Xavier. This Indian suggested sending one of the Pima residents at Tucson to the Gila River to investigate the story. The chief would also send word to his kinsmen at Quitovac to bring the soldier to San Xavier. Finally, the Papago recommended that the Caballero de Croix not be notified until the report could be substantiated. Father Velderrain agreed to all of these suggestions, but Captain Bonilla was not so sure. Returning to Tucson, he interviewed a muleteer from California who had arrived at the presidio five days earlier. This individual reported that when he had passed through the Yuma settlements, all had been well, but as he approached Tucson, Indians told him by signs that the Quechans had killed Rivera and his men. Captain Bonilla decided to take no chances. On August 6, he wrote asking Father Velderrain to have the Papago chief send out his messengers; that same day Bonilla dispatched six men to Arizpe to report the news to Croix.[7]

The commandant-general was stunned. In the last detailed reports from Yuma, Ensign Yslas had been generally optimistic; he even mentioned that the Kohuanas and Halchidomas, too, were asking for missions. On August 1, Croix had written a brief reply to Yslas, telling him to keep the Indians hopeful of future Spanish expansion. Now, he received the "lamentable though uncertain news that the Yumas have destroyed the two new towns of the Río Colorado." Fearing the worst, Croix began "to take steps toward the just punishment of so cruel and treacherous an action."[8]

Apaches had recently attacked the presidio of Santa Cruz de Terrenate, southeast of Tucson, and the Spaniards were preparing a counterstroke. On August 12, Croix ordered the military governor of Sonora, Jacobo Ugarte y Loyola, to gather eighty men from the presidios of Altar, Tucson, Buenavista, and Pitic, along with forty infantrymen of the second company of the Catalonian Volunteers (*Voluntarios de Cataluña*), commanded by Lt. Col. Pedro Fages. If the news from the Colorado River were confirmed, the Spaniards would be sent to fight Quechans rather than Apaches.[9]

Confirmation was not long in coming. On August 18, Captain Bonilla sent another report from Tucson to Croix. Two days before, Bonilla had received the *gobernador* of the Papago village of Quitovac. The Indian brought with him a Spanish soldier named Francisco Xavier Castro. Castro had been with Captain Rivera's command, but had deserted when the bulk of the party had left Yuma. He soon thought better of his desertion and decided to turn himself in at the presidio of Altar. When he reached the village of Quitovac, the headman took him into custody. Soon after, as Castro later reported, several Quechans appeared, "mounted on some horses with the King's brand." The Quechans wanted to kill him, but the Papago headman stopped them.[10] The Papago leader then went to the Colorado River with several of his men, and they had seen the ruins with their own eyes. The Quechans boasted to the Papagos that they had not only wiped out the Spanish towns and missions, but that they also killed Captain Rivera and his men. When asked why, they replied that the Indian interpreters working for the Spaniards told them that the white men were planning to kill them all. The headman concluded his report by stating that the Quechans had invited him and his people to join in resisting the Spaniards, but that he had refused.[11]

Other Indians also circulated word that the Yuma settlements were destroyed. Captain Pedro Tueros, of Altar, had been hearing reports from the Papagos north of his post that the Quechans "had killed the fathers, soldiers, and settlers of the Río Colorado and held captive the women and children." Tueros sent three parties of Pima Indians from Altar out to the Papago country to investigate the rumors. One of these groups had soon returned, reporting that the Papagos were indeed declaring that the Spaniards on the Colorado River were dead and that "Salvador Palma was the instigator of the whole massacre." A second party of Pimas had returned to Altar bearing the same tale, adding that Palma "is very haughty and proclaiming . . . that he will remain . . . waiting for the Spaniards."[12]

On August 31, Tueros forwarded his findings to Military Governor Ugarte. Ominously, the captain reported that two soldiers he had sent from Altar to Yuma with letters for Rivera had not returned after twenty-one days, "and their delay makes me think they may have perished." Tueros concluded, "I no longer doubt the reality of the disaster," and offered himself and his command for an immediate retaliatory strike "for rescuing our people and whatever may have been left of the sacred things and cattle."[13]

The letters from Tueros and Bonilla convinced the caballero that the

Yuma establishments had been exterminated. His honor and that of the king's arms demanded retribution, and on September 8 Croix called a war council *(junta de guerra)* to make plans to punish the Quechans. Joining Croix on the council were Pedro Corbalán, royal intendant and civil governor of Sonora, along with Croix's chief legal and financial adviser, the parsimonious Pedro Galindo y Navarro.[14]

With the legal formalism typical of the Spanish bureaucracy, the three men reviewed the recent news from Bonilla and Tueros, the correspondence from Ensign Yslas, Father Garcés, and Father Díaz, and the 1776 reports of Lieutenant Colonel Anza. Noting that the Quechans had "voluntarily made applications to his Majesty . . . that missionaries might be placed among them and settlers might come and establish themselves in their land," the junta unanimously agreed that in accordance with the laws of the Indies, the Quechans were now "apostates and rebels" and that the council "impose on them the just punishment . . . they deserve."[15]

Having satisfied the royal conscience that hostilities were justified, Croix and the others drew up detailed orders for a campaign to chastise the Quechans. They commanded Lt. Col. Pedro Fages to assemble fifty of his Catalonian Volunteers, sixty presidial troopers from Altar, Buenavista, and Horcasitas, and sixty Indian auxiliaries from San Xavier del Bac, Tucson, Pitic, Caborca, and other villages of the Pimería Alta. With Captain Pedro Tueros, of Altar, as his second in command, Fages was to proceed to Yuma immediately.[16]

Although Croix undoubtedly knew that the Quechans would resist, he permitted himself the hope that they might once again accept Spanish rule. If the Quechans received Fages peacefully and returned their captives and booty, they would not be attacked. But Croix insisted that the leaders of the rebellion were to undergo "a public and exemplary capital punishment . . . in the presence of the rest of the tribe . . . as a warning to prevent them . . . in the future . . . committing like offenses."[17]

The junta also ordered Fages to investigate secretly if the Pimas and Papagos had assisted in the rebellion, taking hostages if necessary to insure their good faith and to secure a clear line of communication and retreat from Yuma. If these tribes had been faithful, the Spaniards would allow them to assist in chastising the Quechans. Should the opportunity present itself, Fages was likewise instructed to enlist aid or take hostages from the Cocopas, Halchidomas, and other tribes along the Colorado River.[18]

Finally, Croix directed Fages upon his arrival at Yuma to notify the governor of California, Felipe de Neve, of the uprising. Croix knew that Neve was at Mission San Gabriel, far removed from the scene of intended hostilities, but on the chance that the governor should "take any steps to which his zeal may prompt him" and send troops from California to assist the expedition, Fages was to cooperate with them in all matters. To insure just such a possibility, Croix immediately sent word of the revolt to Neve himself, warning the governor lest he be caught off guard.[19]

However, Croix's warning was unnecessary: Neve already had first-hand evidence of the events at Yuma. On August 30, a small group of seven soldiers led by Ensign Cayetano Limón reined up at Mission San Gabriel. They had been to the Colorado River and seen the destruction themselves. Rivera and all his men were dead, the towns of La Concepción and Bicuñer burned, and all the inhabitants killed or taken. The following day, Governor Neve sat down and listened intently to Limón's report.[20]

The ensign, who was from the presidio of Buenavista, had been among the escort that accompanied Captain Rivera's cavalcade of soldiers and colonists bound for California. After reaching Yuma, Rivera decided to rest those animals exhausted during the journey and had sent the bulk of his force, including Ensign Limón, on to California. Limón, after delivering his charges to San Gabriel, on August 8 set out to rejoin Rivera at Yuma, accompanied by two corporals and three troopers (one of whom was his son) from Buenavista, and three soldiers from Horcasitas.[21]

Ten days later, Limón's party reached the Indian village of San Sebastián. The headman of the place insisted that Limón should turn back, saying that "there were many Indians on the river and that they had already killed Captain . . . Rivera and all the other people." He declared that the Quechans had also destroyed the party of Corporal Pascual Rivera, which was bringing provisions from the California missions to Yuma. Taken aback, Limón manfully replied that he would nevertheless continue on to the Colorado. The Indian repeated his warnings, recounting that Captain Rivera's body had been thrown into the river and that only the wife of deserter Ysidro Germán was left alive, and she had been carried off by the Halchidomas.[22]

Limón and his men camped overnight at San Sebastián and watered their stock: they were taking seven head of cattle to Captain Rivera for meat on the hoof and each man also had a string of remounts. When they set out at daybreak, an Indian boy again approached the ensign to warn him to head back, telling Limón that Corporal Rivera's supply party had managed to kill eleven of their attackers before they were wiped out. When Limón tried to question the boy further, another Indian came up and jerked the child away by the arm.[23]

At dawn on August 21, Limón and his men reached the Yuma Crossing, where they saw "an extraordinary number of Indians." Four Quechans invited the soldiers to dismount, promising food for the men and pasture for the horses. However, Limón was on his guard and ordered his men to move on. Seeing that the cattle slowed him down, Limón halted the cows near a mesquite tree and detailed troopers Ignacio Leiva, of Buenavista, and Diego de León, of Horcasitas, to guard them. Limón warned the pair to be alert and to stay mounted. If attacked, they were to abandon the cattle and rejoin him and the others, who would stay "within the distance of two gunshots."[24]

Near the river bank, Limón came upon a few deserted jacales. Inside one of them he found torn paper and a broken strongbox. Several bodies lay near the huts, and Limón mistakenly concluded that this had been the site of Captain Rivera's camp. Not realizing that the huts were those of some Quechan families, Limón searched futilely for Rivera's body, finally concluding that the Indians had cast it into the Colorado.[25]

Approaching La Concepción, Limón stationed five men at the foot of the hill while he and Cpl. Agustín Leiva rode up to the town. On entering the square, they found all the buildings burned and the plaza strewn with the dead bodies of the inhabitants, "those that were whole amounting to twelve, not counting many others which were dismembered." Limón noted that the dead "were of both sexes" and that "the majority . . . by their crushed heads . . . had been killed by clubs or stones." Many of the bodies showed signs of being burned, and a few "perished even within the houses."[26]

As they took in the grisly scene, Limón and Corporal Leiva heard gunshots. Wheeling their horses, they raced out of the town and back down the hill. Quechans along both banks of the Colorado were firing arrows and guns at the Spaniards, and after having his men return fire, Limón retreated hastily to where he had left the cattle and the two guards. Though the cattle were still there, both men lay dead, stripped naked, with their heads bashed in. The Quechans pressed in upon the Spaniards, and Limón's situation was desperate. His men were exhausted and thirsty, his horses winded, and he was heavily outnumbered. His only option was to flee back the way he had come.[27]

Abandoning the cattle, Ensign Limón ordered a retreat. The Quechans pursued the Spaniards closely and a running firefight developed. After several hours, the soldiers rode into a hollow, where the Quechans encircled them. A musket ball hit Limón's son and namesake, passing through both his *adarga* (leather shield) and his shoulder. Looking about, he found that the shot had been fired by José, one of the Indian interpreters from the Yuma settlements. The Quechans were close enough for the Spaniards to see that they were led by Salvador Palma, carrying Captain Rivera's shield, and the Halykwamai interpreter Francisco Xavier. Both men taunted Limón and his troops and "shouted at us a thousand insults."[28]

In desperation, the soldiers managed to break through the encircling Indians, but the pursuit continued. At sunset, Limón spied a small mesa. Reaching the top, he said his men turned and stood at bay. For two more hours, the soldiers exchanged fire with the Quechans, but with the night closing in the combat gradually ceased. Limón had his men dismount and saddle fresh horses from their remounts. About eight o'clock, the Spaniards charged down the mesa, heading east. Before dawn, they reached a small pond, where Limón had the horses watered and allowed his men to eat. The Quechans were nowhere to be seen. Eight days later, Limón and his men returned to Mission San Gabriel and reported to Governor Neve. On September 1, the governor forwarded Limón's report to the caballero at Arizpe.[29]

It would be several weeks before the commandant-general would receive Ensign Limón's account, but another eyewitness from Yuma soon appeared. On September 5, a single horseman rode into Altar and was immediately brought to Capt. Pedro Tueros. The rider claimed to have come from the Yuma settlements and that he brought word from Salvador Palma. Upon closer examination, the man turned out to be Pedro Solares, the young soldier from La Concepción. Solares told Captain Tueros that the Quechans had rebelled and destroyed the Colorado River settlements; however, Palma now wished to make peace, and as a sign of good faith had dispatched Solares with horses and seven silver communion patens.[30]

Tueros ignored Palma's offer of peace: it was too late for that. He questioned Solares closely about events at Yuma and what had become of the people. Solares stated that both Spanish towns had been burned, many people killed, and others taken captive by the Quechans. Rivera's command had also been annihilated. Solares even reported that a small detachment bringing cattle from California had been destroyed as well, obviously believing that Ensign Limón and his men had also been killed. Tueros allowed the trooper only a few hours' rest before sending him under escort to Governor Ugarte at the presidio of Pitic. The captain then sent an express to Croix at Arizpe.[31]

The Caballero de Croix's ire rose perceptibly with the final confirmation of the disaster. Governor Ugarte, at Pitic, had assembled the retaliatory strike force under Lieutenant Colonel Fages and was awaiting final word from Croix before dispatching it. On September 16, Croix ordered Ugarte to send the expedition to Yuma and chastise the Quechans "for their treacherous crimes." He directed Fages to "use every possible and suitable means to ransom at any price the men, women and children that remain prisoner." Once the captives were secure, Fages was to force the Quechans, by whatever means necessary, to hand over their three main leaders, Salvador Palma, his brother Ygnacio, and Chief Pablo, along with "the perfidious interpreter Francisco [Xavier]." All were to be tortured and then executed. Croix concluded his directives by stating that after the Spanish captives had been retrieved, "all that has been given for them should be taken away . . . as well as all that . . . they stole from the destroyed towns." Almost parenthetically, the commandant-general added that Fages's dealings with the Quechans should have "no other end in view than that of saving the lives of the King's vassals who are in the power of the Indians."[32]

Lieutenant Colonel Fages set out for Yuma on the same day he received orders from Croix. His command consisted of 40 mounted infantrymen of his own company of the Voluntarios de Cataluña and 40 soldados de cuera from the presidios of Buenavista and Pitic. Moving northwest to Altar, Fages skirmished with renegade Seri Indians, in which five of his men were wounded, one seriously. They captured several Seris and rescued some Pimas whom the Seris had held as slaves. Placing these nineteen women and children on the cantles of their saddles, Fages's troopers continued on to Altar, arriving on September 28.[33] There, 20 more soldados de cuera and 36 Pima Indian auxiliaries joined Fages, bringing his force up to 136 men. Captain Pedro Tueros now became Fages's second in command. The subaltern officers of the expedition included Lieutenant Ignacio de Urrea, of Pitic, Ensign Manuel Antonio Arbizu, of Altar, 1st Sgt. Miguel Palacios, of Pitic, and Sgt. Juan Noriega, of the Catalonian Volunteers. The Franciscan priest Francisco Cenizo, military chaplain of Altar, accompanied the expedition to provide spiritual aid.[34]

Colonel Fages on October 1 ordered the expedition to move out, heading north toward the Gila River, through Papago Indian country. At the village of Tachitoa, more than 100 Papagos "presented themselves to go with us to war against the Yumas." Fages added 40 of the best of these warriors to his troop, giving him a total of 76 Indian auxiliaries. The Spaniards found two Quechans in a nearby village, and the colonel seized them as hostages, "in order to present them to Captain [Salvador] Palma."[35] With his hostages and Papago reinforcements, Fages continued his march, reaching the Gila River, near present-day Gila Bend, ten days after leaving Altar. At this point, 20 Papago warriors from the village of Santa Rosa del Ati joined the expedition.[36]

Proceeding downriver through the land of the Maricopa Indians, the Spaniards reached the Colorado River on October 18. Here Fages and his men were surprised to see a lone figure approaching. It turned out to be Miguel Antonio Romero, the captive soldier from the town of Bicuñer, carrying a letter from Salvador Palma. The Quechan leader had been aware for several days that Fages's force was approaching and he had prepared his people for battle. Palma also made captive Matías de Castro, from the town La Concepción, write a letter dictated by the Quechan leader. In it, Palma told the Spaniards that, if they "came in peace, he was also thus inclined."[37]

Arriving at the Colorado River, Colonel Fages and his men ascended the hill that today the Arizona Territorial Prison State Park occupies. Directly across the river sat the hill on which the town of La Concepción lay. There, the Spaniards saw more than five hundred warriors, "armed with bows, arrows, spears, and some with guns, while many others were coming . . . from neighboring villages." Salvador Palma, who was in command, had wisely placed the river between his people and the Spaniards. The Quechans were obviously prepared for combat, but they made no hostile moves.[38]

Shouting across the narrow confines of the river, Fages asked Palma to negotiate for the release of the Spanish captives. Palma assented, and agreed to a truce. For the next several hours, the Spaniards offered bolts of cloth, blankets, strings of beads, and tobacco to the Quechans, gaining "the return of forty-eight captives men and women, adults and children." Hoping to continue the process, Fages gave Palma a gift of a tricorn hat, "gallooned with silver and having a cockade," along with a shirt and some cigarettes. The Quechan leader reciprocated by sending across the river a large amount of corn, beans, and melons. The Indians promised to return the next day to continue the bartering. With the negotiations concluded for the time being, Fages and his men encamped atop the hill.[39]

As the Spaniards erected their tents, Colonel Fages took a detachment to search for the scene of Captain Rivera's fight. They found the remains of Rivera and his men less than a mile to the east. "The bodies had been consumed," Fages noted, "but that of Moncada was unmistakably identified by a break in one of the shin bones." After gathering up some fragments of torn paper found among the debris, the detachment returned to their hilltop camp.[40]

During the night, Fages interviewed the redeemed captives already secured and began to put together an idea of how many people were still held. On the morning of October 19, he again began ransom negotiations. Over several hours, he sent gifts to the Quechans on their side of the river, and the Indians ferried captive Spaniards to Fages's side. By the end of the day, Fages had redeemed fourteen more prisoners. Several captive families were still intact, but others had been split up among different Quechan villages. When Fages asked about these people, Palma responded that "they were in a village at some distance, and that he himself would send for them and deliver them to us as he had the others."[41]

Sometime during the day, the Spaniards returned to the site of Captain Rivera's last stand, gathered up the skeletal remains, and buried them. After returning to camp, Fages and his men prepared for another round of bargaining with the Quechans, but around ten o'clock that night, an Indian runner entered the camp with news that shattered these plans. The Gila Pimas, Maricopas, and Halchidomas had gathered a force of more than six hundred men and had followed in the wake of the Spanish expedition. Having crossed the Colorado upstream from Yuma, they planned to attack the Quechans in the morning. The allies requested that the Spaniards join in their assault, or at the very least hinder the Quechans from crossing the Colorado. Fages was furious. He had several captives to redeem, and this attack risked their safety. His negotiations with Palma had been without guile, but once hostilities commenced, the Quechans would see the Spaniards' actions as treacherous subterfuge. But the colonel could not sway the warriors of the Maricopa–Gila Pima League, and he reluctantly agreed to support them.[42]

At daybreak, the Spaniards watched as the league's warriors attacked the Quechan villages. Preoccupied with the Spaniards across the river and not expecting their traditional enemies, Palma and his people were caught by surprise. After several hours of fighting, the warriors of the Maricopa–Gila Pima League drove the Quechans from the village near La Concepción, killing fifteen in sight of the white men.[43] About noon, a group of Quechans started to cross the river downstream from the Spanish camp and Fages dutifully sent Ensign Manuel Antonio Arbizu and twenty-five soldados de cuera to thwart the attempt. Arbizu's men killed five warriors and drove back the rest, at the cost of one trooper wounded by an arrow. Then another group of Indians appeared on the opposite bank, and Fages opened fire on them from his encampment, killing another five. Being attacked on all sides, the Quechans fled downstream, leaving their homes to be pillaged and burned by the Pimas, Maricopas, and Halchidomas. Altogether, the Spaniards saw twenty-five Quechans killed, but others fell in the outlying areas and many more were wounded. Fages reported that among the dead was José Antonio, the son of Salvador Palma; Ygnacio Palma was among the wounded. A single Quechan, a blind boy, was taken prisoner by the Spanish.[44]

That afternoon, the forces of the Maricopa–Gila Pima League crossed the Colorado River to join Fages's encampment. They brought with them a captive Spanish woman and her infant daughter, both of whom had escaped during the battle. With this addition, the expedition had rescued sixty-three men, women, and children; at least sixteen others, including five women and several children, remained prisoners. Some families were still separated. Settler Juan José de León and his son had been ransomed, but his wife, Juana Coronado, and two children remained with the Quechans. Juana González, widow of soldier Cayetano Mesa, was freed, but not her two teenage daughters. José Manuel Palomino and his sister María Gertrudis, both under eight years old, had escaped, but their teenage sister, Ignacia, remained a prisoner.[45]

In addition to the captives, the Pimas and their allies also recovered a chasuble, looted from the four dead Franciscans, and gave it to the expedition's chaplain, Father Cenizo. Turning to the rescued prisoners, Cenizo sought any other religious items they may have recovered. Soldier Miguel Antonio Romero brought forth the box containing the silver vials of chrism oil and mass cruets that the carpenter Juan José Miranda had recovered from Salvador Palma's house. The Indian interpreter José Ygnacio Bengochea produced a wine cruet of glass and a small silver bell.[46]

That night, Colonel Fages called together his officers to ask if the expedition should continue with the mission now that hostilities had commenced. He urged them to consider the necessity of adopting "a course agreeable to the service of God and the King, and to the welfare of all." The Quechans had dispersed, and the Spaniards had little likelihood of being able to pursue them effectively or to reopen negotiations for the remaining captives. With these facts before them the officers voted unanimously that they should retreat with the captives already rescued. Fages accepted the decision "though with much pain to me."[47]

The colonel decided that the expedition should withdraw only as far as the Papago village of Sonóitac, some eighty miles from the Yuma Crossing. There, the Spaniards could reequip and reorganize so that they "could yet return to the Colorado and accomplish what had been ordered . . . by the junta de guerra." On October 22, Fages and his men, along with the sixty-four rescued captives, set out. Seeking to save time, the expedition traveled southeast across the rugged Camino del Diablo. Despite the lack of water and a scarcity of pasture for the horses, the Spaniards reached Sonóitac without loss after a difficult six-day journey.[48]

On October 29 and 30, Colonel Fages, along with Captain Tueros, compiled a list of the names and ages of the rescued Spaniards, those killed at La Concepción and Bicuñer, and those who remained prisoners of the Quechans. The two officers then conducted a formal hearing with several of the former captives about the causes and course of the Quechan uprising. Soldiers José Reyes Pacheco, Pedro Solares, and Miguel Antonio Romero, settlers Matías de Castro and Juan José Miranda, and Indian interpreters José de Urrea and José Ygnacio de Bengochea, all testified. Fages and Tueros asked each man, under oath, the same series of questions, among them: What caused the Quechans to attack the settlements? Who were the leaders of the uprising? What were the names of dead settlers and soldiers? What happened to the religious articles, firearms, and other items the Indians had seized? Fages immediately forwarded the transcripts of the interviews and a brief summary of his actions at Yuma to the caballero in Arizpe. The colonel then sent the sixty-four ransomed Spaniards to the presidio of Altar "in company with the party that went for provisions for the troops, so that the planned return to the Colorado might be made."[49]

Two weeks later, the Caballero de Croix convoked a second junta de guerra at Arizpe. The council ordered Fages and his men, now unencumbered with the ransomed colonists, to return to the Colorado River and "attack without losing an instant the faithless and stubborn Yumas, punishing them as their treachery and sedition deserve . . . and seize Captain Salvador Palma and the other ring leaders, . . . that they may immediately suffer capital punishment." Further, Fages was to send word of his actions to Governor Neve of California. If Neve should appear with a force of soldiers, Fages would turn command over to the governor. Finally, with remarkable hindsight, the council commanded that Neve select a location "suitable for the establishment of a presidio . . . and . . . a considerable town to serve as a check on the Yumas."[50]

Remembering the redeemed captives at Altar, the junta de guerra ordered Lt. Andrés Arías Caballero to see to their welfare. The lieutenant was to get clothing to all the survivors and to pay for their travel "to the places, towns or presidios where they may wish to make their home." The soldiers, Pedro Solares and José Reyes Pacheco, of Altar, and Miguel Antonio Romero, of Buenavista, were to return to active duty. Croix stressed that Lieutenant Caballero provide these services "with the economy that they demand, so as not to incur greater expense." The junta concluded its order with the remark that Caballero treat the freed captives "with the pity which is their just due."[51]

On November 23, Fages set out for the Colorado River for a second time. Departing Sonóitac with the same force of soldiers and Indian auxiliaries as on the previous foray, Fages again led his men over the barren Camino del Diablo. At one point, the lack of forage and water for their horses compelled the Spaniards to force-march thirty leagues in just thirty-six hours. Five days after leaving Sonóitac, they reached the Gila River at a place called La Cueva, near present-day Dome, Arizona.[52]

After resting his men and animals for one day, Fages proceeded toward the Colorado. In an attempt to trap the Quechans, he planned an ambitious, nighttime double envelopment. Dividing his command, he sent Captain Tueros with half of the force to cross the Colorado River about one league north of La Concepción. Fages himself, with the remainder of the troops, crossed the Gila River and moved north toward the Colorado across from the destroyed town of Bicuñer. Although two pack mules were drowned in the swollen ford, the colonel and his men succeeded in crossing the Colorado and moved downstream to link up with Tueros's detachment, hoping to trap the enemy between them.[53] However, the Quechans were on their guard, and the Spaniards found the Indian villages empty. By three o'clock in the afternoon, Fages's troops approached the town of La Concepción, where Tueros was waiting. The captain and his men had killed five Quechans and captured three others, a man and two women, but the majority of the tribe had eluded both parties. The expedition soon saw numerous smoke signals rising in every direction as the Quechans massed their forces. Ascending the hill of La Concepción, Fages had his men encamp for the night on the outskirts of the destroyed town.[54]

On December 1, the colonel sent out two parties of soldiers to loot supplies from the Quechan villages and to scout for any members of the tribe. Both parties returned with plundered food, having captured a single Quechan man, who they had bound and led back to camp. On the same day, about thirty Quechan warriors appeared across the Colorado River, on the hill opposite La Concepción. In the same manner as Fages had done during the first expedition, the Indians called out to the Spaniards. The Quechans had not only eluded the Spaniards' plans to envelop them, but had also deftly kept the river between them and the invaders. Fages asked about the captives still held, as well as the whereabouts of Salvador Palma. They replied that the prisoners were with Palma downstream at a place called Santa Eulalia, where he was gathering supplies. The Indians defiantly told Fages that they had allied themselves with several other tribes to fight the Spaniards. "To this," Fages wrote, "we replied disdainfully: let them come; we were enough for them all." The warriors answered, "they [the Quechans] knew they were mortal and not stone." With the mutual braggadocio concluded, the Quechans agreed to bargain for the freedom of the captives the next day.[55]

On the morning of Sunday, December 2, Father Cenizo said mass for the soldiers in the shadow of the ruined town of La Concepción. Fages then ordered a cow slaughtered and "divided among the four detachments." The European Catalonian Volunteers, dressed in their cocked hats and blue-and-yellow regimental coats, presented a marked contrast to the presidial "sons of the country," covered in their leather cueras. The Pima and Papago auxiliaries, almost naked except for their quivers and bows, completed the divergent company mess. While his men breakfasted, Colonel Fages interrogated his prisoners, but obtained little useful information.[56]

At noon, the Spanish sentinels reported spotting two dust clouds on either side of the river. Large numbers of Quechans approached, but they stopped on nearing the Spanish camp. A group of twelve warriors ascended the hill opposite Fages's camp and called out to the white men that they had brought a captive to ransom. Colonel Fages and Father Cenizo offered to exchange the blind Quechan boy taken on the first expedition in October. The Indians agreed, and the prisoners were exchanged. The rescued Spaniard was ten-year-old María Josefa Benítez, whose father, settler Francisco Benítez Plata, had been killed in the uprising; her mother, Juana Reyes, had been retrieved in October. After the exchange, the Quechans departed, promising to return with their remaining captives the next day.[57]

The following morning, Fages laid a trap for the Quechans, stationing thirty soldados de cuera and ten Pima auxiliaries on a small rise north of his camp and another party of fifteen Pimas along the riverbank to the south, "so that we might capture them between the two parties." However, the Quechans again thwarted the Spaniards, staying on the far side of the river. Salvador Palma, his brother Ygnacio, and the interpreter Francisco Xavier led a group of six hundred warriors to the top of the hill opposite La Concepción and shouted across that they had come to bargain. With tension rising, the Quechans castigated Fages for having killed several of their tribe, to which he replied that his men had acted in self-defense. The Indians then declared they wanted peace, but if it came to a fight, they would destroy the Spaniards "on the very spot where they had killed Captain Rivera and his companions." Fages mollified them somewhat "by serious reasoning," and in exchange for the Quechan man recently seized, he ransomed seven captive women. One other Spanish woman remained prisoner, and Fages offered to trade the two Quechan women he still held for her. Palma's men agreed and promised to return with her on the morrow. For the remainder of the day, the Spaniards occupied themselves with the grisly task of gathering up the skeletons that still littered the destroyed town of La Purísima Concepción.[58]

With almost all the Spanish prisoners secured, Fages determined to strike at the Quechans. The following morning, he again set up an ambush. Placing his presidial troopers and Indian auxiliaries on either side of the hill of La Concepción, Fages hoped to draw the Quechans between the two forces during the negotiations and trap them. He stationed the Catalonian Volunteers along the river bank at the foot of the hill to prevent any Quechans from crossing the Colorado and flanking the Spaniards. The signal for the attack was to be sounded by the drum.[59]

The Quechans soon appeared, in two groups. The largest number, led by Salvador Palma and Francisco Xavier, ascended the hill across the river from La Concepción, while Ignacio, son of the dead Chief Pablo, led a smaller band directly toward Fages's trap. Ignacio's men, mostly mounted, approached cautiously. At some distance, they shouted to Fages that they were ready to exchange prisoners. The Spaniards sent forward the two women they held and the Quechans released their last prisoner, María Juliana Sambrano, of Bicuñer, widow of the soldier Esteban Romero. She carried in her arms a newborn infant delivered while she was in captivity.[60]

Fages and Captain Tueros then dragged out the conversation with Ignacio as they slowly moved toward him. But the Spanish drummer mistook the officers' movement as the signal for the attack and abruptly shattered the negotiations with the staccato of the drumroll. Ignacio and his men instantly turned their horses and galloped away. Fages and Tueros ordered the charge and gave chase for more than a league, but Ignacio's men were too fleet; they escaped, many diving into the Colorado and swimming across. Meanwhile, at the sound of the drum, the Catalonian Volunteers at the foot of Concepción hill rose from conceal-ment and fired at Salvador Palma's party across the river. Palma's men scattered in all directions, abandoning three horses. In a very few minutes the action was over.[61]

No doubt frustrated with the failure of the ambush, Colonel Fages dog-gedly kept after the Quechans. The ransomed Spanish women revealed the location of two of Salvador Palma's villages, about seven leagues south of La Concepción. Taking a party of soldados de cuera and Pima warriors, Fages set out at ten o'clock on the night of December 5 to launch a surprise attack on these rancherías. After traveling for several hours, the Spaniards stumbled upon a group of Quechan scouts and in the confu-sion opened fire as the Indians scattered. Pressing on, Fages's men reached the native villages at daybreak; though the campfires still burned, not a single Indian was to be found. The soldiers had no choice but to head back to La Concepción empty-handed.[62]

The following day, Fages sent out several search parties to find the bodies of Fathers Garcés and Barreneche, but to no avail. Then on Decem-ber 7, the colonel decided to head toward Bicuñer and look for the bodies of Fathers Díaz and Moreno, taking with him two of the freed Spanish women who had been residents of the town. Accompanied by Captain Tueros, Ensign Arbizu, thirty-four presidial troopers, and ten Catalonian Volunteers, Fages arrived at the outskirts at dawn. They found the corpse of Father Díaz almost immediately, "still recognizable by the tonsure, which had not yet disappeared." The skeleton of Father Moreno was found behind Bicuñer's church. The skull was missing, but a crucifix and pieces of the gray Franciscan habit were still present. They located the bones of many other residents, and Colonel Fages had these gathered up, burned, and the ashes collected. However, he ordered the remains of the dead Franciscans to be placed in a leather sack, separate from the ashes. Finally, Fages had the "great bell of the town" removed and loaded on a mule.[63]

In the midst of these operations, a soldado de cuera galloped into Bicuñer, carrying word that the Quechans were attacking the main Spanish camp. Fages immediately assembled his soldiers and rode posthaste the ten miles back to camp; however, when he arrived he found that the camp garrison had driven off the Quechans a half hour before, and the only losses it had suffered were nine horses carried off.[64]

Sgt. Juan Noriega, of the Catalonian Volunteers, had been left in command of the camp and Fages ordered him to give his report. Noriega explained that after the colonel's departure, a large number of Quechans, which the sergeant estimated at fifteen hundred, surrounded the camp. Salvador Palma, Ignacio, and Francisco Xavier were again in command. About two hundred mounted warriors attacked the camp from one side, while another three hundred footmen moved around the other. The rest of the Quechans "remained in the plain below the town," constantly sending forward new assault groups.[65]

Noriega had thirty Catalonian Volunteers, about twenty-six soldados de cuera, and the bulk of the ninety-six Pima and Papago auxiliaries in camp. When the attack began, eight or nine presidial troopers were below the hill, outside of camp, guarding the troops' caballada. The Quechans initially succeeded in cutting off the horse herd, but the guards charged into the attackers, killing five and scattering the rest. With an escape route opened, the soldiers drove the herd up the hill and into camp, with the loss of only three animals. Sergeant Noriega then had his men form ranks and opened fire on the advancing Quechans. A few troopers manning the small-caliber cannons, known as swivel guns, or *pedreros*, fired grapeshot into the groups of Quechans gathered on the plains below the camp.[66] After almost two hours of fighting, the Quechans began to waver. At least twenty warriors had been killed and many others wounded. The massed warriors beneath the camp withdrew out of range of the swivel guns, abandoning those assaulting the camp. Seizing the opportunity,

Sergeant Noriega ordered several soldados de cuera to sally out of camp and counterattack. The Quechans broke and fled back down the hill, many diving into the Colorado River and swimming to safety on the other side. Trooper Mendivil rode down upon Ignacio and the interpreter Francisco Xavier, both on foot. The two Indians wrenched Mendivil's lance out of his hands, but he drew his sword and slashed Ignacio across the chest. The two Indians then fled into the brush and Mendivil was unable to follow. Another soldier, named Gamez, set out after Salvador Palma, who was on horseback. Three times Gamez fired his pistol at the kwoxot, and three times the flintlock missed fire. Coming to a clump of trees, Palma quickly dismounted and fled on foot, leaving his horse and the cocked hat Lieutenant Colonel Fages had previously given him in the hands of his exasperated pursuer. At this point, Sergeant Noriega closed his report and the exultant Fages praised his men for their successful action.[67]

For the next two days, the Spaniards rested and recovered from the attack. Colonel Fages saw "many columns of smoke" in the distance and correctly deduced that the Quechans were burning their dead, "along with their personal belongings . . . for this is the custom among the Yuma nation." Remembering his own peoples' customs, Fages had his troopers search through the burned buildings of La Concepción. The bones of the dead settlers were gathered together and cremated; their ashes were then placed in bags, along with those of the people of Bicuñer, to be buried in consecrated ground back in Sonora.[68]

The bodies of Fathers Garcés and Barreneche still had not been found. On Monday, December 10, Fages divided the entire command into two parts to scour the surrounding countryside. The grave of the Franciscans, marked with a small wooden cross, was located sometime during the day. "Captain Don Pedro Tueros had the satisfaction of finding them," Fages reported. "They were not much decayed, especially the body of Father Garcés." Lifting up the cadavers, the expedition then headed north, proceeding all the way to Bicuñer. The bodies of Garcés and Barreneche and the bones of Padres Díaz and Moreno were placed upon the altar of Bicuñer's church, "which, although burned, still had its walls intact." Father Cenizo had candles lit and, together with the entire troop, prayed the rosary before the remains of his fellow Franciscans.[69]

For two more days Colonel Fages had his men search the lands between Bicuñer and Concepción for goods and cattle from the two towns. All the

Quechans' rancherías were deserted and the natives were nowhere to be seen. The Spaniards believed they had all moved downriver to join forces with the Halykwamais. At this point, Fages concluded that the expedition had achieved all that it could—that pursuit of the Quechans would be risky, perhaps futile, with little likelihood of seizing Salvador Palma or any of the other leaders of the uprising. Ten captives had been ransomed and the bodies of the martyred Franciscans secured. Although the Quechans still held a few people, there was no way for Fages to ascertain their whereabouts. It was time to head back to Sonóitac.[70]

On December 13, Fages and his troopers set out over the Camino del Diablo with the rescued prisoners, the remains of the slain missionaries and settlers, and three of the four large church bells. Four days later, they reached Sonóitac without loss. After resting for three days, Fages moved southward again, and on December 22 he disbanded the expedition. Captain Tueros proceeded to his presidio of Altar, taking with him the redeemed captives and "the effects belonging to the King and the missions, the bodies of the four reverend fathers and the ashes of the others who perished at the hands of the perfidious Yumas." Fages took his own Catalonian Volunteers to their quarters at the mission of Pitiquito, where the colonel awaited further orders from the caballero. While he was there, Fages kept his company well in hand. The veteran infantrymen were "instructed in the manual of arms, had the penal laws read to them . . . and underwent inspection of arms."[71]

Before leaving Sonóitac, Fages had sent a brief report of his operations to the caballero. Taken together, the two forays had resulted in the rescue of seventy-four captive men, women, and children and the recovery of the remains of the slain; at least fifty-four Quechans had been killed and many others wounded. However, none of the principal leaders of the uprising had been apprehended, and the Quechans were still defiant. If the Caballero de Croix wished to reassert Spanish control over the Yuma Crossing, future military campaigns would be necessary; therefore, Colonel Fages suggested a combined assault by Spanish forces from Sonora and California. The war against the Quechans was far from over.[72]

10

Fire and Blood

*The Spanish Punitive Expedition, February 1782
to January 1783*

COLONEL FELIPE DE NEVE WAS WORRIED. Ever since he had become
governor of the Californias in 1775, he had labored to strengthen Spain's
hold on the province. With fewer than 150 soldiers spread over a thousand miles and with only sporadic communication with his superiors in
Mexico City, it was a task that would have daunted many. Yet, Neve had
succeeded. By 1781, he had substantially increased the number of soldiers in Alta California, overseen the establishment of the first civilian
settlements in the province, and constructed new presidios and missions
that sought to control and convert the indigenous populations. All of that
was now jeopardized by the war with the Quechans.[1]

Neve had been the first high-ranking Spanish official to become aware
of the uprising at Yuma in the summer of 1781. Ensign Cayetano Limón,
who had barely escaped from the Colorado River with his life in August,

had returned to report personally the disaster to Neve. Realizing that word of the successful revolt might stimulate other tribes to follow suit, Neve took "immediate measures to prevent this news from reaching the ears of the natives of these settlements." He then gathered a substantial force of soldiers outside Mission San Gabriel and issued orders to the presidial commanders at San Diego and Monterey to be on the alert. The show of force worked. The Spanish overawed those California coastal tribes that might have sought to emulate the Quechans.[2]

Once this immediate threat had passed, the governor dispatched word of the uprising to the Caballero de Croix. Satisfied that he had done all he could, Governor Neve continued the duties he had been engaged in before: the establishment of a new presidio and missions along the Santa Bárbara channel. All the while, however, he kept a cautious eye upon the Quechans and the neighboring tribes along the Colorado River.[3]

By December 1781, Neve heard from Teodoro de Croix. Dispatches informed the governor that a punitive expedition would be sent against the Quechans under Lt. Col. Pedro Fages. Croix ordered Neve to proceed to the Colorado to assist in the operation, but these instructions failed to specify a timetable for the expedition and Neve remained unsure as to exactly when Fages would be along the river. As was usual, the lengthy delay in receiving orders from the commandant-general in Arizpe left Neve in the position of acting upon information that was probably no longer reliable. It would not be the first nor the last time that the governor would have to trust his own intuition on how to proceed.[4]

Neve decided to complete the construction of the new presidio of Santa Bárbara before he organized an expedition against the Quechans. In the meantime, he dispatched a small scouting force of twelve men and an interpreter from the San Diego presidio under Ensign José Velásquez to Yuma. If Velásquez found Lieutenant Colonel Fages, he was to assist him; if not, he was to report back to Neve immediately.[5]

In February 1782, Velásquez and his men departed San Diego. They traveled as far as the Kamia Indian settlement of San Sebastián, located about eighty-five miles east of the Colorado River, before receiving any information about Fages. The villagers told Velásquez about "black and white men mounted on horseback, armed, who had come four moons ago. These men had crossed the river . . . and went higher upstream, burning houses, killing some Indians and freeing some captives. Then they went away. Palma escaped into the mountains." It is unclear if

Velásquez and his men continued to Yuma, but they certainly had missed Fages's punitive expedition. Ensign Velásquez returned by the middle of March with his findings, leaving Governor Neve even more in the dark about what to do.[6]

However, on March 26 the situation became clear. While the governor was reconnoitering for a new site for the presidio of Santa Bárbara, word came to him that Don Pedro Fages himself, with thirty-nine soldiers, had arrived that day at Mission San Gabriel. Fages had brought orders placing Neve in command of one of the largest and most complex military operations in years along the frontier. The caballero had determined that the Quechans would pay dearly for their "revolt" against Spain and, Neve would be the instrument of their punishment.[7]

At San Gabriel, Neve spoke with Colonel Fages about the latter's journey. Fages had set out from Sonora on February 27 with ten privates and a sergeant of his company of Catalonian Volunteers and twenty-eight soldados de cuera. From the small mission community of Pitiquito, the detachment headed northwest over the Camino del Diablo en route to Yuma. Twelve days later, they reached the Colorado River and forded without mishap, opposite from the ruined town of San Pedro y San Pablo de Bicuñer. Although watched by a group of about thirty mounted Quechans, the Spaniards were not intimidated. "We stopped for nothing," Fages reported, "taking up our march in column with myself at the head, right through the midst of their villages."[8]

Though the Quechans seemed surprised by the appearance of the colonel and his men, the brazen conduct of the soldiers agitated the Indians even more. Fages recalled that the natives "came out to meet us on the front and rear, as well as on both sides shouting and raising clouds of dust everywhere so that not even they themselves understood each other. But the troop went on in good order, paying no attention at all to this confusion." After riding about twenty miles through Quechan territory, Fages and his men stopped at the Sierra de San Pablo, modern-day Pilot Knob.[9]

Unable to intimidate the Spaniards, the Quechans now attempted to parley, asking where the soldiers were going. Fages replied, "We had come to reestablish ourselves there and make peace. . . . They assented and took leave until the next day when they promised to return and treat concerning the matter." Despite this assurance, Fages noted, "none of the chiefs were among those who did the talking." Perhaps because of this, the colonel remained wary. After several hours rest, Fages stole a nighttime march away from the Indians, riding until his men reached the barrier of the Algodones sand dunes. Successfully overcoming this last obstacle, the remainder of the journey proved uneventful. Fages and his troopers reached San Gabriel two weeks after leaving Yuma.[10]

Colonel Fages provided Neve with a good deal of information that the governor lacked. Fages reported on the results of the two expeditions he had conducted against the Quechans, the nature of the terrain, and the military capabilities of the Indians of the region. All this would prove indispensable to Neve, to fulfill his orders to organize and lead another descent upon the Quechans, subdue them totally, and erect a presidio at the Yuma Crossing.[11]

Neve's orders were the results of the junta de guerra convened at Arizpe by Croix in early January. The council had determined that the governor should lead a combined assault on the Quechans, catching the Indians in a pincers movement between two detachments of troops coming from Sonora and California. The Sonoran contingent would contain more than eighty soldiers and several hundred Indian allies from the Maricopas, Gila Pimas, Pimas Altos, and Papagos. Fages would take half of the Sonoran contingent to contact Neve; the remaining forty soldiers, under the command of Captain Pedro Tueros, would reach the Colorado River by April 1. Governor Neve, with fifty California soldiers along with the men brought by Fages, would rendezvous with Tueros by the same date. Neve's united force would then seek out and destroy the Quechans, capture and execute Salvador Palma and the other leaders, and locate a site for the construction of a presidio and a town to control the crossing.[12]

Four days after the junta de guerra met, Croix wrote a letter modifying the council's decisions in order to give Neve more flexibility. Hearing reports that the Colorado River would be in flood during April and May, and therefore difficult to cross, and that pasturage would be scarce, Croix gave Neve the option of postponing the operation until a more favorable time of year, if he felt so inclined. Appending this note to the orders of the war council, Croix then dispatched Fages to deliver them to the governor.[13]

When the colonel reached Mission San Gabriel, the plans of the junta had been overtaken by events. Both Neve and Fages realized that the Sonoran contingent under Captain Tueros must have already set out for the Colorado River. Believing that he lacked sufficient time to organize an expedition, as well as being preoccupied with the Santa Bárbara presidio, Governor Neve postponed the planned assault. After conferring with

Colonel Fages, the governor decided to launch the attack against the Quechans no later than the middle of September.[14]

There still remained the problem of what to do about Captain Tueros and his Sonoran troopers, undoubtedly already on their way to Yuma. Showing remarkable fidelity and endurance, Lieutenant Colonel Fages volunteered to return immediately to the Colorado River to deliver the change of plans. On April 2, Fages, with ten soldiers who had accompanied him from Sonora and ten from California, departed San Gabriel, exactly one week after he had arrived.[15]

Unknown to him, a Spanish force, substantially larger than either he or Governor Neve realized, waited at Yuma. The caballero in late February had taken steps to increase the number of soldiers from Sonora sent to attack the Quechans. Fages's company of Catalonian Volunteers was replaced by another group of regulars serving on the northern frontier, a piquet of thirty men from the Regiment of the Dragoons of Spain. Sixty soldados de cuera and light troopers from the presidios of Altar, Tucson, Buenavista, and Pitic, along with forty-two Pima auxiliaries from the missions of the Pimería Alta, completed the roster.[16]

The caballero placed the entire force under the command of Capt. José Antonio Romeu, of the Dragoons of Spain, with Capt. Pedro Tueros once again as second in command. The two captains were assisted by Lieutenant Manuel Arbizu, of Pitic, and Ensign Rafael Tovar, of Buenavista, as well as by a young cadet, Don Antonio Urrea, scion of a well-established Sonoran military family. The ninety-five Spaniards of Romeu's command were mounted on a herd of 363 horses and mules and equipped with a "a complete armament of firearms, and also 68 swords and 63 lances." The shortage of blades was partially made up by the addition of a small cannon, or *pedrero*. The forty-two Pima auxiliaries apparently had no animals of their own and were armed only with bows, lances, clubs, and shields.[17]

Departing from the Mission of Caborca on March 18, 1782, Romeu and his men headed over the well-worn trail of the Camino del Diablo, northwest toward the Gila River. The jaded nature of the Spaniards' horse herd made the journey especially difficult. Several times Romeu was forced to leave groups of animals behind at watering holes in order that they might rest and recuperate. Small detachments of soldiers and Pima auxiliaries stayed with the tired beasts before driving them on behind the main party.[18]

On April 1, Captain Romeu and the bulk of his troopers reached the Colorado River, directly opposite from the ruined town of La Concepción. He immediately dispatched a detachment of twenty-six troopers and ten Pimas to reconnoiter for a place to cross the river. Moving north, the Spaniards found a ford called La Capilla, probably across from the visita that Father Garcés had set up to preach to the Quechans. Unable to cross the ford due to high water, the detachment returned, reporting that the Quechan rancherías across the Colorado appeared "totally depopulated."[19]

While these men had been scouting to the north, Romeu and the remaining troopers searched the area of the confluence of the Colorado and Gila Rivers. Once again no signs of the Quechans were found, "not even fresh tracks." With several groups of straggling animals herded by small parties of troopers still many hours behind on the trail, Captain Romeu decided to establish camp on the hill directly across from La Concepción. Anticipating trouble, he ordered his men to "mount, charge and place in battery the pedrero." Tensely, the Spaniards settled in for the night.[20]

At midnight, Romeu dispatched a party of fourteen men under a sergeant to examine the ford of La Capilla. Returning at noon on the following day, the sergeant reported the water at the ford running very fast, and as high as "the side of the saddle tree of a horse." He and his men had seen a large amount of smoke in the distance, but found only one small trail that seemed to have been made by a woman or a child. In the afternoon, the river had fallen somewhat and a good swimmer crossed the ford, finding signs of a native encampment a few miles to the north. With this news, the sergeant and his men returned to camp.[21]

In the meantime, Captain Romeu sent three Pima auxiliaries across the Colorado to examine the environs of La Concepción. The Pimas soon returned, having found many old tracks leading west, toward the ford called Vicular, "at the foot of the sierra called San Pablo, distant four leagues from this encampment." Hoping to catch the Quechans there, the Spaniards quickly planned an attack.[22]

Before daybreak on April 4, Captain Romeu and Captain Tueros led a force of twenty presidial soldiers, eleven Dragoons of Spain, and twenty Pima Auxiliaries, mounted on the most serviceable animals in the horse herd, on a search and destroy mission. Attempting a subterfuge, Romeu and Tueros initially led their men to the northeast, crossing the Colorado at the ford of La Capilla; however, the river was swollen, and after crossing two separate arms of water, a third channel, faster and deeper than the others, thwarted the Spaniards.[23]

Altering their plans, the soldiers recrossed the Colorado and headed back toward their camp. Moving directly toward the Sierra de San Pablo and the ford of Vicular, they came upon fresh tracks heading southeast. Romeu ordered his men to follow at the gallop. After riding eight miles, they deemed the pursuit futile when an Indian auxiliary familiar with the region indicated that the trail led to a mountain "two days distant."[24]

Dejected, the Spaniards moved slowly back to their encampment. Captain Tueros, who had accompanied the previous punitive expeditions, recognized the region as where the Quechans had been residing at that time. Searching among the thick groves of cottonwood and willows that lined the riverbank, Tueros and the other troopers found many cleared fields and several Quechan rancherías, but the huts had been "burned to their uprights" and the fields had not been planted for several months.[25]

By four o'clock in the afternoon, Captains Romeu and Tueros led their men back to their main camp. Suddenly, a group of thirty Indians appeared across the river amid the ruined houses of La Concepción. The Spaniards thought that they had finally located the Quechans, but the Indians shouted that they were Kohuanas and wanted to talk to the white men. Eventually, sixteen Indians, including a Kohuana "captain" and one member of the Halchidoma tribe, crossed the Colorado, to be "well received" by Romeu.[26]

The Kohuana chief informed the Spaniards that the Quechans "had abandoned their lands at the end of the previous month." The Quechans knew that troops were coming from Sonora "to join with those from California" and, to avoid the soldiers, they had abandoned their homeland en masse and invaded the territory of the Halchidomas "with the idea to finish them off." The Mohaves, close kinsmen of the Quechans, and the Kamia Indians, who inhabited the areas northwest of Yuma, joined in this invasion. Together, these "three tribes concluded to batter and to exile from their lands" the Halchidomas, allowing the Quechans to "afterwards establish themselves amongst . . . their ancient friends."[27]

Before leaving their traditional lands, the Quechans deposited some of their people and many of their animals and goods among their neighboring allies. The Kohuana chief informed Captain Romeu that some Kamia Indians guarded the Quechans' fields near the ford of Vicular and the Sierra de San Pablo, having "much provision, mules, horses and clothes like those which we carried." The Halykwamai tribe also supported the Quechans by granting shelter to several families.[28]

For the Kohuanas, the appearance of Captain Romeu's expedition offered an opportunity to enrich themselves at their neighbors' expense, as well as to relieve the pressure on their friends, the beleaguered Halchidomas. On April 8, a chieftain named José Antonio, "one of those baptized in the City of Mexico in company with the treacherous Salvador Palma," appeared at the Spanish camp. Over the next two days, José Antonio and other Kohuana leaders attempted to entice the Spaniards into attacking the Halykwamais. The Kohuanas cleverly pointed out the abundance of horses and mules possessed by the Halykwamais and noted that the Spaniards' animals were "in a bad state." Romeu commented that the Kohuanas made these observations "perhaps to see if they could excite our covetousness."[29]

The pressure on Romeu to act increased on April 11, when the Kohuanas escorted into camp a Halchidoma envoy. The man "said that his tribe desired that we should go and help them against the Yumas." The envoy reported that the Quechans were upriver from the Spanish position and that, together with the Kamias and Mohaves, they were attacking his people. The Halchidoma assured the Spaniards that, if the soldiers intervened, his people would provide "many supplies and abundant fields of wheat and corn, already in season." Tactfully, Romeu replied that he could not leave the Yuma Crossing because he was waiting for orders from the governor of California, but he promised to relay the Halchidoma's request to his superiors, along with those things "most favorable for them."[30] The following day, a large group of Kohuanas, along with their families, arrived near the Spanish camp, saying that they were going to place themselves between the white men and the Halykwamais for mutual protection. Romeu remained uncertain as how to treat this move.

On April 13, "at eight in the morning Lt. Col. Don Pedro Fages arrived at the other bank of the river with twenty soldados de cuera of the Provinces of Sonora and California."[31] Fages had reached the Yuma Crossing twelve days after leaving San Gabriel. Cautiously entering La Concepción, he was immediately seen by Romeu's troops across the river. Fages, with two men, went "to the top of a cliff which overlooks the landing place of the town, where I saluted Captains Don Joseph Romeu and Don Pedro Tueros and the other officers of the expedition." Romeu had a

Kohuana Indian swim across and retrieve the orders that Fages carried from Governor Neve. Upon opening them, Romeu succinctly summarized the governor's orders: "Suspend all operations against the Yumas until a more opportune time."[32]

Captain Romeu then ordered the construction of "a small raft that they formed with some lassos and headstalls from the troopers horse gear." Ever vigilant, Lieutenant Colonel Fages hesitated at first to leave his small command unattended, but at the insistence of Romeu "and of the other officers, I crossed to where their camp was, having set the troop in order . . . so as to be able to cooperate in case of any movement by the enemy . . . and inasmuch as our arrival caused marked rejoicing, we passed the remainder of the day and night in pleasure, without any event whatsoever."[33]

The next morning, Fages recrossed the Colorado River; by noon, he had started his return journey to Mission San Gabriel. Captain Romeu, too, prepared to return, in his case to Sonora, but on the following day an embassy of four Indians, one Gila Pima, one Maricopa, and two Halchidomas, arrived, "asking help in order to dislodge from the lands of the latter, the Yumas, who had possessed themselves of them." The Indians reported that the Halchidomas had lost many of their cultivated fields, and they were in danger of starving. Several Kohuanas joined the discussion, and in view of the situation, Romeu delayed his departure.[34]

A Halchidoma chieftain, accompanied by five warriors, came to the Spanish camp the next day. He repeated his peoples' request for immediate aid from the white men, but proudly denied that his tribe had been defeated by the Quechans, boasting instead that, although the Halchidomas had lost some stores of beans, "they had been recompensed with . . . *pinole* [corn meal] . . . *panochas* [sugar] and *cigarros*" taken from their attackers. Despite the chief's braggadocio, Romeu continued to be unsure if the Halchidomas were winning or losing against the Quechans, especially after the Gila Pima and Maricopa envoys also called for the Spaniards to join the fray.[35]

Captain Romeu clearly could not intervene. His supplies were low, and the orders from Governor Neve bid him to leave the Yuma area immediately. Hoping to fan the flames of tribal enmity, the captain assured the representatives of the Kohuanas, Halchidomas, Maricopas, and Gila Pimas that he "would return before the coming of the cold to succor them and to castigate or exterminate" the Quechans. He then urged the Indian envoys to maintain "the spirit of union among the four nations against the traitorous Yumas" and warned them that "they knew the superiority of our arms and of our great resolution."[36]

On April 17, Captain Romeu and his command broke camp and moved down the Gila River to head for home. Several Kohuanas and Halchidomas accompanied the Spaniards for the next two days. They assured the white men that they would seek aid from the Maricopas and Gila Pimas for a united attack upon the Quechans. Satisfied that he had secured the support of these four tribes, Romeu continued his journey back to Caborca, where he arrived at the end of the month.[37]

After disbanding the expedition, Captain Romeu and the piquet of the Dragoons of Spain continued on to Altar with Captain Tueros and his troopers. From this presidio, Romeu sent a copy of his diary of the expedition to Teodoro de Croix at Arizpe. The caballero received this document on May 6 and, after reviewing it and other reports, issued orders calling for another junta de guerra in ten days, designed to organize and launch the fourth Spanish punitive campaign against the Quechans.[38]

On the appointed day, Croix, Royal Intendent and Civil Governor Pedro Corbalán, and Asesor Pedro Galindo y Navarro sat down to draw up plans to finish off the Quechans once and for all. After reviewing the latest communications from Governor Neve and various military officers in Sonora, the junta agreed with the California governor's proposal to attack the Quechans no later than September 15. As before, troops from Sonora and California would rendezvous at the Yuma Crossing, trapping the Quechans between them. The combined forces would then crush the Indians, execute Palma and the other leaders, and select a site for establishing a new presidio and town.[39]

Again, the junta ordered Neve to assume overall command of the expedition, with Fages as his second. The California contingent would consist of seventy troopers, including the eleven Catalonian Volunteers and twenty-eight presidial soldiers who had escorted Fages to Mission San Gabriel the previous March. Captains José Romeu and Pedro Tueros again were given command of the Sonoran contingent, composed of the same mixed force of the Dragoons of Spain and presidial soldiers. Forty Gila Pimas and Papagos and twenty Pimas Altos would supplement the Sonoran troopers.[40]

Governor Neve also had authorization to recruit up to eighty Indians from the friendly tribes along the Colorado River, preferably the Kohuanas, led by Chief José Antonio. To assure the assistance of these tribes, the junta ordered the expedition to be outfitted with gifts to the value of 300 pesos, including "red and blue bayeta, blankets, . . . striped *rebozos*, . . . glass beads, tie ribbons, and some fine red Naples linen." Neve was also given the option of handing to the allied tribes any booty taken from the Quechans.[41]

Determined to meet any contingency, the junta ordered the expedition thoroughly equipped. To ford the Colorado River, the Sonoran detachment carried a large variety of tools for constructing rafts, including "twelve axes, twelve mattocks, six crow bars . . . and some ship's rope." For added firepower, the expedition's arsenal included two cannons from the presidio of Altar, "with their gun carriages, gunners ladles, rammers, wormers, some match, lead and cannon balls." Finally, an entire, fresh remount herd was provided, including two hundred horses and forty mules to be transferred to the California troopers. With this, the junta de guerra concluded on May 17. Copies of its resolutions were immediately dispatched to Governor Neve in California and the Sonoran military commanders.[42]

All through the spring and summer of 1782, the Spaniards prepared for the projected campaign. During the same period, the Quechans were also organizing their war effort. The destruction of the Spanish settlements at Yuma resulted in the outbreak of a general war between the members of the Quechan League and the Maricopa–Gila Pima League. Determined to forestall any future Spanish presence along the Colorado River, the Quechans launched a series of attacks on those tribes that had supported the white men or that stood between them and their allies.[43]

As noted by Captain Romeu, the Quechans, Mohaves, and the Kamias had joined together and attacked the Halchidomas. The latter tribe suffered so many losses that they appealed for aid from the tribes of the Maricopa–Gila Pima League. However, the Quechan effort to dispossess the Halchidomas of their lands failed and, sometime during the summer of 1782, the Quechans returned to the confluence of the Gila and Colorado Rivers, their traditional homeland. Finding the Kohuanas there, the Quechans and their allies proceeded to assault the squatters, driving them out. Pursuing the defeated Kohuanas, the Quechans occupied a large section of territory south of the Sierra de San Pablo, establishing new rancherías and raising crops.[44]

By late August, the Spanish forces in Alta California and Sonora completed their preparations and were ready for another punitive descent on the Colorado River. No doubt alerted to the impending operation, the nations of the Quechan League and their opponents in the Maricopa–Gila Pima League girded themselves for the conflict.

On August 21 and 26, Fages and Neve moved out in two successive waves from Mission San Gabriel to attack the Quechans. While Fages commanded the specified thirty-nine troopers, Neve had gathered only nineteen California soldiers from the presidios of Monterey and San Diego, under the direction of Ensign José Velásquez. Uniting their detachments southeast of San Gabriel, the combined force moved toward the Yuma Crossing.[45] However, on September 4, near the Kamia Indian village of San Sebastián, eighty-five miles northeast of their destination, a courier brought dispatches that affected the entire campaign. By an order of the Caballero de Croix dated July 12, 1782, Neve had been promoted to inspector-general of the Interior Provinces of New Spain, a position he was to assume immediately. By the same order, Fages was designated to succeed Neve as governor of the Californias.[46]

Undoubtedly taken aback by these sudden changes, Neve nevertheless observed the formalities of having the transfer of command officially witnessed by Ensign Velásquez and sergeants Miguel Rivera, of the Catalonian Volunteers, and Mariano Verdugo, of the presidio of Monterey. For the next three days, the new inspector-general composed a set of instructions and delivered them, along with "several papers and documents relating to the government," to Fages. He then formally acknowledged the colonel as "the provisional governor of the said peninsula of the Californias." On September 11, Fages returned to San Diego to assume his duties as governor. Neve and the remainder of the expedition continued toward the Colorado River.[47]

Five days later, the California detachment reached the Yuma Crossing and ascended to the ruined town of La Concepción. Immediately across the river from them, they saw the Sonoran detachment of 108 men commanded by Captains Romeu and Tueros, which had arrived one day before the Californians. Wasting no time, General Neve ordered several rafts to be constructed and the forces to be united. For the next several days, the Spaniards tried to link up, but were hampered because "the strong current and the eddy that formed at the landing hindered the course of the rafts." By September 20, however, Captain Romeu, two ensigns, "and forty men with one pedrero were transferred from the south to the north bank."[48]

Over the following three days, Neve and his officers were surprised by the arrival of six or seven hundred Halchidomas and Maricopas, eager to join the Spaniards in attacking the Quechans. Six chieftains crossed over to La Concepción to parley with Neve. With some difficulty, he managed to deploy the motley group of warriors on either bank of the Colorado. In the meantime, Spanish scouts reported that the Quechans had moved several days before to the region near the ruined town of Bicuñer.[49]

Determined to strike the enemy, Neve and Captain Romeu, with sixty troopers and twelve Pima auxiliaries, set out on September 23 at 10:30 P.M. Several hours later, they came upon a group of four hundred Halchidomas and Maricopas. "I was obliged," Neve later wrote, "to make a short halt . . . to prevent their joining or mingling with the troops." After sending the Indians to join their compatriots at La Concepción, the Spanish force continued forward, but upon reaching Bicuñer, found the area abandoned.[50]

Deciding to go in pursuit, before sunrise Neve and his men moved south toward the lands of the Kohuanas. By the afternoon, the Spaniards neared the Laguna de Santa Eulalia, some twenty-five miles south of the Sierra de San Pablo, where they came upon a series of fresh tracks. Following the signs, the soldiers shortly thereafter discovered "a confused crowd" of Halchidomas, Maricopas, and even some Kohuanas, huddled "at the edge of a dense underbrush." Beyond, the Spaniards saw a large lagoon, abutting an arm of the Colorado River, in the midst of which lay a large village. The Quechans had been found.[51]

As Felipe de Neve prepared his men for an attack on the village, a group of five mounted Quechan scouts were seen shadowing the Spanish column. Neve immediately ordered Ensign Tovar, eight troopers, and ten Pima auxiliaries to pursue the enemy scouts and to outflank the village. The governor ordered Tovar to locate a path through the lagoon and into the village, but not to engage the enemy. As Tovar and his men rode out, some Halchidomas and Kohuanas, apparently on their own initiative, followed in their wake.[52]

Turning to the large group of Halchidoma and Maricopa warriors milling about the underbrush, Neve managed with a great amount of difficulty to organize them for an attack on the Quechan village. "I succeeded in getting some of them to advance," he later wrote, "but they retreated shortly thereafter, and fled from the attacking enemy."[53]

Unable to mount a serious frontal assault upon the village, Neve heard gunfire coming from the flank: Ensign Tovar, contrary to orders, had attacked the scouts he was trailing. The Quechan riders "sought safety in the river and were crossing a very large muddy lagoon" toward the village. Neve was furious: the chance of a surprise flank attack had been lost. "Confronted with the question of having disobeyed my orders," the general fumed, "[Tovar] told me that the enemy had attacked him. . . . [and] he considered the critical moment lost."[54]

Neve realized that the Quechans were now firmly in place along all sides of the village; in addition, they had taken up good defensive positions on both banks of the river and the adjacent lagoon. "Because they had taken refuge in the woods so near the river, obstacles impassable to our troops," Neve conceded, "they could mock our every effort."[55]

The Spaniards also now realized that the large group of Halchidoma, Kohuana, and Maricopa warriors had no stomach for a major fight. "I wanted to detach 400 Indians from the friendly tribes that surrounded us," Neve recalled, "because I had become distrustful of them, having seen certain inconsistencies, such as the fact that those who had accompanied Alférez Tovar had not shot a single arrow." With obvious frustration, Neve ordered his men to form up and return to their main base at La Concepción.[56]

Upon their arrival, the Spaniards found that there had been a great deal of excitement since they had left. Captain Tueros had been left in command of the camp and, during the day, several Halchidomas reported to him that the Quechans were coming to attack "in great numbers." As the Spanish encampments were on opposite hills divided by the Colorado, Tueros faced the problem of defending both places simultaneously. Dividing his forces as best he could, he was "obliged to order that the horses be assembled close to both camps and preparations had been made to repel the attackers." With the return of General Neve and his detachment, the report of a planned attack proved false. Given their performance so far, many of the Spanish officers probably questioned the military value of their Indian allies.[57]

On September 25, however, the faith of the Spaniards was partially restored when two Kohuana leaders appeared with an ambitious plan. Under the command of Chief José Antonio, the Kohuanas proposed to move their warriors to the south side of the Colorado and follow the river downstream until they reached the Quechan village. The Spaniards on the north bank would parallel the Kohuana movement. Together the combined forces would drive the Quechans out of their fortified village and into the open, where they would be destroyed.[58]

Felipe de Neve approved the plan, scheduling the combined assault in three days. To the Kohuanas, the general "explained what they should carry out and that they should return to their tribe to prepare to attack." To support the Indians, he assembled a picked detachment of forty presidial troopers and Dragoons of Spain and twelve Pima auxiliaries. Captain Romeu commanded the strike force, assisted by Lieutenant Arbizu and Sgt. Diego López, of Romeu's piquet of Dragoons.[59]

Before sunrise on September 28, Romeu and his assault force moved out, following the course of the Colorado River due west. Past the Sierra de San Pablo, the river turned south, and by midmorning the detachment approached the site of the Quechan ranchería. But Chief José Antonio and the Kohuanas were nowhere to be seen, and Romeu's men found themselves unsupported. To make matters worse, the Quechans had improved their defensive preparations by removing many of their noncombatants. The Spaniards were later informed that Salvador Palma, "accompanied by the old men, some women, and children . . . had taken shelter in the rough hills of Bicuñer." With their families safely to the north of the Spanish invaders, the Quechan warriors, under command of Palma's brother, Ygnacio, and probably accompanied by a substantial force of allied Mohaves and Kamias, prepared to give battle.[60]

Although outnumbered and bereft of the promised support of the Kohuanas, Captain Romeu refused to retreat. Forming his men, Romeu charged directly into the Quechan village, scattering the Indian defenders. The Spanish vanguard, led by Cpl. Francisco López, of Altar, and four scouts, did great execution. Galloping back and forth across the village, López and his squad "continued to trample down the Indians . . . they lanced and cut down many."[61]

Stunned by the charge of the Spanish horsemen, the Quechans and their allies dove into the waters surrounding most of the village, some into the lagoon, others into the Colorado River. Many, "with water up to their chests," swam to the opposite bank of the river as the Spaniards fired at them; however, the cool of the early morning had left the lagoon "covered by a . . . mist or vapors that it exhaled," which obstructed vision.

Blinded by the fog, "two soldados de cuera cast themselves headlong" into the lagoon and were "scarcely able to get out with their lances and adargas." Both troopers lost "their horses, fully saddled and equipped," and as they slogged in the mire "made a target for the enemy." Though one was badly wounded by an arrow in the chest, the two men escaped.[62]

The Quechans soon recovered from the Spanish charge and now fought "with agility and tenacity." Impressed by this defense, Romeu and his men questioned if the opposing warriors were actually Quechans or from "more warlike nations," such as the Mohaves or Kamias. Of whatever tribe, the Indian defenders proved formidable opponents.[63]

Having cleared the village, Romeu's men moved around the perimeter of the lagoon, probing for a weakness. The captain soon realized that the Quechan warriors were ensconced around the lagoon and on the river banks "among the forest and thickets." Along with the dense vegetation, Romeu found that the Indians were further camouflaged by "a dense amount of vapors that . . . allowed the enemy . . . to conceal themselves." Forming his troopers in two ranks, Romeu ordered them to fire volleys into "those small intervals in the mist" that his men could see through. The Spaniards for an hour and a half "fired by ranks . . . particularly into the lagoon and opposite bank."[64]

The volleys were ineffective and the Quechans began to taunt the Spaniards. Gathering themselves together, the Indians advanced toward Romeu and his men and "presented themselves in action for attack." Seizing the opportunity, the captain and his troopers executed a series of feigned retreats. Taking the bait, the Quechans rushed after the soldiers, only to be caught by a devastating countercharge after being sucked out into the open. Captain Romeu and his men, with "lance thrusts and saber slashes, and also firing," inflicted great loss on the Indians.[65]

However, the Quechans could execute some tactics of their own. Using their superior numbers, they dispatched groups of warriors to envelope both of Romeu's flanks. They also launched a feint attack against the Spaniards' horse herd, and Romeu, fearing the loss of his caballada, ordered his men to form up for a genuine retreat. Slowly falling back, the Spaniards continued to fire volleys into the advancing warriors.[66] After a short while, word came that the caballada had not been attacked. Instantly, Romeu turned his men about and charged the pursuing Quechans. Again, the Spaniards lanced many Indians, but only one was cut down and killed, the majority regaining the safety of the lagoon and the thick brush along the banks of the Colorado.[67]

A lull now came upon the battlefield. In an attempt to intimidate the Quechans, Romeu directed his troopers to occupy and loot the village. "With the scorn that they deserve," the Spaniards, in full view of the Quechans across the river, "refreshed themselves with some watermelons and with their luscious pinole." After an hour of feasting in front of the enemy, Romeu commanded his men to cut the heads off of all the dead Indians they could find; the severed heads, however, were afterwards lost, "due to the carelessness of those carrying them," and only a single ear remained of these grisly trophies to be presented later to General Neve.[68]

The Quechans' losses during the battle had been severe. Spanish scouts found "at least forty" dead Indians in and around the village, and later reports speculated that "surely this fate befell Ygnacio, brother of Salvador Palma." Captain Romeu also recalled that "in the lagoon and opposite bank the enemy [dead] were heaped together." He assumed these were all victims of his men's volley fire, and did not include those killed "with the lance and sword." The Spaniards could not determine the number of wounded Quechans, but maintained that it was probably larger than those slain.[69]

As the mist surrounding the lagoon showed no signs of lifting, and with the Quechans still defiant, Romeu felt he had done all he could, and broke off the engagement. His men had fired more than eight hundred cartridges against the enemy, and his ammunition supply was low. Two horses had been killed and six wounded, and the remainder of the herd were exhausted. Although only four troopers had been wounded, one was in serious condition with a flint arrowhead lodged in his chest, and the captain "dared not make an incision and draw it out." To make matters worse, the Spaniards' Indian auxiliaries were clearly intimidated by the number of Quechans, as only two of them had actually joined in the fighting. The fear that they might desert, coupled with everything else, convinced Captain Romeu to return to the base camp.[70]

The day after the battle, General Neve decided he should send the California contingent back to their posts. The lack of forage for the animals had taken its toll, and forty-nine animals had been lost from the Californians' caballada since they had left San Gabriel. "Day by the horse herd was deteriorating," Neve declared. "The continuing loss and the deaths of the animals led me to decide that the California troops should be withdrawn together with some of the fresh horses." The following day, Ensign Velásquez and the nineteen troopers from San Diego and Monterey returned to their posts, having been given seventy-eight fresh horses and mules from the Sonoran herd. However, the eleven Catalonian Volunteers and twenty-eight presidial soldiers who had escorted Colonel Fages to California the preceding March remained with General Neve.[71]

The diminution of his forces increased the general's dejection and frustration at not being able to defeat the Quechans decisively. Immediately thereafter, Felipe de Neve gave up; on October 1, he and his men crossed to the south bank of the Colorado to unite with Romeu's command. Neve had finally decided "that the . . . expedition ought to send its troops back to their designated posts." The next night, he left the Yuma Crossing with half the men, followed twenty-four hours later by Captain Romeu and the remainder.[72]

But Neve then had second thoughts. Hoping that the Quechans might still be brought to battle, he "decided to pursue them until greater punishment had been inflicted." Within five days of leaving, the Spaniards returned to the Colorado. The general dispatched captains Romeu and Tueros with a force of sixty-one soldiers and twelve Pima auxiliaries to reconnoiter the regions north and south of the Yuma Crossing to see if the Quechans had returned to their traditional homelands.[73] Finding the area abandoned, Romeu and Tueros then headed southwest into the lands of the Kohuanas. The Spaniards had received a report that the Quechans were "at the place of the big house." But on approaching the prehistoric ruins of the *casa grande,* located somewhere south of the Sierra de San Pablo, the soldiers found the place empty. Neve later wrote that the Quechans' "departure from the river was the only thing that could be ascertained, since the . . . bank of the river was followed toward the west for some eighteen leagues but not a single Indian was found."[74]

Felipe de Neve finally accepted the inevitable: the forces under his command had killed at least forty Indians and wounded many more, but they had not taken any of the principal tribal leaders; the Quechans had not been subdued. Incapable of inflicting any more damage, on October 12, 1782, Neve officially ended the campaign and headed back to Sonora. Five days later, the Spaniards reached the Papago village of Sonóitac, where they rested and watered their stock. Taking advantage of the lull, Neve hurriedly composed an account of the campaign for the caballero.[75]

Seeking to explain his failure to subdue the Quechans, the general spread the blame wherever he could. "Previous campaigns," he claimed, "hindered the attainment of favorable results" and prevented him from administering "the just punishment of the ringleaders and the rebelling Yuma tribe . . . and keeping communication to the river free." Neve also maintained that the nature of the terrain worked against the Spaniards, noting that "the troops cannot remain without destroying their horses in a short time because of the lack of pasturage." With notable understatement, General Neve concluded his report by observing that "the capture of ringleaders in a countryside where one cannot pursue them because of the shelter it affords, is difficult."[76]

For the next several weeks, Neve busied himself with the disbanding of the expedition, sending the troopers back to their garrisons and distributing the horses and mules among them. Then on January 3, 1783, in the town of Arizpe, Croix called a final junta de guerra to consider if any more action should be taken against the Quechans. Like the previous war councils, this meeting included the caballero, Governor Corbalán, and Asesor Galindo, plus General Neve and Captain Tueros as newcomers. All of them knew that it would be the opinions of Felipe de Neve that would determine what course the council would take.[77]

Wasting no time, Neve declared that the crown must consider the attempt to settle the Yuma Crossing as having failed. The Quechans were now implacably hostile to the Spaniards, and without their support a settlement or mission could not be successful. Furthermore, in Neve's opinion the lands around the Colorado River were too barren and sterile, filled with salt marshes and sand dunes. In addition, as all necessary supplies would have to be carried from Sonora, a presidio at Yuma would prove inordinately expensive.[78] Taking their tenor from Neve, the other members of the junta pointed out the need to muster all Spanish forces against the Apaches and the ever-rebellious Seris; a presidio along the Colorado would divert manpower desperately needed elsewhere. Should the Spaniards need to use the Yuma Crossing, a well-armed party of thirty men would be sufficient to force their way through, even in the face of hostile Quechans.[79]

On January 27, Teodoro de Croix, commandant-general of the Interior Provinces, forwarded the findings of the junta de guerra to José de Gálvez and the king in Madrid. As a presidio and settlements along the Colorado River would excessively burden the royal treasury, and as they would prove of little practical military value, the council recommended the abandonment of all attempts to control the region. The following August, King Charles III formally approved the council's decision.[80]

After a year and a half of intensive effort and a great effusion of blood, the Spanish crown, with a mere shuffling of papers, officially declared the war against the Quechans to be over. For the Caballero de Croix, General Neve, and many other Spanish leaders, putting more effort into controlling the Yuma Crossing would not be worth the expense. No one bothered to ask the survivors of the destroyed settlements of La Concepción and Bicuñer the cost of their enslavement or the value of their dead relatives.[81]

Epilogue

The Shadow of Death, 1784 to 1796

FOR SALVADOR PALMA and the Quechan people, the Spanish crown's decision to suspend operations against them meant very little. Although Palma seems to have reestablished his position as kwoxot among the tribe, the alliance he had fostered with the white men resulted in an enormous loss of life. Out of a population estimated at between three thousand and five thousand, approximately two hundred people had been killed and perhaps twice as many wounded and crippled. In addition, others had been captured and enslaved. Overall, casualties may have approached one-fifth of the tribe. The Quechans paid a high price to regain their independence and to drive the Spaniards from their lands. And still the killing went on.[1]

Marshaling their allies the Kamias and the Mohaves, the Quechans avenged themselves on those tribes who had aided the Spaniards, especially the Halchidomas, Kohuanas, Maricopas, and Gila Pimas. These attacks in turn activated the system of intertribal alliances among the nations of the Quechan and Maricopa–Gila Pima Leagues, triggering an unrelenting series of wars that would last for more than half a century.[2]

Several tribes suffered extensively. In 1785, a Spanish scouting expedition found evidence of devastating Quechan attacks deep into the lands of the Kohuanas, along a tributary of the Colorado later known as the Río Hardy, fifty miles south of the Sierra de San Pablo. For the Halchidomas, the situation was even worse. Caught between the Quechans to the south, the Mohaves to the north, and the Kamias to the west, the Halchidomas suffered raids and attacks from all sides. As the wars continued year after year, the enormous casualties incurred forced the Kohuanas and Halchidomas away from the Colorado River, along the Gila, where they were gradually absorbed by the more powerful nations. By the middle of the nineteenth century, both peoples, along with the Halykwamais, had ceased to exist as independent tribal groups.[3]

As the nations of the Quechan and Maricopa–Gila Pima Leagues killed and enslaved each other, the representatives of the Spanish crown struggled with the consequences of their failure to construct settlements at the Yuma Crossing. For many of them, the establishment of who was to blame for the debacle was of great concern. General Felipe de Neve was among the most vociferous in portioning out guilt. Neve's inability to defeat the Quechans decisively stuck in his craw, and no doubt he felt it reflected poorly on him. Further, the closing of the overland supply route from Sonora jeopardized the development of Alta California, for which he had worked so long and hard. Casting about for a scapegoat, Neve pinned the blame squarely on the shoulders of Father Garcés and Juan Bautista de Anza, now a colonel. However, while the Franciscan had paid with his life, Anza's career advanced as a result of the Yuma enterprise. He, therefore, became the special object of Neve's scorn.[4]

Upon reviewing the origins of the Yuma enterprise, Neve came to the conclusion that Anza had misrepresented the true nature of the Quechans and of the Yuma Crossing for settlement. The general believed that Anza had overestimated the fertility of the land and the docility of the Indians. In Neve's opinion, these distortions had been the catalyst for the entire sad affair. The fact that Anza had provided, in actuality, a sober and accurate assessment of the Quechans and recommended a formidable military force to subdue them did not change the opinion of Felipe de Neve.[5]

After Neve succeeded Teodoro de Croix as commandant-general of the

Interior Provinces on February 18, 1783, his animus increased. In a calculated snub, he forbade Anza to call himself the discoverer of the road to California, and he repeatedly denigrated Anza's tenure as governor of New Mexico. But Neve had little time left to torment Anza or to do anything else: a year and a half later, Neve fell ill on a journey to Chihuahua City. After lingering for several days, he died on August 21, 1784, at the age of fifty-seven.[6]

Much of Neve's ire could be traced to the attitude of Teodoro de Croix. The caballero sought to excuse his own failures in designing the Yuma settlements by faulting both Anza and Garcés, although his criticism was far less damning. In a report to José de Gálvez of February 28, 1782, in the midst of the punitive expeditions, Croix summed up his opinion of Anza and Garcés: "I think that the pretty notions they presented to the government about the Yuma nation were more the products of religious zeal, a desire to serve, and love, on the part of the first for laudable labors, and on the part of the second for apostolic labors, than of reality."[7]

The "pretty notions" that Croix complained of led him to believe that the Quechans were different from other Indians, and that Salvador Palma actually possessed authority over his people. All of this had been an illusion. The Quechans, in Croix's words, were "more or less treacherous, inconstant, stubborn and wild," while Palma "has no more authority than any Apache *capitancillo*." In addition, the caballero exculpated himself by citing the base treachery of the interpreter Francisco Xavier, who had spread lies about Spanish intentions and who had been encouraged in his machinations by the ambitions of Ygnacio Palma. Finally, there had been "the extravagant greed" of the Quechans themselves, which no amount of Spanish goods could quench.[8]

To some degree, all of Croix's excuses were true. Furthermore, the blame he received for the interminable delays that plagued the start of the Yuma project were not all of the caballero's making. The devastations caused by the Apaches, Comanches, and other Indian peoples hostile to the Spanish had been far more pressing, from a military viewpoint, than the planned expansion toward the Gila and Colorado Rivers. Given the enormous problems and vast distances of the Interior Provinces, Croix's inability to deal quickly with Yuma had been to a large extent inevitable.[9]

The true failure of the Caballero de Croix lay in the makeup of his plans once he decided to move on the issue. Regardless of the nature of Salvador Palma's authority, or of the attitude of the Quechan people,

Croix had been extremely foolhardy in establishing settlements without the protection of an adequate military force. Viceroy Bucareli, Garcés, Anza, and others had repeatedly pointed out that a presidio ought to be the cornerstone for any effort along the Colorado River. The caballero chose to ignore these warnings. And considering that Croix had direct evidence of the results of policies similar to his in the failed 1773 attempt to found a mission among the Seris, his decision was even less defensible than that of the earlier disaster.[10]

In reality, Teodoro de Croix made economy the underlying principle in his plans for Yuma. Seconded in this sentiment by his asesor, Pedro Galindo y Navarro, Croix determined to establish a cost-effective settlement, rather than an adequate military presence along the Colorado. Indeed, in reports to José de Gálvez and Charles III, Croix bragged of the reduced expenses to the exchequer resulting from his "military colonies."[11]

The caballero also did not apply his own military experience to the Yuma problem. Throughout the Interior Provinces, he had witnessed the inability of presidios to assist each other because they were too far apart. As a result, one of his primary accomplishments as commandant-general was to realign these posts in positions that allowed for mutual support. Yet at Yuma, Croix sent out a feeble force of only twenty soldiers and twenty untrained civilians and placed them in one of the most isolated positions on the frontier, more than 150 miles from the nearest presidio.[12]

Croix never acknowledged these failures; nor did they diminish his reputation with his superiors. Overall, the king felt Croix's tenure as commandant-general was a success. The caballero proved himself a competent administrator and he had succeeded in containing the hostile Indians of the Interior Provinces. When a much more serious Indian revolt threatened Spanish power, Charles III dispatched him to deal with another array of hostile natives. In 1783, Teodoro de Croix was promoted to lieutenant general and appointed the new viceroy of Peru in the wake of the devastating revolt of Tupac Amaru. For the next five years, Croix instituted a sweeping series of reforms that healed much of the damage caused by the insurrection. By the time he returned to Spain, his wise and just policies had left Peru better governed than it had been in more than a century.[13]

If the crown failed to find fault with the actions of Croix in regard to Yuma, the Franciscans of the Santa Cruz College in Querétaro were not so forgiving. They knew that Croix's niggardly handling of the financial and military support for the settlements had contributed to their failure. But the Franciscans were convinced that, overall, Croix's refusal to form traditional missions, with political, economic, and spiritual authority vested in the missionaries, doomed the project from its inception.[14]

In 1792, Father Juan Domingo de Arricivata, writing of the events at Yuma, declared that Croix's decision to deprive Father Garcés and his companions of their traditional powers flew in the face of more than two hundred years of Franciscan experience in converting Indians. "It is evident," he wrote, "how far from conforming to . . . doctrines which the missionaries know as elementary principles of their ministry" were Croix's regulations for the two "mission-pueblos" along the Colorado River.[15]

To Father Arricivata and his brothers at the college, Asesor Pedro Galindo y Navarro, who had played a large role in actually drafting the regulations for the Yuma settlements, was even more culpable than the caballero. They maintained that when Fathers Garcés and Díaz attempted to get Croix to modify the regulations, Galindo squelched the padres' objections. "It is the misfortune of superiors," Arricivata noted, "to have associated with them certain impolitic schemers who with plausible flatteries make them disregard the character of those who give them information." For the Querétaran fathers, the asesor's "new rules" were designed only for economy, not the conversion of the Indians. "In making the regulations," Padre Arricivata bitterly concluded, "their legislator might rightfully be given the name of 'artificer of death.' "[16]

Father Diego Miguel Bringas de Manzaneda y Encinas echoed these sentiments. In an attempt to revive crown support for a new missionary effort toward the Gila River, in 1796 Father Bringas sought to demonstrate why the efforts of Padre Garcés and his companions had failed. Like Father Arricivata before him, Bringas found that "the causes for the failure . . . reduce substantially to the way in which the foundation was directed."[17] Bringas castigated Galindo y Navarro for insisting on new regulations for the Yuma settlement: "The Asesor dictated the conditions and methods of setting them up. This was against the laws, against custom, against experience." "The result . . . [was that] the barbarians ruined the two pueblos, cruelly beating to death . . . the missionaries . . . as well as many other persons." Chidingly, Bringas added: "Thus the government discovered how important it is to take the advice of practical missionaries." Concluding on a somewhat more charitable note, Padre

Bringas suggested a motive for Croix's and Galindo's Yuma regulations: "Their own zeal and salutary intentions suggested to them that a novelty would be more efficacious than the method accredited by experience."[18]

More than political infighting triggered the efforts of these two priests to hold government officials accountable for the Yuma disaster: there were also serious theological considerations. Father Garcés and his companions had died under circumstances suggestive of martyrdom. After the revolt, the Franciscans of the Santa Cruz College examined the situation of their fallen brothers in close detail, scenting the odor of sanctity.[19]

Soon after the conclusion of the initial punitive expeditions, Father Francisco Antonio de Barbastro, the college's president for the missions of the Pimería Alta, wrote to Lt. Col. Fages on February 4, 1782. Barbastro hoped to prove that Father Garcés and his compañeros "were free of being even the remote cause of disturbances which brought about the ruin of the new missions." To do this, Barbastro prepared for Fages a series of questions, closely examining the behavior of the four dead missionaries. More importantly, the padre sought to discover "if any circumstances are known which might indicate that their deaths were holy before the Lord."[20]

Fages's response was more than Barbastro and his fellow Franciscans hoped for. After interviewing the survivors, the colonel declared that the Yuma missionaries "acted virtuously and with exemplary modesty and charity. They were dedicated to the holy purpose of attracting the Indians to the knowledge of the Faith. . . . In no way did they contribute to the causes of the revolt and the ruin of . . . the missions." Overall, Fages declared, Father Garcés and the others had labored with "apostolic fervor."[21]

The mortal remains of the four dead priests provided evidence of sanctity as well. Fages stated that when he and his men found the bodies of the slain missionaries, the conditions of the corpses "did not indicate that such a long time had passed." The remains of Fathers Garcés and Barreneche were especially fresh, "and were almost incorrupt." Several redeemed Spanish captives also reported "that in the pueblo of San Pedro y San Pablo de Bicuñer they had heard sweet songs and at night it seemed to them that the friars were walking as in procession around the church in whose vicinity the venerable remains of . . . Fathers . . . Díaz and . . . Moreno were discovered."[22]

Colonel Fages's reports gave impetus to the belief of the friars of the Santa Cruz College that their slain brethren were martyrs for the faith.

After the bodies had been recovered, the remains of the fallen missionaries had been transported to the mission of San Pedro y San Pablo de Tubutama. There, they were laid to rest under the main altar, after a formal ceremony attended by almost all the Franciscans in the Pimería Alta, as well as many others.[23]

After the internment, Father President Barbastro continued gathering information, determined to press the cause of martyrdom. Several years passed before the college's superiors decided to bring the bodies of Garcés, Díaz, Barreneche, and Moreno back to Querétaro. As objects of veneration, the relics of the slain priests might exhibit further signs of sanctity. In 1793, after some difficulty, Father Barbastro informed his superiors in Querétaro that he had finally managed to arrange for the transfer of "the bones of our brothers. . . . They will be carried by the muleteer, Félix, who leaves . . . from the village of San Miguel de Horcasitas with orders to deliver his cargo to the college."[24]

After a lengthy journey, the entire community of the Santa Cruz College and many citizens of Querétaro turned out on July 18 and 19, 1794, to reinter the bones of the four Yuma missionaries in a series of solemn ceremonies. As it was the thirteenth anniversary of their deaths, the Franciscans prepared two laudatory sermons, one in Latin and one in Spanish, in honor of Garcés, Díaz, Barreneche, and Moreno.[25]

Father José María Carranza delivered the Latin eulogy on the afternoon of July 18. The following morning, Father Bringas gave a stirring sermon in Spanish. Both speakers praised the heroic virtues of the four Yuma martyrs, likening their lives and deaths to the words of St. Paul: "Christ shall be magnified in my body, whether it be by life or by death. For me to live is Christ and to die is gain." The speakers were so moving and so effective that their sermons were remembered for many years, and Padre Bringas's was eventually published in its entirety.[26]

Yet, while the Franciscans praised the merits and honored the memory of their slain brothers, the inescapable fact remained that the cause for which they had perished remained unfulfilled. Father Garcés had dreamed of advancing the northern frontier to the Colorado and Gila Rivers, Christianizing and bringing peace to the natives of the region and forging a permanent link between Sonora and California. These had been the forces that lay behind Spain's attempt to settle the Yuma Crossing. None of the goals would ever be achieved.[27]

Still, the Spaniards did not totally cease their efforts to establish a secure overland route to California. In 1785, Pedro Fages, now governor of the province, led an expedition from Baja California to search for a road into Sonora that crossed the Colorado River south of the Yuma Crossing. He found some promising trails, but his efforts were wasted when, in the following year, Viceroy Bernardo de Gálvez suspended all contact with the tribes of the region. "Under no circumstances," Gálvez ordered Spanish officials, "should you take measures either contrary or favorable to the Yumas and other tribes of the Río Colorado." The long war against the Apaches was building to a crescendo, and Gálvez wanted all Spanish forces massed against the primary enemy. As for the Quechans, the viceroy conceded, "it is necessary to forget those Indians for the present, hiding our injuries until safe opportunity comes for satisfying them."[28]

For ten years, the Spaniards heeded Gálvez's instructions. Then, in 1796, a renewal of interest in opening a road between Sonora and California emerged. Dominican fathers had been pushing a chain of missions up the long, barren peninsula of Baja California for many years. As they moved northward, the possibility of supplying their missions from Sonora beckoned, as it had for Father Kino and the long-vanished Jesuits at the end of the seventeenth century.[29] As a result, in October of that year José Joaquín de Arillaga, the lieutenant governor of California, commanded an exploring expedition to the region between the mountains of northeastern Baja California and the mouth of the Colorado River. Arillaga and his men reached the river a few miles above where it emptied into the Gulf of California. The Cocopas of the vicinity proved friendly, and when Arillaga inquired about the Quechans and "Captain Palma" he was told that the kwoxot still lived.[30]

However, as they headed northwest along the Río Hardy, the Spaniards were attacked by several Kamia Indian groups. Casualties occurred on both sides. Arillaga prudently decided to withdraw from the region and by the end of the month had returned to San Diego. In his report to his superiors, Arillaga noted that because of the continuing hostility of the natives along the Colorado, a road to Sonora would require at least two presidios with large detachments of troops. No action was ever taken to put these plans into effect.[31]

The explorations of Arillaga marked the last serious attempt on the part of the Spaniards to establish themselves along the Colorado River; the road between Sonora and California was forever closed to them. As a result, the growth of the settlements in Alta California was permanently stunted and the province remained isolated, weak, and vulnerable. The same fate befell the northern reaches of the Pimería Alta, where Hispanic influence in what was to become Arizona remained limited to the regions south of the Gila River.[32] However, all of these consequences waited upon the future. As Spain's power waned toward the end of the eighteenth century, her failure to control the Yuma Crossing faded into the shadows. The twilight of empire obscured and marginalized events in the Interior Provinces as the kingdoms of Europe were dismantled by the republics of the new world.

But for the Quechans and other peoples, the forces unleashed by the attempt were inexorable. For more than a decade Spanish leaders had dreamed, planned, and finally set in motion a great expansion of the northern frontier, designed to strengthen their hold on the land, to push forward "the rim of Christendom," and to bring peace to the bellicose tribes along the Gila and Colorado. But in the end, all they had done was to incite new wars and to spread the shadow of death.

Notes

Preface

1. Beilharz, *Felipe de Neve*, 121.
2. Chapman, *Founding of Spanish California*, ix, 418.
3. Weber, *Spanish Frontier in North America*, 264.
4. Ibid., 258.

Chapter 1. Wayfarers and Rivalries

1. Maughan, "Francisco Garcés," 67–70.
2. Ibid., 68; Forbes, *Warriors of the Colorado*, 145.
3. Maughan, "Francisco Garcés," 68–70.
4. Ibid., 76; Francisco Garcés, "Diario que se ha formado con la ocasion de la entrada que hice a los vecinos Gentiles . . . [1771]," Archivo General de la Nación (AGN), Historia 396 and California 36 (hereafter cited as Garcés "Diario 1771").
5. Maughan, "Francisco Garcés," 69.
6. Ibid., 70–74; Garcés, "Diario 1771."
7. Maughan, "Francisco Garcés," 1–4, 44–47.
8. Ibid., 3–4.

9. Ibid., 74; Bannon, *Spanish Borderlands Frontier*, 49–53; Weber, *Spanish Frontier in North America*, 82–84.

10. Curiously, Kino's discovery of the peninsularity of California failed to persuade even members of his own order, and throughout the first half of the eighteenth century some Jesuits continued to believe that California was an island. Dunne, *Black Robes in Lower California*, passim; Bannon, *Spanish Borderlands Frontier*, 67–71, 143–46; Chapman, *Founding of Spanish California*, 18–19.

11. Bannon, *Spanish Borderlands Frontier*, 143–46; Chapman, *Founding of Spanish California*, 18.

12. Dunne, *Jacobo Sedelmayr*, 35–36, 51; Dunne, *Black Robes in Lower California*, 207–18, 318–34, 375–87; Bannon, *Spanish Borderlands Frontier*, 148–52; Chapman, *Founding of Spanish California*, 28–44.

13. Aiton, "Spanish Colonial Reorganization," 273–74; Bobb, *Viceregency of Antonio María Bucareli*, 85–87; Fagg, *Latin America*, 238; Petrie, *King Charles III of Spain*, 137–50; Weber, *Spanish Frontier in North America*, 198–99.

14. Aiton, "Spanish Colonial Reorganization," 273–74. Bobb, *Viceregency of Antonio María Bucareli*, 85–87; Petrie, *King Charles III of Spain*, 137–50; Weber, *Spanish Frontier in North America*, 198–99.

15. Archer, *Army in Bourbon Mexico*, 8–21; Bobb, *Viceregency of Antonio María Bucareli*, 116–20, 173, 185; Fagg, *Latin America*, 217–18, 229, 238–39; Torres-Ramirez, *Alejandro O'Reilly en las Indias*, passim.

16. Fagg, *Latin America*, 238–41; Navarro García, *Don José de Gálvez*, passim; Weber, *Spanish Frontier in North America*, 236–42.

17. Weber, *Spanish Frontier in North America*, 204–12; Navarro García, *Don José de Gálvez*, 47–69, 98–114; Bannon, *Spanish Borderlands Frontier*, 170–71.

18. Weber, *Spanish Frontier in North America*, 237–39; Bobb, *Viceregency of Antonio María Bucareli*, 156–59; Navarro García, *Don José de Gálvez*, 90, 156–58.

19. Weber, *Spanish Frontier in North America*, 212–14.

20. Kessell, *Friars, Soldiers, and Reformers*, 8; Weber, *Spanish Frontier in North America*, 242.

21. Fagg, *Latin America*, 174–78, 181–85; Ricard, *Spiritual Conquest of Mexico*, passim; Matson and Fontana, *Friar Bringas Reports to the King*, 10–16.

22. Matson and Fontana, *Friar Bringas Reports to the King*, 16–17; Weber, *Spanish Frontier in North America*, 94–96, 306; Kessell, "Anza Damns the Missions," 53–63.

23. Kessell, *Friars, Soldiers and Reformers*, 5–6, 14–15; Matson and Fontana, *Friar Bringas Reports to the King*, 14–16.

24. Matson and Fontana, *Friar Bringas Reports to the King*, 15–16.

25. Fagg, *Latin America*, 222–23; Kessell, *Friars, Soldiers, and Reformers*, 12–24; Weber, *Spanish Frontier in North America*, 242; McCarty, *Spanish Frontier in the Enlightened Age*, passim.

26. Kessell, *Friars, Soldiers, and Reformers*, 17–18, 42–45; McCarty, *Spanish Frontier in the Enlightened Age*, 1–9, 53–60.

27. Kessell, *Friars, Soldiers, and Reformers*, 17–18, 42–45; McCarty, *Spanish Frontier in the Enlightened Age*, 1–9, 53–60.

28. Forbes, *Warriors of the Colorado*, passim.

29. Ibid.

30. Ibid., 3–36.

31. Ibid., 83–95.

32. Ibid., 102–7.

33. When Father Eusebio Kino made his journeys to the Yuma Crossing between 1700 and 1702, he cultivated and maintained friendly relations with the Quechans and their neighbors; ibid., 117–24; Navarro García, *Don José de Gálvez*, 44–46. Officer, "Kino and Agriculture in the Pimería Alta," 287–306.

34. Dunne, *Jacobo Sedelmayr*, 61–64, 70–72; Forbes, *Warriors of the Colorado*, 136–39.

35. Unfortunately, the Spanish impact was not limited to new crops and livestock. As had happened since Indians and Europeans had come together, Old World diseases preceded direct contact. During the seventeenth and eighteenth centuries, periodic epidemics swept the Colorado River region, killing an unknown number of native peoples. Forbes, *Warriors of the Colorado*, 128–35; Kroeber and Fontana, *Massacre on the Gila*, 63–65; Sheridan, "Kino's Unforeseen Legacy," 157–63.

36. Forbes, *Warriors of the Colorado*, 76–78, 133–35; Kroeber and Fontana, *Massacre on the Gila*, 65, 104–8, 130–31, 140; Sheridan, "Kino's Unforeseen Legacy," 157–63.

37. Forbes, *Warriors of the Colorado*, 42, 80–81; Kroeber and Fontana, *Massacre on the Gila*, 33–35, 101–10, 136–38.

38. Forbes, *Warriors of the Colorado*, 80–81; Kroeber and Fontana, *Massacre on the Gila*, 33–35, 101–10, 136–38.

39. Forbes, *Warriors of the Colorado*, 80–81; Kroeber and Fontana, *Massacre on the Gila*, 33–35, 101–10, 136–38.

40. Forbes, *Warriors of the Colorado*, 80–81; Kroeber and Fontana, *Massacre on the Gila*, 33–35, 101–10, 136–38. Two other groups of Yumans, the Kohuanas and the Halykwamais, were located between the Quechans and the Cocopas. Both tribes fluctuated in their support between the two leagues, supporting various tribes within each league at different times. By the end of the eighteenth century, the Kohuanas allied themselves with the Cocopas and the Halykwamais chose the Quechans. By the mid-nineteenth century, both groups were annihilated or assimilated during the endless wars between the two leagues.

41. Forbes, *Warriors of the Colorado*, 77–78, 81, 134; Kroeber and Fontana, *Massacre on the Gila*, 35–38, 128–31.

42. Forbes, *Warriors of the Colorado*, 78, 134; Kroeber and Fontana, *Massacre on the Gila*, 35–38, 128–31.

43. Kessell, *Friars, Soldiers, and Reformers*, 8–9, 14–15; Weber, *Spanish Frontier in North America*, 239–42.

Chapter 2. The Gate Unlocked

1. Kessell, "Making of a Martyr," 181–83; Arricivata, *Crónica seráfica y apostolica*, 540–41. Copies of this work can be found at the Arizona Historical Society, Tucson,

and University of Arizona Library, Tucson. June 16, 1783, Certificate of Baptism and Confirmation for Garcés attested by Fr. Pedro Alemán, Civezza Collection 201:5.

2. Kessell, "Making of a Martyr," 183–84; Arricivata, *Crónica seráfica y apostolica*, 540–41.

3. Kessell, "Making of a Martyr," 185–88; Arricivata, *Crónica seráfica y apostolica*, 540–41.

4. Kessell, *Friars, Soldiers, and Reformers*, 15–17; Alger, *Little Flowers of St. Francis of Assisi*, passim; Kessell, "Making of a Martyr," 189–90.

5. Kessell, *Friars, Soldiers, and Reformers*, 15–17; McCarty, *Spanish Frontier in the Enlightened Age*, 5–9.

6. McCarty, *Spanish Frontier in the Enlightened Age*, 11, 18–23, 27–35; Kessell, *Friars, Soldiers, and Reformers*, 21–23.

7. McCarty, *Spanish Frontier in the Enlightened Age*, 46–50; Kessell, *Friars, Soldiers, and Reformers*, 23–25. The term *Rim of Christendom* is taken from the title of Herbert Bolton's biography of Father Kino, *Rim of Christendom*.

8. McCarty, *Spanish Frontier in the Enlightened Age*, 2, 47–50. Dobyns, *Spanish Colonial Tucson*, 26–35, 133–41, describes the demography and population shifts of these two communities. Sheridan, "Kino's Unforeseen Legacy," 151–64.

9. Maughan, "Francisco Garcés," 42–53.

10. Ibid.

11. Ibid. 59–60; Chapman, *Founding of Spanish California*, 146–47.

12. Navarro García, *Don José de Gálvez*, 168–78; Chapman, *Founding of Spanish California*, 153; Kessell, *Friars, Soldiers, and Reformers*, 93.

13. Navarro García, *Don José de Gálvez*, 168–78; Weber, *Spanish Frontier in North America*, 242–46.

14. Maughan, "Francisco Garcés," 60, 87; Chapman, *Founding of Spanish California*, 147, 153; Kessell, *Friars, Soldiers, and Reformers*, 93.

15. Navarro García, *Don José de Gálvez*, 168–78; Weber, *Spanish Frontier in North America*, 241–43, 248.

16. Navarro García, *Don José de Gálvez*, 168–78; Weber, *Spanish Frontier in North America*, 248; McCarty, *Spanish Frontier in the Enlightened Age*, 86–88, 98–99, 102–3.

17. McCarty, *Spanish Frontier in the Enlightened Age*, 103–5; Navarro García, *Don José de Gálvez*, 200–205; Kessell, *Friars, Soldiers, and Reformers*, 55; Weber, *Spanish Frontier in North America*, 248.

18. Maughan, "Francisco Garcés," 60–65.

19. Ibid.

20. Ibid., 56, 58, 60–65; Kessell, *Friars, Soldiers, and Reformers*, 55; McCarty, *Spanish Frontier in the Enlightened Age*, 104.

21. Maughan, "Francisco Garcés," 76–78; Kessell, *Friars, Soldiers, and Reformers*, 62–63.

22. Francisco Garcés, "Diario desde ocho de Agosto con la ocasion de la visita de los proximos Gentiles, que practique para poder dar noticia del actual estado, y propocion para adelantar y propagar nuestra Santa Fe y dominios del Rey nuestro Señor,"

Bolton Transcript 234, Bancroft Library, University of California, Berkeley, quoted in Maughan, "Francisco Garcés," 66. This is Garcés's introduction to the 1771 diary submitted to Bucareli.

23. Garcés's fate had been a mystery to both his fellow Franciscans and the Spanish military. There had been reports that he was being held against his will and others that he had gotten himself killed. Captain Anza, the commander of the presidio of Tubac, circulated among the tribes that if Garcés was not sent back soon, and in one piece, his troopers would come and punish the culprits. Garcés, "Diario 1771"; Maughan, "Francisco Garcés," 65–75, and Fr. Esteban de Salazar to Fr. Mariano Antonio de Buena y Alcalde, Tubutama, November 13, 1771, Archivo General de las Indias (AGI), Audencia de Guadalajara (Guad.) 512, quoted ibid, 75; Kessell, *Friars, Soldiers, and Reformers*, 62.

24. Kessell, *Friars, Soldiers, and Reformers*, 93–94; Chapman, *Founding of Spanish California*, 24–29, 145–46, 149–55.

25. Chapman, *Founding of Spanish California*, 145–46, 154–55.

26. Maughan, "Francisco Garcés," 90–103.

27. Ibid., 103–4

28. Forbes, *Warriors of the Colorado*, 149–50; Maughan, "Francisco Garcés," 105, 108.

29. Maughan, "Francisco Garcés," 108.

30. "Font's Complete Diary of the Second Anza Expedition," *Anza's California Expeditions*, ed. Bolton (hereafter, *ACE*), 4:80. A year later, Bolton published volume 4 of *Anza's California Expeditions* as an individual work under the title *Font's Complete Diary: A Chronicle of the Founding of San Francisco*. "Anza's Complete Diary, 1774," 2:33, 38; "Anza's Diary from Tubac to San Gabriel, 1774," 2:157, both in *ACE*; Coues, *On the Trail of a Spanish Pioneer*, 201–3.

31. "Font's Complete Diary," ed. Bolton, 4:80; "Anza's Complete Diary, 1774," 2:33, 38; and "Anza's Diary from Tubac to San Gabriel, 1774," 2:157, both in *Anza's California Expeditions*, ed. Bolton.

32. "Anza's Complete Diary, 1774," 2:1–2, "Díaz's Diary from Tubac to San Gabriel, 1774," 2:247–48, 258–59, and "Garcés's Diary from Tubac to San Gabriel, 1774," 2:309, all in *ACE*.

33. "Anza's Complete Diary, 1774," 2:37–42; "Díaz's Diary from Tubac to San Gabriel, 1774," 2:258–59; and "Garcés's Diary from Tubac to San Gabriel, 1774," 2:321–22, all in *ACE*.

34. "Palma to Bucareli, Mexico, November 11, 1776," in *ACE*, 5:367–68. An official copy of the original letter can be found in AGN, Provincias Internas (hereafter PI), 23.

35. Forbes, *Warriors of the Colorado*, 62–74; Kroeber and Fontana, *Massacre on the Gila*, 40–46.

36. Forbes, *Warriors of the Colorado*, 62–74; Kroeber and Fontana, *Massacre on the Gila*, 40–46.

37. Forbes, *Warriors of the Colorado*, 62–74; Kroeber and Fontana, *Massacre on the Gila*, 40–46.

38. Forbes, *Warriors of the Colorado,* 72–74, 173–74.

39. "Anza's Complete Diary, 1774," 2:42–46; "Díaz's Diary from Tubac to San Gabriel, 1774," 2:262–63, 267–69; and "Garcés's Diary from Tubac to San Gabriel, 1774," 2:322–24, all in *ACE.*

40. "Anza's Complete Diary, 1774," 2:57–96, "Díaz's Diary from Tubac to San Gabriel, 1774," 2:270–88, and "Garcés's Diary from Tubac to San Gabriel, 1774," 2:325–47, all ibid.

41. "Anza's Complete Diary, 1774," 2:115–17, ibid.; Maughan, "Francisco Garcés," 117.

42. Chapman, *Founding of Spanish California,* 358.

43. "Anza's Complete Diary, 1774," 2:121, in *ACE.*

44. "Anza's Complete Diary, 1774," 2:121, and "Palma to Bucareli, Mexico, November 11, 1776," 5:366–68, both ibid; Forbes, *Warriors of the Colorado,* 156–57.

45. "Anza's Complete Diary, 1774," 2:121, in *ACE.*

Chapter 3. The Gospel on the River

1. Chapman, *Founding of Spanish California,* 286–91; Maughan, "Francisco Garcés," 125–26, 128.

2. Chapman, *Founding of Spanish California,* 288, 291; Maughan, "Francisco Garcés," 126, 133, 135.

3. Chapman, *Founding of Spanish California,* 292–94; Maughan, "Francisco Garcés," 126–28.

4. "Garcés and Díaz to Bucareli, Ures, March 21, 1775", in *ACE,* 5:279–81, 286–290; Maughan, "Francisco Garcés," 119–24, 135–37.

5. According to Bucareli, Garcés was to "examine the sites [for missions] . . . and to ascertain the spirit and disposition of the natives toward the catechism and toward vassalage to our sovereign." "Bucareli to Garcés, Mexico, January 2, 1775," in *ACE.* Chapman, *Founding of Spanish California,* 294–300; Maughan, "Francisco Garcés," 128–32. However, Salvador Palma had continued to show a favorable disposition to the Spaniards. He traveled to the presidio of Altar several times to trade horses and to ask for Spanish assistance in attacking his enemies. Bernardo de Urrea to Antonio María de Bucareli, Altar, February 22 and October 21, 1774, and February 16 and September 11, 1775, AGN PI, 237.

6. "Anza's Diary of the Second Anza Expedition, 1775–1776," in *ACE,* 3:1–2.

7. "Anza's Diary of the Second Anza Expedition, 1775–1776," 3:36–38, and "Font's Complete Diary of the Second Anza Expedition," 4:68–69, both in *ACE.*

8. "Font's Complete Diary of the Second Anza Expedition " 4:70–72, ibid.

9. "Anza's Diary of the Second Anza Expedition, 1775–1776," 3:39–40; and "Font's Complete Diary of the Second Anza Expedition," 4:73–74, both ibid.

10. "Font's Complete Diary of the Second Anza Expedition," 4:76–80, ibid.

11. "Font's Complete Diary of the Second Anza Expedition," 4:79, ibid.; Coues, *On the Trail of a Spanish Pioneer,* 1:154–56.

12. Kessell, *Friars, Soldiers, and Reformers*, 112–17; "Diary Written on the Colorado River by Father Fray Thomas Eixarch," in *ACE*, 3:311–12; Coues, *On the Trail of a Spanish Pioneer*, 1:161–62.

13. Kessell, *Friars, Soldiers, and Reformers*, 114–15; "Diary Written on the Colorado River by Father Fray Thomas Eixarch," 3:311, in *ACE*; Coues, *On the Trail of a Spanish Pioneer*, 1:162–63.

14. "Diary Written on the Colorado River by Father Fray Thomas Eixarch," 3:311, in *ACE*.

15. Ibid., 312–15.

16. Ibid., 315–20

17. Ibid., 322–23.

18. Ibid., 332–34; Maughan, "Francisco Garcés," 152–54. Coues, *On the Trail of a Spanish Pioneer*, 1:173–200, contains Garcés's account of this journey.

19. "Diary Written on the Colorado River by Father Fray Thomas Eixarch," 3:338–39, 341, 343, 355–56 in *ACE*; Maughan, "Francisco Garcés," 152–55; Coues, *On the Trail of a Spanish Pioneer*, 1:203–5, 208–11.

20. "Diary Written on the Colorado River by Father Fray Thomas Eixarch," 3:324, in *ACE*.

21. Ibid., 347–50.

22. Ibid., 340.

23. Ibid., 345.

24. Ibid., 355, 359–61.

25. Ibid., 364–69.

26. Ibid., 369–71, 375.

27. Ibid., 372, 377–78.

28. Ibid., 376.

29. Ibid., 378, 380–81; Forbes, *Warriors of the Colorado*, 168, 174.

Chapter 4. Hopes and Promises

1. "Diary Written on the Colorado River by Father Fray Thomas Eixarch," 3:319–20, "Font's Complete Diary of the Second Anza Expedition," 4:486, and "Anza's Diary of the Second Anza Expedition, 1775–1776," 3:38–40, all in *ACE*.

2. "Font's Complete Diary of the Second Anza Expedition," 4:486–87, ibid.

3. "Font's Complete Diary of the Second Anza Expedition," 4:488–89; "Anza's Diary of the Second Anza Expedition" 3:177–78, ibid.

4. "Font's Complete Diary of the Second Anza Expedition," 4:488–89, and "Anza's Diary of the Second Anza Expedition" 3:177–78, both ibid.

5. "Anza's Diary of the Second Anza Expedition", 3:177, 181, ibid.

6. Ibid. 3:181, 184.

7. Maughan, "Francisco Garcés," 183–84; Francisco Garcés "Diario que se ha formado el Padre Fray Francisco Garcés, Hijo del Colegio de la Santa Cruz de Querétaro en el viaje hecho este año de 1775. . . ." AGN, Historia 24 (hereafter cited as Garcés,

"Diario 1775–1776"). This diary is translated in its entirety by Coues, *On the Trail of a Spanish Pioneer*. For Garcés's reception by the Quechans see ibid. 2:430.

8. Coues, *On the Trail of a Spanish Pioneer*, 2:436.

9. Garcés had also suggested settlers at Yuma to his superiors at the Santa Cruz College of Querétáro. Francisco Garcés to Fr. Ramualdo Cartagena, Ures, March 1775, Civezza Collection 201:22; "Garcés and Díaz to Bucareli, Ures, March 21, 1775," *ACE*, 5:276–90; Maughan, "Francisco Garcés," 122–24, 133–37.

10. February 14, 1776–September 17, 1776, Garcés, "Diary 1775–1776," trans. in Coues, *On the Trail of a Spanish Pioneer*, at 1:213–312, 2:313–440.

11. Francisco Antonio Barbastro, "Compendio de lo más notable que han trabajado en Sonora los hijos del colegio de la Santa Cruz de Querétáro," Babiácora, September 10, 1788, Civezza Collection 202:35; and Garcés to Cartagena, March 1775; Maughan, "Francisco Garcés," 134, 137, 140. Garcés alternately suggested moving the Altar presidio to the Colorado River, thirty leagues northeast of the Yuma Crossing. "Garcés and Díaz to Bucareli, Ures, March 21, 1775," *ACE*, 5:276–90.

12. Santiago, *Red Captain*, passim.

13. Maughan, "Francisco Garcés," 137, 140; Barbastro, "Compendio de lo más notable."

14. Maughan, "Francisco Garcés," 126–27, 184.

15. "Garcés to Bucareli, San Xavier del Bac, September 14, 1776," in *ACE*, 5:319–20; Maughan, "Francisco Garcés," 185.

16. Maughan, "Francisco Garcés," 185.

17. Ibid., 187; Garcés to Father Juan Diego Ximenes Pérez, San Xavier, September 24, 1776, Civezza Collection 201:17.

18. "Bucareli to Gálvez, Mexico, October 27, 1776," 5:363–64, and "Bucareli to Gálvez, Mexico, November 26, 1776," 5:395–97, both in *ACE*.

19. "Bucareli to Gálvez, Mexico, October 27, 1776," 5:363–64, and "Bucareli to Gálvez, Mexico, November 26, 1776," 5:395–97, both ibid.

20. "Palma to Bucareli, Mexico, November 11, 1776," 5:365–76, ibid.

21. Ibid.

22. Ibid.; Forbes, *Warriors of the Colorado*, 177.

23. "Arangoyte to Bucareli, Mexico, November 18, 1776," in *ACE*, 5:379–82.

24. "Anza to the Viceroy, Mexico, November 20, 1776," ibid., 5:383–94.

25. Ibid., 5:384–85.

26. Ibid., 5:386–88.

27. Ibid., 5:389–90.

28. Ibid., 5:393–94.

29. Maughan, "Francisco Garcés," 132–33, 188, 196; Kessell, *Friars, Soldiers, and Reformers*, 85, 126.

30. Kessell, *Friars, Soldiers, and Reformers*, 126; Maughan, "Francisco Garcés," 188.

31. Father Francisco Garcés to Father Juan Diego Ximenes Pérez, San Ignacio, December 25, 1776, Civezza Collection 201:18; Maughan, "Francisco Garcés," 189–90.

32. Navarro García, *Don José de Gálvez*, 157–60, 275; Weber, *Spanish Frontier in North America*, 224–27; Thomas, *Teodoro de Croix*, 16–17.

33. Garcés to Ximenes Pérez, December 25, 1776; Maughan, "Francisco Garcés," 189–90.

34. Maughan, "Francisco Garcés," 190–96; (Francisco Garcés), "Reflecciones al Diario anterior, Tubutama, January 3, 1777, AGN, Historia 24, and trans. in Coues, *On the Trail of a Spanish Pioneer*, at 2:441–502.

35. Coues, *On the Trail of a Spanish Pioneer*, 2:441–54.

36. Ibid., 2:454–55.

37. Ibid., 2:455–57.

38. For the garrison on the Río de la Asunción, Father Garcés recommended a force of fifty leather-jacket soldiers (*soldados de cuera*), eighty dragoons, and fifty convicts, "and if more, so much the better." Coues, *On the Trail of a Spanish Pioneer*, 2:457–67.

39. Ibid., 2:467–69.

40. Ibid., 2:469–92; Weber, *Spanish Frontier in North America*, 254–56.

41. Coues, *On the Trail of a Spanish Pioneer*, 2:493–94.

42. Ibid., 495–96.

43. Ibid., 497–99.

44. Ibid., 500–2.

45. Garcés to Father Juan Diego Ximenes Pérez, Tubutama, January 3, 1777, Civezza Collection 201:19; Maughan, "Francisco Garcés," 196.

46. Cutter, *Defenses of Northern New Spain*, 24–25; Thomas, *Teodoro de Croix*, 17–18; Chapman, *Founding of Spanish California*, 390.

47. Cutter, *Defenses of Northern New Spain*, 20–27; Bobb, *Viceregency of Antonio María Bucareli*, 143–52; Santiago, *Red Captain*, 75–76.

48. Bobb, *Viceregency of Antonio María Bucareli*, 143–52.

49. "Gálvez to Bucareli, El Pardo, February 3, 1777," 5:399; "Gálvez to Bucareli, February 10, 1777," 5:401; "Gálvez to Bucareli, El Pardo, February 14, 1777," 5:406–7; and "Gálvez to Croix, El Pardo, February 14, 1777," 5:408–9, all in *ACE*.

50. "Baptism of Captain Palma, Chief of the Yuma Indians, and Three Others of His Tribe, Mexico, February 13, 1777," 5:402–5, and "Bucareli to Gálvez, Mexico, February 24, 1777," 5:410–12, both ibid.

51. Ibid. (both "Baptism" and "Bucareli to Gàlvez").

52. "Bucareli to Gálvez, Mexico, February 24, 1777," 5:410–12, ibid.; José Dario Arguello, "Informe q[u]e el Then[ien]te Dn. José Arguello presenta al Sor. Gobernador Dn. Diego de Borica en virtud de su superior Or[de]n del numbero de naciones de Yndios gentiles q[u]e sitan las marjenas del Río Colorado . . . ," Monterey, February 28, 1797, in Arguello Documents, Bancroft Library, University of California, Berkeley.

53. Juan Bautista de Anza to Antonio Bucareli, Durango, April 3, 1777, AGN, PI, 237; Kessell, *Friars, Soldiers, and Reformers*, 131.

54. Juan Bautista de Anza to Antonio Bucareli, Horcasitas, May 22 and September 24, 1777, both in AGN, PI, 237.

55. Palma's property was described later by José Dario Arguello in his "Informe q[u]e el Then[ien]te Dn. José Arguello," Arguello Documents, Bancroft Library.

Chapter 5. Voices Crying in the Wilderness

1. Cutter, *Defenses of Northern New Spain*, passim; Bobb, *Viceregency of Antonio María Bucareli*, 143–55; Thomas, *Teodoro de Croix*, 20–35; Chapman, *Founding of Spanish California*, 386–95; Navarro García, *Don José de Gálvez*, 281–93.

2. Maughan, "Francisco Garcés," 208–10. There is some indication that Croix may have spoken with Salvador Palma himself before the Quechan leader departed Mexico City in March 1777. Arricivata *Crónica seráfica y apostolica*, 493, trans. in Roberts, "Spanish Missions at Yuma," (hereafter, "SMY"), at 311.

3. Croix's orders are quoted in Bobb, *Viceregency of Antonio María Bucareli*, 145; Thomas, *Teodoro de Croix*, 19, 22–27.

4. Bobb, *Viceregency of Antonio María Bucareli*, 148–52; Thomas, *Teodoro de Croix*, 27, 30–31; Chapman, *Founding of Spanish California*, 392–95.

5. Bobb, *Viceregency of Antonio María Bucareli*, 152–53; Thomas, *Teodoro de Croix*, 35–39; Bannon, *Spanish Borderlands Frontier*, 183–84.

6. Francisco Garcés to Fr. Diego Ximenez, Tucson, February 18, 1778, Civezza Collection 201:20; Maughan, "Francisco Garcés," 216–17.

7. Forbes, *Warriors of the Colorado*, 181; Maughan, "Francisco Garcés," 213–14.

8. Arricivata, *Crónica seráfica y apostolica*, 492–93, trans. in Roberts, "SMY," at 310–11; Maughan, "Francisco Garcés," 214–15.

9. Maughan, "Francisco Garcés," 215. The quote is from Arguello, "Informe q[u]e el Then[ien]te Dn. José Arguello," trans. in Forbes, *Warriors of the Colorado* at 181.

10. The quote is from Arricivata, *Crónica seráfica y apostolica*, 492–93, trans. in Roberts, "SMY," at 310–11; Maughan, "Francisco Garcés," 215; Thomas, *Teodoro de Croix*, 141–42; Capt. Pedro Tueros to Teodoro de Croix, San Miguel (de Horcasitas), January 22, February 3 and 28, 1779, AGI Guad. 517.

11. Tueros to Croix, January 22, February 3 and 28, 1779; Navarro García, *Don José de Gálvez*, 301; Thomas, *Teodoro de Croix*, 43, 141–42.

12. Tueros to Croix, January 22, 1779; Navarro García, *Don José de Gálvez*, 301; Thomas, *Teodoro de Croix*, 43.

13. Tueros to Croix, February 3, 1779.

14. Tueros to Croix, February 3 and 28, 1779.

15. Maughan, "Francisco Garcés," 215; Tueros to Croix, January 22, February 3 and 28, 1779.

16. Teodoro de Croix to Francisco Antonio Barbastro, Chihuahua, February 5, 1779; Croix to Francisco Garcés, Chihuahua, February 5, 1779; Croix to Pedro Corbalán, Chihuahua, February 5, 1779; Croix to Capt. Pedros Tueros, Chihuahua, February 22, 1779, all in AGI Guad. 277 and 517. The quote is from Arricivata, *Crónica seráfica y apostolica*, 493, trans. in Roberts, "SMY," at 311.

17. Maughan, "Francisco Garcés," 137, 140, 217–18; "Anza to the Viceroy, Mexico, November 20, 1776," 5:383–84, in *ACE*; Coues, *On the Trail of a Spanish Pioneer*, 2:455–56.

18. Weber, *Spanish Frontier in North America*, 226–27; Kessell, *Friars, Soldiers, and Reformers*, 136–37.

19. Maughan, "Francisco Garcés," 218; Kessell, *Friars, Soldiers, and Reformers,* 24, 89.

20. "Testimonio de Habito y Profession de Fé . . . Fr. Juan Marcelo Díaz," certified copy dated December 11, 1783, 202:32; "Certificate of Baptism and Confirmation of Juan Díaz," certified copy dated October 29, 1783, 201:23, both in Civezza Collection; Arricivata, *Crónica seráfica y apostolica,* 529–35.

21. Maughan, "Francisco Garcés," 135–59, 188; Kessell, *Friars, Soldiers, and Reformers,* 24, 89, 94–97.

22. Arricivata, *Crónica seráfica y apostolica,* 493–94; Kessell, *Friars, Soldiers, and Reformers,* 75, 80; Maughan, "Francisco Garcés," 218–19.

23. Maughan, "Francisco Garcés," 218–19. Garcés is quoted in Arricivata, *Crónica seráfica y apostolica,* 494, trans. in Roberts, "SMY," at 314–15.

24. Francisco Garcés to Pedro Tueros, Altar, March 23, 1779, AGI Guad. 277 and 517.

25. Ibid.

26. Ibid.

27. Ibid.

28. Ibid.

29. Francisco Garcés to Teodoro de Croix, Altar, March 23, 1779, AGI Guad. 277 and 517.

30. Ibid.

31. Pedro Tueros to Francisco Garcés, Altar, April 14, 1779, from a certified copy dated April 29, 1779, AGI Guad. 277 and 517.

32. Ibid.

33. Pedro Corbalán to Teodoro de Croix, Arizpe, May 15, 1779; Fr. Juan Díaz, "Cuenta y cargo y data . . . , Caborca, June 8, 1779," AGI Guad. 277 and 517.

34. Díaz, "Cuenta y cargo y data . . . , Caborca, June 8, 1779."

35. Arricivata, *Crónica seráfica y apostolica,* 495; Arguello's service record is attached to Roque de Medina, "Revista pasada por el Ayudante Inspector Dn. Roque de Medina a la compañía de Cavalleria que guarnece el Expresado Presidio, Santa Gertrudis del Altar," July 5, 1779, a copy of which is included in Caballero de Croix to José de Gálvez, Arizpe, December 23, 1780, AGI Guad. 277 (hereafter cited as "Revista de Santa Gertrudes de Altar," July 5, 1779).

36. Arricivata, *Crónica seráfica y apostolica,* 495; Arguello's service record, in "Revista de Santa Gertrudes de Altar," July 5, 1779.

37. Arricivata, *Crónica seráfica y apostolica,* 495. The Garcés quote is from Francisco Garcés to Teodoro de Croix, Puerto de la Concepción, September 2, 1779, AGI Guad. 277 and 517.

38. Arricivata, *Crónica seráfica y apostolica,* 495.

39. Garcés to Croix, September 2, 1779.

40. Ibid.

41. Francisco Garcés to Pedro Corbalán, Puerto de la Concepción, September 2, 1779, AGI Guad. 277 and 517; Chapman, *Founding of Spanish California,* 405.

42. Garcés to Croix, September 2, 1779, AGI Guad. 277 and 517; Chapman, *Founding of Spanish California*, 404–5.

43. Garcés to Croix, September 2, 1779, AGI Guad. 277 and 517.

44. Ibid.

45. Ibid.

46. Ibid.

47. Ibid.

48. Ibid.

49. Ibid.; Arricivata, *Crónica seráfica y apostolica*, 495, trans. in Roberts, "SMY," at 316.

50. Arricivata, *Crónica seráfica y apostolica*, 495–96, trans. in Roberts, "SMY," at 318.

51. Arricivata, *Crónica seráfica y apostolica*, 495, trans. in Roberts, "SMY," at 316–17.

52. Arricivata, *Crónica seráfica y apostolica*, 496, trans. in Roberts, "SMY," at 319.

53. Arricivata, *Crónica seráfica y apostolica*, 497, trans. in Roberts, "SMY," at 321.

54. Arguello, "Informe q[u]e el Then[ien]te Dn. José Arguello," trans. from Arguello Documents, Bancroft Library; Francisco Garcés to Teodoro de Croix, Puerto de la Concepción, November 6, 1779, AGI Guad. 277 and 517. However, Garcés was unable to conduct an adequate census of the entire tribe because they were scattered about "as this is the harsh time for their crops."

55. Arguello, "Informe q[u]e el Then[ien]te Dn. José Arguello," Forbes trans.

56. Ibid., trans. from Arguello Docs. Bancroft Library.

57. Garcés to Croix, November 6, 1779, AGI Guad. 277 and 517.

58. Ibid.

59. Arguello, "Informe q[u]e el Then[ien]te Dn. José Arguello," Forbes trans.

60. Forbes, *Warriors of the Colorado*, 66–74, 181–82.

61. Garcés to Croix, November 6, 1779, AGI Guad. 277 and 517.

62. Ibid.

63. Ibid.

64. Ibid.

65. Ibid.; Chapman, *Founding of Spanish California*, 405–7.

66. Garcés to Croix, November 6, 1779 AGI Guad. 277 and 517; Chapman, *Founding of Spanish California*, 405–7.

67. Garcés to Croix, November 6, 1779; Chapman, *Founding of Spanish California*, 405–7. For the sexual habits of the Quechans, see Forbes, *Warriors of the Colorado*, 54–56.

68. Garcés to Croix, November 6, 1779, AGI Guad. 277 and 517; Chapman, *Founding of Spanish California*, 405–7.

69. Arguello, "Informe q[u]e el Then[ien]te Dn. José Arguello," trans. from Arguello Docs., Bancroft Library; Arricivata, *Crónica seráfica y apostolico*, 497, trans. in Roberts, "SMY," at 322; "Revista de Santa Gertrudis de Altar, July 5, 1779"; Garcés to Croix, November 6, 1779.

70. Garcés to Croix, La Purísima Concepción, December 27, 1779, AGI Guad. 277 and 517; Chapman, *Founding of Spanish California,* 407.

71. Garcés to Croix, December 27, 1779.

72. Ibid.

73. Ibid.

74. Ibid.

75. Ibid.

Chapter 6. The Knight's Gamble

1. Thomas, *Teodoro de Croix,* 43–44. Aside from a substantial church complex, Arizpe in 1791 had "130 poorly constructed houses, placed without any direction or order. . . . The majority of the homes are built of adobe. . . . All are poorly constructed, low roofed and sagging, without light and covered with brush and earth." Salmón, "1791 Report on the Villa de Arizpe," 13–28.

2. Thomas, *Teodoro de Croix,* 39–43; Weber, *Spanish Frontier in North America,* 225–26.

3. Thomas, *Teodoro de Croix,* 39–45; Kessell, *Friars, Soldiers, and Reformers,* 135; Bannon, *Spanish Borderlands Frontier,* 184.

4. Bannon, *Spanish Borderlands Frontier,* 184–85; Weber, *Spanish Frontier in North America,* 226–27.

5. Arricivata, *Crónica seráfica y apostolica,* 497, trans. in Roberts, "SMY," at 322–23; Maughan, "Francisco Garcés," 225.

6. Arricivata, *Crónica seráfica y apostolica,* 497, trans. in Roberts, "SMY," at 322–23; Maughan, "Francisco Garcés," 225. The quote is from Matson and Fontana, *Friar Bringas Reports to the King,* 86.

7. Fr. Juan Díaz to Teodoro de Croix, Arizpe, February 12, 1780, AGI Guad. 277 and 517; Chapman, *Founding of Spanish California,* 407.

8. Díaz to Croix, February 12, 1780; Chapman, *Founding of Spanish California,* 407.

9. Díaz to Croix, February 12, 1780; Chapman, *Founding of Spanish California,* 407.

10. Díaz to Croix, February 12, 1780; Chapman, *Founding of Spanish California,* 407.

11. In the Spanish Empire, colonial officials often evaded difficult royal orders by invoking the formula of *"Obedezco, pero no cumplo,* I obey, but do not comply." Meyer and Sherman, *Course of Mexican History,* 153.

12. Thomas, *Teodoro de Croix,* 207–19.

13. Navarro García, *Don José de Gálvez,* 281; Thomas, *Teodoro de Croix,* 20, 43, 217.

14. The first draft of Croix's "Instrucción que previene las reglas para el estableci-miento de las pueblos de Españoles, e Indias sobre las margenes del Río Colorado en territorio del Nación Yuma" is dated from Arizpe, February 17, 1780. A revised draft, essentially unchanged, was drawn up on March 3, 1780. The final order was dated March 7, 1780. All are found in AGI Guad. 277 and 517. In addition, a copy of the final March 7, 1780, decree is in Civezza Collection 202:33, and is also translated in its entirety in Matson and Fontana, *Friar Bringas Reports to the King,* at 96–105, under

the title of "Instructions on the Rules for the Establishment of Two Pueblos of Spaniards and Indians on the Banks of the Colorado River in the Territory of the Yuma Nation." In the document, Croix referred to the settlements as both pueblos and military colonies. Thomas, *Teodoro de Croix*, 221.

15. Matson and Fontana, *Friar Bringas Reports to the King*, 97, 102, 104–5.

16. Ibid., 97, 105.

17. Ibid.

18. Thomas, *Teodoro de Croix*, 221–22.

19. Ibid., 219–22. Regarding the origins of the plan for two pueblos at Yuma, Franciscan chronicler Fr. Juan Domingo Arricivata, writing a dozen years after the event, laid the blame for the idea clearly on the shoulders of Croix and Asesor Galindo y Navarro, labeling the latter "an artisan of death." Arricivata, *Crónica seráfica y apostolica*, 499, trans. in Roberts, "SMY," at 326. However, Charles Edward Chapman rejected this interpretation, asserting that the idea "resulted primarily" from the suggestions of Garcés and Díaz. Chapman, *Founding of Spanish California*, 410. Jack Forbes, on the other hand, maintained that the idea was essentially "Croix's plan," and that it "was as good an example of what might be termed 'humanitarian imperialism' as one could find, and it may have been the only approach that had a chance of success with the Quechans." Forbes, *Warriors of the Colorado*, 187–88. Regardless of its origin, Garcés's biographer, Scott Jarvis Maughan, saw the plan as "a radical departure from past practice." Maughan, "Francisco Garcés," 226. John L. Kessell, *Friars, Soldiers, and Reformers*, 140, labeled the plan "unprecedented."

20. Fr. Juan Díaz to Teodoro de Croix, Arizpe, February 19, 1780, AGI Guad. 277 and 517; Chapman, *Founding of Spanish California*, 408–9.

21. Díaz to Croix, February 19, 1780; Chapman, *Founding of Spanish California*, 408–9.

22. Pedro Galindo y Navarro to Croix, Arizpe, February 29, 1780, AGI Guad. 277 and 517; Chapman, *Founding of Spanish California*, 408–9.

23. Matson and Fontana, *Friar Bringas Reports to the King*, 102–3.

24. Ibid., 102–4.

25. Thomas, *Teodoro de Croix*, 214; Chapman, *Founding of Spanish California*, 411–12.

26. Matson and Fontana, *Friar Bringas Reports to the King*, 101–2

27. Medina, "Revista de Santa Gertrudis de Altar, July 5, 1779." I have translated the Spanish term *alférez* into its English equivalent, *ensign*, employing its original meaning of a standard bearer. The position of alférez was not equivalent to that of second lieutenant. Regular officers of that rank were known as *sub-tenientes*. Instead, *alférez* hearkened back to the early sixteenth century, when the first presidial companies were formed. At that time, the position of standard bearer held a tactical responsibility second only to the captain of the company. By the eighteenth century, the alférez had evolved into the most junior commissioned officer among the presidial forces. For a discussion of this and other ranks, the reader can consult D. José Almirante, *Diccionario Militar: Entimológico, Histórico, Tecnológico*.

28. Medina, "Revista de Santa Gertrudis de Altar, July 5, 1779"; Santiago, *Red Captain*, 36–40, 50.

29. Santiago Yslas to the Commandant-General, San Miguel de Horcasitas, March 1778; Santiago Yslas to Juan Bautista de Anza, San Miguel de Horcasitas, March 26, 1778, both in AGI Guad. 277. The Montijo family owned a large portion of farm land, oxen, cattle, and a herd of more than two hundred horses. Don Manuel de Azuela, lieutenant of the Horcasitas militia, and Don Salvador Rodríguez, a leading citizen, testified that they had known Sergeant Montijo and his family for many years and that they were of good standing and repute. Azuela and Rodríguez to Juan Bautista de Anza, San Miguel de Horcasitas, March 28, 1778; Don Phelipe Montijo (to Juan Bautista de Anza), San Miguel de Horcasitas, March 30, 1778, all in AGI Guad. 277. In translating María Ana Montijo's recollection of the Yuma settlements, Fr. Kieran McCarty listed her name as Montielo. However, other documents unavailable to Fr. McCarty clearly show that her family name was Montijo. McCarty, "The Colorado Massacre of 1781," 221–25.

30. Medina, "Revista de Santa Gertrudis de Altar, July 5, 1779.

31. Ibid.

32. Matson and Fontana, *Friar Bringas Reports to the King*, 96–105.

33. Ibid., 97–105; Kessell, *Friars, Soldiers, and Reformers*, 141.

34. Teodoro de Croix to Fr. Juan Díaz, November 8, 1780, AGI Guad. 277 and 517, trans. in Roberts, "SMY," at 14; Matson and Fontana, *Friar Bringas Reports to the King*, 100–101; Kessell, *Friars, Soldiers, and Reformers*, 141.

35. It is unclear if the number of farm animals promised to the settlers was similarly guaranteed to the soldiers of the two pueblos. Croix's instructions called for a minimum of fifty oxen, one hundred cows, fifty bulls, and one hundred mares for the settlers, with another fifty cows, four bulls, two hundred sheep, and eight rams supplied by the missions for the common fund. Yslas was, therefore, short by a total of 150 cows, oxen, and horses. Matson and Fontana, *Friar Bringas Reports to the King*, 100, 103.

36. Fr. Juan Díaz to Teodoro de Croix, Tubutama, September 12, 1780, AGI Guad. 277 and 517, trans. in Roberts, "SMY," at 11–13.

37. Ibid.

38. Biographical information on Barreneche can be found in Arricivata, *Crónica seráfica y apostolica*, 547–54, and Pazos, "El V.P. Fr. Juan Antonio Joaquín de Barreneche," 463–70.

39. Arricivata, *Crónica seráfica y apostolica*, 547.

40. Matson and Fontana, *Friar Bringas Reports to the King*, 86 n.73; Pazos, "El V.P. Fr. Juan Antonio Joaquín de Barreneche," 465.

41. Pazos, "El V.P. Fr. Juan Antonio Joaquín de Barreneche," 466.

42. Ibid., 463, 465.

43. Arricivata, *Crónica seráfica y apostolica*, 502, trans. in Roberts, "SMY," at 334–35.

44. Ibid.

45. Fr. Juan Díaz to Teodoro de Croix, Purísima Concepción del Río Colorado, November 8, 1780, AGI Guad. 277 and 517, trans. in Roberts, "SMY," at 15–19.

46. Ibid.

47. Ibid.

48. Ibid.

49. Forbes, *Warriors of the Colorado*, 74, 189.

50. Pazos, "El V.P. Fr. Juan Antonio Joaquín de Barreneche," 458–60.

51. Ibid.

52. Ibid.

53. Forbes, *Warriors of the Colorado*, 189–90.

54. Francisco Garcés to Teodoro de Croix, Purísima Concepción del Río Colorado, December 30, 1780, AGI Guad. 277 and 517, trans. in Roberts, "SMY," at 8–9.

55. Forbes, *Warriors of the Colorado*, 190.

Chapter 7. The Respectable Union

1. Coues, *On the Trail of a Spanish Pioneer*, 1:145–46.

2. Santiago Yslas to Teodoro de Croix, La Limpia Concepción, December 30, 1780, in AGI Guad. 277 and 517, trans. in Roberts, "SMY," at 25–27.

3. Ibid.

4. Ibid.

5. Santiago Yslas to Teodoro de Croix, Pueblo de la Concepción de los nuevos Establecimientos del Río Colorado, January 17, 1781 (one of four letters, all of the same date) in AGI Guad. 277 and 517, trans. in Roberts, "SMY," at 33–34.

6. For the garrisons at Yuma, see Medina, "Revista de Santa Gertrudis de Altar, July 5, 1779," and Roque de Medina, "Revista . . . de San Agustín del Tucson, May 3, 1779," enclosed in El Cavallero de Croix to José de Gálvez, Arizpe, December 23, 1780, AGI Guad. 277; Dobyns, *Spanish Colonial Tucson*, 153, 155, provides details on the age and racial makeup of the troopers from Tucson. I have compiled the number of residents in each town after comparing (1) "Statements that Don Pedro Fages . . . Obtained from the captives Pacheco, Solares, Romero, Castro, Miranda, Bengochea, Urrea, at Sonóitac, October 29, 1781," certified copy dated October 1783, Monterey, signed by Fages, Civezza Collection 201:26 (hereafter cited as Fages, "Statements from the captives"); (2) List of captives and killed found in "Copia a la letra de las Diligencias practicadas sobre la sublevacion de los Yndios Yumas del Río Colorado, por el Teniente Coronel Don Pedro Fages, Año de 1781," certified copy, Monterey, signed by Fages, Civezza Collection 201:26 (hereafter cited as Fages, List of captives and killed); (3) McCarty, "Colorado Massacre of 1781," 221–25. The two documents in the Civezza Collection are translated in Roberts, "SMY," at 130–66.

7. For the location of the Bicuñer mission, see Yates, "Locating the Colorado River Mission San Pedro y San Pablo de Bicuñer," 123–30.

8. Yslas to Croix, January 17, 1781 (another of the four letters; see note 5), trans. in Roberts, "SMY," at 40.

9. Medina, "Revista de Santa Gertrudis de Altar, July 5, 1779," and "Revista de

San Agustín del Tucson, May 3, 1779"; Dobyns, *Spanish Colonial Tucson*, 153, 155; Fages, "Statements from the captives"; Fages, List of captives and killed; McCarty, "Colorado Massacre of 1781," 221–25.

10. Fee de Habito y de Profesion del Reverendo Fray Mathias Moreno, April 29, 1783, Civezza Collection 202:29; Arricivata, *Crónica seráfica y apostolica*, 536–40.

11. Una carta notable del V.P. Fr. José Moreno, año de 1781, Civezza Collection 202:29. This letter is printed in Burrus, *Diario del Capitan Commandante Fernando de Rivera y Moncada*, 2:640–43.

12. Kessell, *Friars, Soldiers, and Reformers*, 88–89, 98, 100.

13. Kessell, *Friars, Soldiers, and Reformers*, 100; Matson and Fontana, *Friar Bringas Reports to the King*, 59.

14. Kessell, *Friars, Soldiers, and Reformers*, 100; Matson and Fontana, *Friar Bringas Reports to the King*, 108.

15. Garcés to Croix, December 30, 1781, trans. in Roberts, "SMY," at 8–9.

16. This letter is printed in Pazos, "El V.P. Fr. Juan Antonio Joaquín de Barreneche," 460–61.

17. Ibid.

18. Ibid.

19. Ibid.

20. Yslas to Croix, January 17, 1781 (one of the four letters; see note 5), all in AGI Guad. 277 and 517; Arricivata, *Crónica seráfica y apostolica*, 503, both trans. in Roberts, "SMY," at 34, 337.

21. Arricivita, *Crónica seráfica y apostolica*, 503, trans. in Roberts, "SMY," at 337.

22. Yslas to Croix, January 17, 1781 (two of the four letters; see note 5), trans. in Roberts, "SMY," at 29, 33–34.

23. Yslas to Croix, January 17, 1781 (one of the four letters), trans. in Roberts, "SMY," at 34.

24. Ibid.

25. Ibid.

26. Teodoro de Croix to Juan Díaz, Arizpe, January 12, 1781; Teodoro de Croix to Santiago Yslas, Arizpe, January 12, 1781; Teodoro de Croix to Francisco Garcés, Arizpe, January 28, 1781; Teodoro de Croix to Santiago Yslas, Arizpe, February 22, 1781, three letters, all AGI Guad. 277 and 517 and all trans. in Roberts, "SMY," at 10, 20–22, 28, 30, 36.

27. Croix to Díaz, January 12, 1781, trans. in Roberts, "SMY," at 20–21.

28. Ibid.; Croix to Yslas, January 12, 1781, trans. in Roberts, "SMY," at 22.

29. Croix to Garcés, January 28, 1781, trans. in Roberts, "SMY," at 10.

30. Croix to Yslas, February 22, 1781, trans. in Roberts, "SMY," at 30.

31. Croix to Díaz, January 12, 1781, and Croix to Yslas, February 22, 1781, both trans. in Roberts, "SMY," at 20, 28.

32. Santiago Yslas to Teodoro de Croix, Pueblo de La Concepción, March 23, 1781, AGI Guad. 277 and 517, trans. in Roberts, "SMY," at 23–24.

33. Ibid.

34. Forbes, *Warriors of the Colorado*, 191–93.

35. Information on the physical appearance of the village of La Purísima Concepción is provided in the descriptions of the ruins found on the site by U.S. military officers and others associated with the establishment of Ft. Yuma between 1849 and 1852. See especially Heintzelman, *Report of July 15, 1853*, and Bartlett, *Personal Narrative*, 2:161, both quoted in Coues, *On the Trail of a Spanish Pioneer*, 1:149, 150.

36. Pazos, "El V.P. Fr. Juan Antonio Joaquín de Barreneche," 461–62; Garcés to the Guardian and Directory, March 23, 1781, La Purísima Concepción del Río Colorado, Civezza Collection 201:5.

37. Garcés to Guardian and Directory, March 23, 1781; the portions referred to here are quoted in Arricivata, *Crónica seráfica y apostolica*, 497, which is translated in Roberts, "SMY," at 321–22; Maughan, "Francisco Garcés," 239–43.

38. Garcés to Guardian and Directory, March 23, 1781; these portions are quoted in Arricivata, *Crónica seráfica y apostolica*, at 505, trans. in Roberts, "SMY," at 342–43; Maughan, "Francisco Garcés," 239–43.

39. Pazos, "El V.P. Fr. Juan Antonio Joaquín de Barreneche," 461–62; Garcés to Guardian and Directory, March 23, 1781; these portions are quoted in Arricivata, *Crónica seráfica y apostolica*, 505, trans. in Roberts, "SMY," at 342–43; Maughan, "Francisco Garcés," 239–43.

40. Pazos, "El V.P. Fr. Juan Antonio Joaquín de Barreneche," 461–62; Garcés to Guardian and Directory, March 23, 1781; Maughan, "Francisco Garcés," 239–43.

41. Pazos, "El V.P. Fr. Juan Antonio Joaquín de Barreneche," 461–62; Garcés to Guardian and Directory, March 23, 1781; these portions are quoted in Arricivata, *Crónica seráfica y apostolica*, 495, trans. in Roberts, "SMY," at 317–18; Maughan, "Francisco Garcés," 239–43.

42. Garcés to Guardian and Directory, March 23, 1781; Maughan, "Francisco Garcés," 239–43.

43. Pazos, "El V.P. Fr. Juan Antonio Joaquín de Barreneche," 461–62.

44. Ibid.

45. Ibid.

46. Garcés to the Guardian and Directory, March 23, 1781.

47. Ibid.

48. Ibid.

49. Ibid.

50. Ibid.; Maughan, "Francisco Garcés," 238–43.

51. Santiago Yslas to Teodoro de Croix, May 28, 1781, Pueblo de La Concepción, one of two letters, AGI Guad. 277 and 517, trans. in Roberts, "SMY," at 37–38.

52. Ibid.

53. Yslas to Croix, May 28, 1781, one of two letters, trans. in Roberts, "SMY," at 31–32.

54. Fages, "Statements from the captives," and Arricivata, *Crónica seráfica y apostolica*, 504, both trans. in Roberts, "SMY," at 145, 149, 160, 163, 339–40; Forbes, *Warriors of the Colorado*, 195.

55. Arricivata, *Crónica seráfica y apostolica*, 504, tanslated in Roberts, "SMY," 339; Forbes, *Warriors of the Colorado*, 195.

56. Forbes, *Warriors of the Colorado*, 74, 195.

57. Palou, *Historical Memoirs of New California*, 4:200–201; Fages, "Statements from the captives," trans. in Roberts, "SMY," at 160, 163; Forbes, *Warriors of the Colorado*, 194–95.

58. Fages, "Statements from the captives," trans. in Roberts, "SMY," at 140, 150, 159–60, 163–64; Forbes, *Warriors of the Colorado*, 200. The soldier José Cayetano Mesa had adopted a Halchidoma Indian named José Ygnacio de Bengochea, who originally came to Yuma as a servant to Father Moreno. Bengochea was another *nifora* war-slave who had been raised in the presidio of Altar and understood Quechans. Upon arriving at Yuma he had left Moreno's service to act as an interpreter for the Spaniards while living with his new guardian. In later testimony, Bengochea claimed to have heard Francisco Xavier, Ygnacio Palma, Salvador Palma, and others say "that when the soldiers went to San Gabriel for provisions they asked that a troop should come from the peninsula and that likewise Ensign Commandant Yslas had requested soldiers from the Province of Sonora that together they might exterminate the Yumas, and that the latter before the two . . . troops could arrive resolved on the uprising that took place." Fages, "Statements from the captives," trans. in Roberts, "SMY," at 159–60.

59. Forbes, *Warriors of the Colorado*, 198–200.

60. Ibid., 194–95, 198–200.

61. Ibid., 199.

62. Ibid., 74, 197, 200.

63. Palou, *Historical Memoirs of New California*, 4:200–201; Fages, "Statements from the captives," trans. in Roberts, "SMY," at 140, 150, 159–60, 163–64; Forbes, *Warriors of the Colorado*, 197, 200.

Chapter 8. The Fury of the Yumas

1. Palou, *Historical Memoirs of New California*, 4:201; Forbes, *Warriors of the Colorado*, 195, 198–200; Ives, *José Velásquez*, 16, 157.

2. Forbes, *Warriors of the Colorado*, 195–96; Arguello, "Informe q[u]e el Then[ien]te Dn. José de Arguello" in Arguello Documents, Bancroft Library; Burrus, *Diario del Capitan Rivera y Moncada*, 497–99.

3. Forbes, *Warriors of the Colorado*, 194–95, 198–200; Arricivata, *Crónica seráfica y apostolica*, 503, trans. in Roberts, "SMY," at 338.

4. "Account that Ensign Cayetano Limón Gave the Governor of the Californias of the Gallant Fight he had with the Yumas, Mission San Gabriel, August 21, 1781," AGI Guad. 517 (hereafter cited as Account of Limón), trans. in Roberts, "SMY," at 119.

5. Arguello, "Informe q[u]e el Then[ien]te Dn. José Arguello," Arguello Documents, Bancroft Library.

6. Account of Limón, trans. in Roberts, "SMY," at 119–20.

7. Account of Limón; Felipe de Neve, "Statement of the Number and Kinds of Animals Which were with Captain Don Fernando de Moncada on the Río Colorado,"

and "List of the Soldiers and Recruits who Remained at the Río Colorado with Captain Don Fernando Rivera y Moncada and who were Killed by the Heathen Indians that Inhabit that Region" (hereafter cited as Neve, "List of Soldiers and Recruits"), San Gabriel, September 1, 1781, all in AGI Guad. 517, and all trans. in Roberts, "SMY," at 120, 122–23; Forbes, *Warriors of the Colorado*, 197.

8. Forbes, *Warriors of the Colorado*, 197, 200–201; Fages, "Statements from the captives," trans. in Roberts, "SMY," at 138, 140, 145, 155.

9. Arricivata, *Crónica seráfica y apostolica*, 507, trans. in Roberts, "SMY," at 347.

10. Ibid.

11. Fages, "Statements from the captives," Arricivata, *Crónica seráfica y apostolica*, 507, trans. in Roberts, "SMY," at 136, 138, 145–46, 155–56, 161, 165, 347; "Sermon de Bringas de Manzaneda," in Burrus, *Diario del Capitan Rivera y Moncada*, 640–41.

12. Fages, "Statements from the captives," and Fages, List of captives and killed, both trans. in Roberts, "SMY," at 130, 136, 145–46.

13. Fages, Statements from captives. trans. in Roberts, "SMY," at 155–56.

14. McCarty, "Colorado Massacre of 1781," 222; Arricivata, *Crónica seráfica y apostolica*, 506, trans. in Roberts, "SMY," at 346.

15. McCarty, "Colorado Massacre of 1781," 222; Arricivata, *Crónica seráfica y apostolica*, 507, and Fages, "Statements from the captives," both trans. in Roberts, "SMY," at 149–50, 346.

16. McCarty, "Colorado Massacre of 1781," 222–23; Arricivata, *Crónica seráfica y apostolica*, 507, trans. in Roberts, "SMY," at 346.

17. McCarty, "Colorado Massacre of 1781," 223.

18. Ibid., 222; Arricivata, *Crónica seráfica y apostolica*, 507, trans. in Roberts, "SMY," at 346.

19. McCarty, "Colorado Massacre of 1781," 223; Arricivata, *Crónica seráfica y apostolica*, 506, 507, trans. in Roberts, "SMY," at 346.

20. Arricivata, *Crónica seráfica y apostolica*, 507, and Fages, "Statements from the captives," both trans. in Roberts, "SMY," at 140, 150.

21. Arricivata, *Crónica seráfica y apostolica*, 507–8, and Account of Limón, both trans. in Roberts, "SMY," at 120, 348–49.

22. Arricivata, *Crónica seráfica y apostolica*, 507–8, Neve, "List of Soldiers and Recruits," and Fages, List of captives and killed, all trans. in Roberts, "SMY," at 123, 130, 134, 348–49.

23. Arricivata, *Crónica seráfica y apostolica*, 507, and Fages, "Statements from the captives," both translated in Roberts, "SMY," at 146, 156, 161, 165, 347.

24. Fages, List of captives and killed, and Fages, "Statements from the captives," both trans. in Roberts, "SMY," at 135–36, 138–39, 146, 156, 161, 165.

25. Fages, List of captives and killed, and Fages, "Statements from the captives," both trans. in Roberts, "SMY," at 130–36, 138–39, 146, 156, 161, 165.

26. McCarty, "Colorado Massacre of 1781," 223; Arricivata, *Crónica seráfica y apostolica*, 507, trans. in Roberts, "SMY," at 347.

27. McCarty, "Colorado Massacre of 1781," 223; Account of Limón, trans. in Roberts, "SMY," at 117.

28. McCarty, "Colorado Massacre of 1781," 223.

29. Fages, List of captives and killed, and Fages, "Statement of captives," both trans. in Roberts, "SMY," at 117, 131, 150; McCarty, "Colorado Massacre of 1781," 223.

30. McCarty, "Colorado Massacre of 1781," 223.

31. Ibid.; Arricivata, *Crónica seráfica y apostolica*, 507, trans. in Roberts, "SMY," at 348.

32. Arricivata, *Crónica seráfica y apostolica*, 507–8, trans. in Roberts, "SMY," at 348–49.

33. Ibid., and Fages, List of captives and killed, both trans. in Roberts, "SMY," at 130, 133–34, 348–49.

34. Account of Limón, and Felipe de Neve to Teodoro de Croix, San Gabriel, September 1, 1781, AGI Guad. 517, both trans. in Roberts, "SMY," at 118, 120, 124–27.

35. Arricivata, *Crónica seráfica y apostolica*, 508, trans. in Roberts, "SMY," at 350–51.

36. Ibid., trans. in Roberts, "SMY," at 349–50; McCarty, "Colorado Massacre of 1781," 223–24; Burrus, *Diario del Capitan Rivera y Moncada*, 667 n72.

37. Arricivata, *Crónica seráfica y apostolica*, 508, trans. in Roberts, "SMY," at 349–50; Maughan, "Francisco Garcés," 248; McCarty, "Colorado Massacre of 1781," 223–24.

38. Arricivata, *Crónica seráfica y apostolica*, 508, and Fages, List of captives and killed, both trans. in Roberts, "SMY," at 131, 135, 350; McCarty, "Colorado Massacre of 1781," 223–24.

39. Arricivata, *Crónica seráfica y apostolica*, 508, trans. in Roberts, "SMY," at 350; McCarty, "Colorado Massacre of 1781," 224–25.

40. Arricivata, *Crónica seráfica y apostolica*, 508, trans. in Roberts, "SMY," at 350; McCarty, "Colorado Massacre of 1781," 224.

41. Arricivata, *Crónica seráfica y apostolica*, 508, trans. in Roberts, "SMY," at 350; McCarty, "Colorado Massacre of 1781," 224.

42. Arricivata, *Crónica seráfica y apostolica*, 508, trans. in Roberts, "SMY," at 350–51.

43. Fages, "Statements from the captives," trans. in Roberts, "SMY," at 150, 156; McCarty, "Colorado Massacre of 1781," 224.

44. Fages, "Statements from the captives," trans. in Roberts, "SMY," at 150, 156.

45. Arricivata, *Crónica seráfica y apostolica*, 508, trans. in Roberts, "SMY," at 350; McCarty, "Colorado Massacre of 1781," 225.

46. Arricivata, *Crónica seráfica y apostolica*, 508–9, trans. in Roberts, "SMY," at 351.

47. Ibid., 509, trans. in Roberts, "SMY," at 351–52; McCarty, "Colorado Massacre of 1781," 224–25.

48. Arricivata, *Crónica seráfica y apostolica*, 509, trans. in Roberts, "SMY," at 352; McCarty, "Colorado Massacre of 1781," 222–25.

49. Fages, "Statements from the captives," trans. in Roberts, "SMY," at 141–42.

50. Ibid., trans. in Roberts, "SMY," at 150–51, 156.

51. Ibid., trans. in Roberts, "SMY," at 151–54, 156–57.

52. Ibid., in Roberts at 141, 146.

53. Fages, List of captives and killed, trans. in Roberts, "Spanish Mission at Yuma," at 130–36.

54. Thomas, *Teodoro de Croix*, 221.

Chapter 9. Ransom and Retribution

1. Thomas, *Teodoro de Croix*, passim.

2. Ibid., 214.

3. Ibid., 221–22.

4. Fr. Juan Bautista de Velderrain to Capt. Juan Manuel de Bonilla, Tucson, August 6, 1781; Capt. Juan Manuel de Bonilla to Fr. Juan Bautista de Velderrain, Tucson, August 6, 1781; and Capt. Juan Manuel de Bonilla to Teodoro de Croix, August 6, 1781, all in AGI Guad. 517, and all trans. in Roberts, "SMY," at 59–64; Kessell *Friars, Soldiers, and Reformers*, 143; Matson and Fontana, *Friar Bringas Reports to the King*, 63.

5. Velderrain to Bonilla, August 6, 1781, trans. in Roberts, "SMY," at 59.

6. Bonilla to Croix, August 6, 1781, trans. in Roberts, "SMY," at 62–64.

7. Velderrain to Bonilla, August 6, 1781; Bonilla to Velderrain, August 6, 1781; and Bonilla to Croix, August 6, 1781, all trans. in Roberts, "SMY," at 59–64.

8. Teodoro de Croix to Santiago Yslas, Arizpe, August 1, 1781; and Teodoro de Croix to Jacobo Ugarte y Loyola, Arizpe August 12, 1781, both in AGI Guad. 517, and both trans. in Roberts, "SMY," at 39, 66–67.

9. Croix to Ugarte y Loyola, August 12, 1781, trans. in Roberts, "SMY," at 66–67; Sanchez, *Spanish Bluecoats*, 70.

10. Capt. Juan Manuel de Bonilla to Teodoro de Croix, Tucson, August 18, 1781, in AGI Guad. 517, and trans. in Roberts, "SMY," at 70–72. Castro was listed as killed in a report later compiled by Alta California Governor Felipe de Neve, who obviously did not know that he had deserted prior to the attack. Neve, "List of Soldiers and Recruits," trans. in Roberts, "SMY," at 123.

11. Bonilla to Croix, August 18, 1781, trans. in Roberts, "SMY," at 70–72.

12. Capt. Pedro Tueros to Jacobo Ugarte y Loyola, Altar, August 31, 1781, AGI Guad. 517, trans. in Roberts, "SMY," at 76–78.

13. Ibid.

14. Junta de Guerra y Real Hacienda, Arizpe, September 9, 1781, trans. in Roberts, "SMY," at 81–90.

15. Ibid.

16. Ibid

17. Ibid.

18. Ibid.

19. Teodoro de Croix to Felipe de Neve, Arizpe, September 11, 1781, AGI Guad. 517, trans. in Roberts, "SMY," at 95–97.

20. Account of Limón, trans. in Roberts, "SMY," at 114–21; Palou, *Historical Memoirs of New California*, 4:201–2; Ives, *José Velásquez*, 16–18.

21. Account of Limón, trans. in Roberts, "SMY," at 114; Ives, *José Velásquez*, 16–18.

22. Account of Limón, trans. in Roberts, "SMY," at 114–21.

23. Ibid., at 115–16, 120.

24. Ibid, at 115–16.

25. Ibid., at 120.

26. Ibid., at 117.

27. Ibid.

28. Ibid., at 118.

29. Ibid., at 118–19; Felipe de Neve to Teodoro de Croix, San Gabriel, September 1, 1781, AGI Guad. 517, trans. in Roberts, "SMY," at 124–27.

30. Capt. Pedro Tueros to Teodoro de Croix, Altar, September 9, 1781, AGI Guad. 517; Fages, "Statements from the captives"; and Arricivata, *Crónica seráfica y apostolica*, 509, all trans. in Roberts, "SMY," at 99–101, 141–42, 352. Captain Tueros identified the soldier as Francisco Xavier Valdes, of the presidio of Buenavista, but neither the list of dead and captured that Pedro Fages later compiled nor Gov. Felipe de Neve's list of troopers and recruits under Rivera y Moncada shows a soldier with this name. Pedro Solares was interviewed by Fages at Sonóitac in October of 1781 along with other survivors from Yuma. At that time Solares specifically stated he had been sent by Salvador Palma to Altar. In my opinion, Tueros did interview Pedro Solares, but mistakenly identified him as Francisco Valdes. Fages, List of captives and killed; Neve, "List of the Soldiers and Recruits," both trans. in Roberts, "SMY," at 123, 130–36.

31. Tueros to Croix, September 9, 1781, trans. in Roberts, "SMY," at 99–101.

32. Jacobo Ugarte y Loyola to Teodoro de Croix, Pitic, September 11, 1781, and Teodoro de Croix to Jacobo Ugarte y Loyola, Arizpe, September 16, 1781, AGI Guad. 517, both in Roberts, "SMY," 103–7.

33. Pedro Fages to Teodoro de Croix, Pitic, September 11, 1781, AGI Guad. 517; trans. in Roberts, "SMY," at 111–12; Ives, "Retracing the Route of the Fages Expedition of 1781," 49–60; Ives, *José Velásquez*, 18–20. For an alternate translation of the campaign, see Priestley, "Colorado River Campaign, 1781–1782," 135–62.

34. Fages to Croix, September 11, 1781, trans. in Roberts, "SMY," at 111–12; Ives, "Retracing the Route of the Fages Expedition of 1781," 49–60.

35. Ives, "Retracing the Route of the Fages Expedition of 1781," 60–62.

36. Ibid., 62–63

37. Ibid., 63–65; Burrus, *Diario del Capitan Rivera y Moncada*, 508–509.

38. Ives, "Retracing the Fages Expedition," 65–66.

39. Ibid., 66

40. Ibid.

41. Ibid.

42. Ibid.

43. Ibid., 66–67.

44. Ibid.

45. Ibid., 67; Fages, List of captives and killed, trans. in Roberts, "SMY," at 130–34; Priestley, "Colorado River Campaign," 155–61.

46. Ives, "Retracing the Fages Expedition," 67; Fages, "Statements from the cap-

tives," trans. in Roberts, "SMY," at 157–59; Priestley, "Colorado River Campaign," 156–59.

47. Ives, "Retracing the Fages Expedition," 67–68; Priestley, "Colorado River Campaign," 156–59.

48. Ives, "Retracing the Fages Expedition," 68–70; Priestley, "Colorado River Campaign," 156–59.

49. Fages, List of captives and killed, and Fages "Statements from the captives"; and Pedro Fages to Teodoro de Croix, Sonóitac, October 29, 1781, all trans. in Roberts, "SMY," at 130–76; Ives, "Retracing the Fages Expedition," 70; Priestley, "Colorado River Campaign," 160–61.

50. Junta de Guerra y Real Hacienda, Arizpe, November 15, 1781, and Teodoro de Croix to Felipe Neve, Arizpe, November 15, 1781, both AGI Guad. 517, and both trans. in Roberts, "SMY," at 177–86.

51. Junta de Guerra y Real Hacienda, November 15, 1781, and Teodoro de Croix to Andrés Arías Caballero, Arizpe, November 15, 1781, both in AGI Guad. 517, and both in Roberts, "SMY," 177–88.

52. Ives, "Retracing the Fages Expedition," 157–58; Priestley, "Colorado River Campaign," 161–95.

53. Ives, "Retracing the Fages Expedition," 158–70; Priestley, "Colorado River Campaign," 161–95.

54. Ives, "Retracing the Fages Expedition," 158.

55. Ibid., 158–59.

56. Ibid., 159.

57. Ibid., 159–60; Fages, List of captives and killed, trans. in Roberts, "SMY," at 132–33, 136.

58. Ives, "Retracing the Fages Expedition," 160.

59. Ibid., 161.

60. Ibid.; Fages, List of captives and killed, trans. in Roberts, "SMY," at 133, 135.

61. Ives, "Retracing the Fages Expedition," 161.

62. Ibid., 161–62.

63. Ibid., 162–63; Matson and Fontana, *Friar Bringas Reports to the King,* 109–10.

64. Ives, "Retracing the Fages Expedition," 163.

65. Ibid.

66. Ibid.

67. Ibid., 163–64.

68. Ibid., 165.

69. Ibid., 165–66; Matson and Fontana, *Friar Bringas Reports to the King,* 110.

70. Ives, "Retracing the Fages Expedition," 166–67; Pedro Fages to Teodoro de Croix, Sonóitac, December 20, 1781, AGI Guad. 517, trans. in Roberts, "SMY," at 196. According to the list he had compiled in October, Fages recorded that there were sixteen captives still held by the Quechans before the second expedition. These included seven women, seven children (at least two of whom were boys), José Antonio, "a Pima Indian who was with the deceased Padre Garcés," and an unnamed servant of Captain Rivera. Fages says several times that he rescued "ten captive women," al-

though the first person ransomed was a ten-year-old girl. Of the sixteen captives listed by Fages on October 29, 1781, ten were women or girls, and it seems that these were the redeemed individuals of the second expedition. Fages, List of captives and killed, trans. in Roberts, "SMY," at 130–36.

Thus, by Fages's own count there were still six captives yet to be freed when he left Yuma after his second foray, four of which seem to have been children. It is possible that Fages did not include the four children in his total for the second expedition. Conversely, they may have been integrated into Quechan society or sold as slaves to other tribes. However, it seems unlikely that Fages would omit recording the release of adult males, all of whom were not accounted for, including Captain Rivera's servant (assuming the servant was a man), and Garcés's Pima servant José Antonio.

Ensign Cayetano Limón reported that in the skirmish he had with the Quechans in August 1781 his son was shot "by an Indian named José, who was serving as an interpreter." Since the only other interpreter named José, a Kohuana Indian named José Urrea, was ransomed by Fages, Ensign Limón's report may indicate that the Pima, José Antonio, joined the Quechans. Account of Limón, trans. in Roberts, "SMY," at 118.

71. Ives, "Retracing the Fages Expedition," 168–70.

72. Fages to Croix, December 20, 1781, trans. in Roberts, "SMY," at 196.

Chapter 10. Fire and Blood

1. Beilharz, *Felipe De Neve*, 124–25, 130.

2. Neve to Croix, September 1, 1781, trans. in Roberts, "SMY," at 124–27; Beilharz, *Felipe De Neve*, 124–25; Forbes, *Warriors of the Colorado*, 205–6.

3. Beilharz, *Felipe De Neve*, 115–18.

4. Ibid., 124–25; Ives, *José Velásquez*, 158–60.

5. Beilharz, *Felipe De Neve*, 115–18; Ives, *José Velásquez*, 158–60; Forbes, *Warriors of the Colorado*, 214.

6. Ives, *José Velásquez*, 158–60.

7. Ives, "From Pitic to San Gabriel in 1782," 242–43.

8. Ibid., 225–31.

9. Ibid., 230–31.

10. Ibid., 230–42.

11. Beilharz, *Felipe De Neve*, 126–27.

12. Ibid.; Teodoro de Croix to José de Gálvez, Arizpe, February 28, 1782, AGI Guad. 517.

13. Croix to Gálvez, February 28, 1782; Beilharz, *Felipe de Neve*, 126–27.

14. Croix to Gálvez, February 28, 1782; Beilharz, *Felipe de Neve*, 126–27.

15. Ives, "Retracing Fages' Route from San Gabriel to Yuma," 141–60.

16. José Antonio Romeu, "Diario de ocurrencias que he seguido desde el dia 18 de Marzo de 1782 en que se reunieron las tropas del destacamento que devia hallarse le 1 de Abril de este año en las margenes del Río Colorado . . . ," AGI Guad. 277 (hereafter cited as "Diario de ocurrencias"). The Regiment of the Dragoons of Spain had been

created in Mexico City in 1764, composed of twelve companies of forty men each. Along with its sister unit, the Dragoons of Mexico, the two regiments were among the first Spanish regular army units (*tropas veteranas*) formed in New Spain. A hundred-man detachment of the Dragoons of Spain took part in the Cerro Prieto campaign against the Seris in 1767–1771. In 1773, a piquet of fifty men was sent to serve in Nueva Vizcaya (modern Chihuahua). In 1779, the piquet was transferred to Sonora, where they stayed until sometime after 1785. During this period, the unit was one of only three groups of regulars in the Interior Provinces, the others being the eighty-man Second Company of the Catalonian Volunteers, and a fifty man piquet of the Dragoons of Mexico. See Navarro García, *José de Gálvez*, 150–52, 229, 332. An inspection of the piquet of the Dragoons of Spain was done by Adj. Insp. Maj. Roque de Medina in January 1782, immediately prior to the operation at Yuma. Medina, "Revista de Inspeccion de Piquette de Dragones de España," April 28, 1782, AGN, PI, 79.

17. Romeu, "Diario de ocurrencias."

18. Ibid.

19. Ibid.

20. Ibid.

21. Ibid.

22. Ibid. The ford of Vicular, or Bicular, was located at the base of modern Pilot Knob, on a site later referred to by American and Mexican forty-niners as "the emigrant ferry." Near this spot, American ferrymen, including Theodore Foster, established a stockade that in 1850 was dubbed Fort Defiance. Woodward, *Journal of Lt. Thomas W. Sweeney*, 138–39, 226–30.

23. Romeu, "Diario de ocurrencias."

24. Ibid.

25. Ibid.

26. Ibid.

27. Ibid.

28. Ibid.

29. Ibid.; "Baptism of Captain Palma, Chief of the Yuma Indians, and Three Others of His Tribe, Mexico, February 13, 1777," 5:403–4, in *ACE*.

30. Romeu "Diario de ocurrencias."

31. Ibid.; Ives, "Retracing Fages' Route from San Gabriel to Yuma," 152–53.

32. Romeu, "Diario de ocurrencias"; Ives, "Retracing Fages' Route from San Gabriel to Yuma," 152–53.

33. Romeu, "Diario de ocurrencias"; Ives, "Retracing Fages' Route from San Gabriel to Yuma," 152–53.

34. Romeu, "Diario de ocurrencias"; Ives, "Retracing Fages' Route from San Gabriel to Yuma," 152–53.

35. Romeu, "Diario de ocurrencias."

36. Ibid.

37. Ibid. The Spaniards were also joined by a Pima Indian named Eusebio, who had run away from the mission of Caborca two years earlier with a woman from one of

the Colorado River tribes. Eusebio and his companion had been living with an un-identified tribe, possibly the Cocopas, several days' journey to the south of the Yuma Crossing.

38. Teodoro de Croix to Jacobo Ugarte y Loyola, Arizpe, May 6, 1782; Junta de Guerra, Arizpe, May 16 and 17, 1782; and Teodoro de Croix to Felipe de Neve, Arizpe, May 18, 1782, all AGI Guad. 277.

39. Junta de Guerra, May 16 and 17, 1782; Croix to Neve, May 18, 1782.

40. Junta de Guerra, May 16 and 17, 1782; Croix to Neve, May 18, 1782.

41. Junta de Guerra, May 16 and 17, 1782; Croix to Neve, May 18, 1782.

42. Junta de Guerra, May 16 and 17, 1782; Croix to Neve, May 18, 1782.

43. Forbes, *Warriors of the Colorado*, 81, 216, 221–22

44. Ibid.; Romeu, "Diario de ocurrencias."

45. Ives, *José Velásquez*, 161–63; Beilharz, *Felipe de Neve*, 127.

46. Ives, *José Velásquez*, 161–63; Beilharz, *Felipe de Neve*, 127, 135. Neve's new position also came with his promotion to brigadier general, by which rank I will refer to him henceforth.

47. Ives, *José Velásquez*, 161–63; Beilharz, *Felipe de Neve*, 127, 156–72.

48. Ives, *José Velásquez*, 164; Forbes, *Warriors of the Colorado*, 218.

49. Ives, *José Velásquez*, 165.

50. Ibid.

51. Ibid.

52. Ibid.

53. Ibid.

54. Ibid.

55. Ibid., 166.

56. Ibid.

57. Ibid.

58. Ibid.

59. Ibid.

60. Romeu's account of the action is summarized in Felipe de Neve, "Extracto," January 23, 1783, and is included in a packet of documents from Teodoro de Croix to José de Gálvez, February 28, 1782, AGI Guad. 517. Ives, *José Velásquez*, 166.

61. Neve, "Extracto."

62. Ibid.

63. Ibid.

64. Ibid.

65. Ibid.

66. Ibid.

67. Ibid.

68. Ibid.

69. Ibid.

70. Ibid.

71. Ives, *José Velásquez*, 166–67; Beilharz, *Felipe De Neve*, 128.

72. Ives, *José Velásquez*, 167; Beilharz, *Felipe De Neve*, 128.

73. Ives, *José Velásquez*, 167; Forbes, *Warriors of the Colorado*, 219.

74. Ives, *José Velásquez*, 167; Forbes, *Warriors of the Colorado*, 219.

75. Ives, *José Velásquez*, 167–68.

76. Ibid.

77. Chapman, *Founding of Spanish California*, 414; Navarro García, *Don José de Gálvez*, 395–96; Forbes, *Warriors of the Colorado*, 220.

78. Chapman, *Founding of Spanish California*, 414; Forbes, *Warriors of the Colorado*, 220; Beilharz, *Felipe De Neve*, 128–29.

79. Chapman, *Founding of Spanish California*, 414; Beilharz, *Felipe De Neve*, 128–29.

80. Chapman, *Founding of Spanish California*, 414; Navarro García, *Don José de Gálvez*, 395–96; Beilharz, *Felipe De Neve*, 128–29.

81. Chapman, *Founding of Spanish California*, 414; Navarro García, *Don José de Gálvez*, 395–96; Beilharz, *Felipe De Neve*, 128–29.

Epilogue

1. The total number of casualties sustained by the Quechans between July 1781 and October 1783 is difficult to determine; however, approximations can be made. In the initial attacks on the Spanish settlements of July 17–19, 1781, there were undoubtedly Quechans killed and wounded, most probably in action against Rivera y Moncada's entrenched command. An estimate of twenty-five Quechans killed and a like number wounded seems reasonable. In the two punitive expeditions led by Pedro Fages between September and December 1781, at least fifty-nine Quechans were confirmed slain by the Spaniards, with more killed, wounded, and captured by their Indian allies. Captain Romeu's abortive third expedition of March and April 1782 seems to have inflicted no loss on the Quechans, while Felipe de Neve's assault of September 1782 reported at least forty Quechans killed.

However, in referring to this last campaign, the Franciscan historian Juan Domingo Arricivata recorded that the Spaniards "killed one-hundred and eight Indians, took eighty-five prisoners of both sexes, liberated ten Christians that were held captive and took from the Indians one thousand and forty eight horses." It seems likely that Neve would have reported such substantial numbers in his initial report to Croix, but there is no record of this.

It is possible that the figures reported by Arricivata were compiled sometime after the conclusion of the campaign, in which case they may have been inflated. The reference to the ten Christians liberated may indicate the six individuals Pedro Fages did not list as ransomed after his two expeditions, or it may indicate that some of the Spaniards reported killed in the insurrection were in fact still held captive. On the other hand, it may also refer to Christian Indian neophytes from the missions of the Pimería Alta, living with, traded to, or captured by the Quechans. Such was the case with Eusebio, the Pima Indian runaway from Caborca, discovered by Captain Romeu along the Colorado River in April of 1782. Arricivata, *Crónica seráfica y apostolica*,

514; Romeu, "Diario de ocurrencias"; Forbes, *Warriors of the Colorado*, 210–14; Ives, *José Velásquez*, 163.

2. Forbes, *Warriors of the Colorado*, 80–82, 234.

3. Ibid., 80–82, 222–24, 234, 251–56; Ives, *José Velásquez*, 191–93.

4. Chapman, *Founding of Spanish California*, 414–16; Beilharz, *Felipe De Neve*, 128.

5. Chapman, *Founding of Spanish California*, 414–16; Beilharz, *Felipe De Neve*, 128.

6. Chapman, *Founding of Spanish California*, 414–16; Beilharz, *Felipe De Neve*, 135–36.

7. Croix to Gálvez, February 28, 1782, AGI Guad. 517, and also quoted in Kessell, *Friars, Soldiers, and Reformers*, 145–46.

8. Ibid.

9. Kessell, *Friars, Soldiers, and Reformers*, 146; Bannon, *Spanish Borderlands Frontier*, 186–87.

10. Kessell, *Friars, Soldiers, and Reformers*, 146; Chapman, *Founding of Spanish California*, 409–10, 413; Matson and Fontana, *Friar Bringas Reports to the King*, 107.

11. Thomas, *Teodoro de Croix*, 218–22; Chapman, *Founding of Spanish California*, 409.

12. Bannon, *Spanish Borderlands Frontier*, 184–85; Weber, *Spanish Frontier in North America*, 225–26.

13. Fisher, *Last Inca Revolt*, 388–90.

14. Arricivata, *Crónica seráfica y apostolica*, 498–502, trans. in Roberts, "SMY," at 323–34; Matson and Fontana, *Friar Bringas Reports to the King*, 105–7.

15. Arricivata, *Crónica seráfica y apostolica*, 502, trans. in Roberts, "SMY," at 334.

16. Arricivata, *Crónica seráfica y apostolica*, 498–99, trans. in Roberts, "SMY," at 323–26.

17. Matson and Fontana, *Friar Bringas Reports to the King*, 96.

18. Ibid., 86–87, 96.

19. Ibid., 108 n.81.

20. Ibid., 107–11.

21. Ibid.

22. Ibid.

23. Cullimore, "A California Martyr's Bones," 16; Kessell, *Friars, Soldiers, and Reformers*, 145.

24. Cullimore, "A California Martyr's Bones," 18.

25. Ibid., 17–19; Burrus, *Diario de Capitan Rivera y Moncada*, 533–675, contains Father Bringas's sermon in its entirety.

26. Cullimore, "A California Martyr's Bones," 17–19; Burrus, *Diario de Capitan Rivera y Moncada*, 533–675. The quotation from St. Paul is from Philippians 1:21, 22.

27. Forbes, *Warriors of the Colorado*, 257; Weber, *Spanish Frontier in North America*, 258.

28. Forbes, *Warriors of the Colorado*, 222–25; Ives, *José Velásquez*, 179–99.

29. Forbes, *Warriors of the Colorado*, 226–25; Chapman, *Founding of Spanish California*, 428–30.

30. Forbes, *Warriors of the Colorado,* 228–34; Chapman *Founding of Spanish California,* 430–34.

31. Forbes, *Warriors of the Colorado,* 228–34; Chapman *Founding of Spanish California,* 430–34.

32. Chapman *Founding of Spanish California,* 416–18, 428–34; Weber, *Spanish Frontier in North America,* 258, 264–65; Beilharz, *Felipe de Neve,* 121.

Bibliography

Primary Sources

Manuscripts
Archivo General de las Indias. Audencia de Guadalajara. Seville, Spain.
Legajos 277, 517 (microfilm, Bancroft Library, University of California, Berkeley).
Archivo General de la Nación, Mexico City, Mexico.
Californias 36 (microfilm, Arizona Historical Society, Tucson).
Historia 24, 396 (microfilm, Arizona Historical Society, Tucson).
Provincias Internas 23, 79, 237 (microfilm, Arizona Historical Society, Tucson).
Bancroft Library, University of California at Berkeley.
Arguello, José Dario, 1792–1815. Documents. MSS C-A 308: 2.
Pontificio Ateneo Antoniano, Vatican, Rome, Italy.
Civezza, Fr. Marcellino da, Collection (microfilm no. 305, University of Arizona Library, Tucson).

Published Works
Arricivata, P., Fr. Juan Domingo. *Crónica seráfica y apostólica del colegio de propaganda fide de la Santa Cruz de Querétaro en la Nueva España, dedicada al Santísimo Patriarca El Señor San Joseph.* Mexico City: Don Felipe Zuñiga y Ontiveros, 1792.

Bartlett, John Russell. *Personal Narrative of Explorations and Incidents in Texas, New Mexico, California, Sonora, and Chihuahua.* 2 vols. New York: D. Appleton, 1854.

Bolton, Herbert Eugene, ed. *Anza's California Expeditions.* 5 vols. 1930. Reprint New York: Russell and Russell, 1966.

———, ed. *Font's Complete Diary: A Chronicle of the Founding of San Francisco.* Berkeley: University of California Press, 1931.

Burrus, Ernest J., S.J., ed. *Diario del Capitan Commandante Fernando de Rivera y Moncada con un Apendice Documental.* 2 vols. Madrid: Ediciones José Porrua Turanzas, 1967.

Coues, Elliott, trans. and ed. *On the Trail of a Spanish Pioneer: The Itinerary of Francisco Garcés in His Travels through Sonora, Arizona and California, 1775–1776.* 2 vols. New York: Francis P. Harper, 1900.

Cutter, Donald C., trans. and ed. *The Defenses of Northern New Spain: Hugo O'Conor's Report to Teodoro de Croix, July 22, 1777.* Dallas: Southern Methodist University Press and De Golyer Library, 1994.

Dunne, Peter Masten, trans. *Jacobo Sedelmayr, Missionary, Frontiersman, Explorer in Arizona and Sonora: Four Original Manuscript Narratives, 1744–1751.* Tucson: Arizona Pioneers' Historical Society, 1965.

Heintzelman, Major Samuel P. *Report of July 15, 1853.* 34th Cong., 3rd sess. 1857. H. Exec. Doc. 76.

Ives, Ronald L., ed. "From Pitic to San Gabriel in 1782: The Journey of Don Pedro Fages." *Journal of Arizona History* 9 (Winter 1968): 222–44.

Ives, Ronald L., ed. "Retracing Fages' Route from San Gabriel to Yuma, April 1782." *Arizona and the West* 17 (Summer 1975): 141–60.

Ives, Ronald L., ed. "Retracing the Route of the Fages Expedition of 1781." 2 parts. *Arizona and the West* 8 (Spring and Summer 1966): 49–70, 157–70.

Kessell, John L., ed. "Anza Damns the Missions: A Spanish Soldier's Criticism of Indian Policy, 1771." *Journal of Arizona History* 13 (Spring 1972): 53–63.

McCarty, Kieran, O.F.M., trans. and ed. "The Colorado Massacre of 1781: Maria Montielo's Report." *Journal of Arizona History* 16 (Autumn 1975): 221–25.

Matson, Daniel S., and Bernard L. Fontana. *Friar Bringas Reports to the King: Methods of Indoctrination on the Frontier of New Spain, 1726–1797.* Tucson: University of Arizona Press, 1977.

Palou, Fray Francisco, O.F.M. *Historical Memoirs of New California.* Trans. and ed. Herbert Eugene Bolton. 4 vols. Berkeley: University of California Press, 1926.

Pazos, Manuel R., O.F.M. "El V.P. Fr. Juan Antonio Joaquín de Barreneche, matrizado por los Indios Yumas del Río Colorado el 19 de julio de 1781: Algunas cartas originals. Relaciones contemporáneas de su vida." *Archivo Ibero-Americano* 1 (1941): 455–73.

Priestley, Herbert I., ed. "The Colorado River Campaign, 1781–1782: Diary of Pedro Fages." *Academy of Pacific Coast History Publications* 3 (May 1913): 135–233.

Salmón, Roberto Mario, trans. "A 1791 Report on the Villa de Arizpe." *Journal of Arizona History* 24 (Spring 1983): 13–28.

Woodward, Arthur, ed. *The Journal of Lt. Thomas W. Sweeney 1849–1853.* Los Angeles: Westernlore Press, 1956.

Secondary Sources

Unpublished
Maughan, Scott Jarvis. "Francisco Garcés and New Spain's Northwestern Frontier, 1768–1781." Ph.D. diss., University of Utah, 1968.

Published
Aiton, Arthur. "Spanish Colonial Reorganization under the Family Compact." *Hispanic American Historical Review* 12 (August 1932): 269–80.
Alger, Abby Langdon, ed. *The Little Flowers of St. Francis of Assissi.* Mount Vernon, Va.: Peter Pauper Press, n.d.
Archer, Christon I. *The Army in Bourbon Mexico, 1760–1810.* Albuquerque: University of New Mexico Press, 1977.
Almirante, D. José. *Diccionario Militar: Entimológico, Histórico, Tecnológico.* Madrid: Imprenta y Litografía del Depósito de la Guerra, 1869.
Bannon, John Francis. *The Spanish Borderlands Frontier, 1513–1821.* New York: Holt, Rinehart and Winston, 1970.
Beilharz, Edwin A. *Felipe de Neve, First Governor of California.* San Francisco: California Historical Society, 1971.
Bobb, Bernard E. *The Viceregency of Antonio María Bucareli in New Spain 1771–1779.* Austin: University of Texas Press, 1962.
Bolton, Herbert Eugene. *Rim of Christendom: A Biography of Eusebio Francisco Kino, Pacific Coast Pioneer.* New York: MacMillan, 1936.
Chapman, Charles Edward. *The Founding of Spanish California: The Northwestward Expansion of New Spain.* New York: MacMillan, 1916.
Cullimore, Clarence. "A California Martyr's Bones." *California Historical Quarterly* 33 (1954): 13–21.
Dobyns, Henry F. *Spanish Colonial Tucson.* Tucson: University of Arizona Press, 1976.
Dunne, Peter Masten. *Black Robes in Lower California.* Berkeley: University of California, 1952.
Fagg, John Edwin. *Latin America: A General History.* New York: MacMillan, 1977.
Fisher, Lillian Estelle. *The Last Inca Revolt, 1780–1783.* Norman: University of Oklahoma Press, 1966.
Forbes, Jack D. *Warriors of the Colorado: The Yumas of the Quechan Nation and Their Neighbors.* Norman: University of Oklahoma Press, 1965.
Ives, Ronald L. *José Velásquez: Saga of Borderland Soldier.* Tucson: Southwest Mission Research Center, Arizona State Museum, 1984.
Kessell, John L. *Friars, Soldiers, and Reformers: Hispanic Arizona and the Sonora Mission Frontier, 1767–1856.* Tucson: University of Arizona Press, 1976.
——. "The Making of a Martyr: The Young Francisco Garcés." *New Mexico Historical Review* 45 (Autumn 1970): 181–96.

Kroeber, Clifton B., and Bernard L. Fontana. *Massacre on the Gila: An Account of the Last Major Battle between American Indians, with Reflections on the Origin of War.* Tucson: University of Arizona Press, 1986.

McCarty, Kieran, O.F.M. *A Spanish Frontier in the Enlightened Age: Franciscan Beginnings in Sonora and Arizona, 1767–1770.* Washington, D.C.: Academy of American Franciscan History, 1981.

Meyer, Michael C., and William L. Sherman. *The Course of Mexican History.* 2d edn. New York: Oxford University Press, 1983.

Navarro García, Luis. *Don José de Gálvez y la Commandancia General de los Provincias Internas del Norte de Nueva España.* Seville, Spain: Escuela de Estudios Hispano-Americanos de Sevilla, 1964.

Officer, James E. "Kino and Agriculture in the Pimería Alta." *Journal of Arizona History* 34 (Autumn 1993): 287–306.

Petrie, Sir Charles. *King Charles III of Spain: An Enlightened Despot.* London: Constable, 1971.

Ricard, Robert. *The Spiritual Conquest of Mexico: An Essay on the Apostalate and Evangelizing Methods of the Mendicant Orders in New Spain 1523–1572.* Berkeley: University of California Press, 1966.

Roberts, Elizabeth E. "Spanish Missions at Yuma, 1779–1781: A Translation of Original Documents." M.A. thesis, University of California, Berkeley, 1920.

Sanchez, Joseph P. *Spanish Bluecoats: The Catalonian Volunteers in Northwestern New Spain, 1767–1810.* Albuquerque: University of New Mexico Press, 1990.

Santiago, Mark. *The Red Captain: The Life of Hugo O'Conor, Commandant Inspector of the Interior Provinces of New Spain.* Tucson: Arizona Historical Society, 1994.

Sheridan, Thomas E. "Kino's Unforeseen Legacy: The Material Consequences of Missionization." *The Smoke Signal* 49 and 50 (Spring and Fall 1988): 151–60.

Thomas, Alfred Barnaby, ed. and trans. *Teodoro de Croix and the Northern Frontier of New Spain, 1776–1783.* Norman: University of Oklahoma Press, 1941.

Torres-Ramirez, Bibiano. *Alejandro O'Reilly en las Indias.* Seville, Spain: Escuela de Estudios Hispano-Americano de Sevilla, 1969.

Weber, David J. *The Spanish Frontier in North America.* New Haven, Conn.: Yale University Press, 1992.

Yates, Richard. "Locating the Colorado River Mission San Pedro y San Pablo de Bicuñer." *Journal of Arizona History* 13 (Summer 1972): 123–30.

Index

About the Author

During his fifteen years with the Arizona Historical Society at its Yuma and Tucson branches, Mark Santiago has become familiar with the Spanish period of the southwestern United States. While studying the history of the Yuma region, he became interested in the role of the Spanish military, not only in the borderlands area but also throughout the world.

Santiago has published *The Red Captain: The Life of Hugo O'Conor, Commandant Inspector of the Interior Provinces of New Spain* (Arizona Historical Society, 1994) and articles and review essays in the *Journal of Arizona History*. He has also served as a consultant on several documentaries on Arizona history and has appeared in the public television series *The Desert Speaks*.

Arizona has been his home since childhood, and he received his B.A. (1981) and M.A. (1983) degrees from the University of Arizona, in Tucson. He is married to Dawn Moore Santiago, a fellow historian/editor, and they have three sons, Edward, Alexander, and Justin. Currently, he is the collections manager for the Arizona Historical Society, Tucson, and he continues his research into various aspects of eighteenth-century Spanish military history.